D0458073

George Clooney

DEC 05 2012

George Clooney

George Clooney

An Actor Looking for a Role

Mark Browning

 PRAEGER

AN IMPRINT OF ABC-CLIO, LLC
Santa Barbara, California • Denver, Colorado • Oxford, England

Copyright 2012 by Mark Browning

All rights reserved. No part of this publication may be reproduced, stored in a retrieval system, or transmitted, in any form or by any means, electronic, mechanical, photocopying, recording, or otherwise, except for the inclusion of brief quotations in a review, without prior permission in writing from the publisher.

Library of Congress Cataloging-in-Publication Data

Browning, Mark, 1966–
   George Clooney : an actor looking for a role / Mark Browning.
     p. cm.
   Includes bibliographical references and index.
   ISBN 978–0–313–39621–2 (hard copy : alk. paper) — ISBN 978–0–313–39622–9 (ebook)
1. Clooney, George—Criticism and interpretation. I. Title.
PN2287.C546B76   2012
791.4302′8092—dc23   2012010975

ISBN: 978–0–313–39621–2
EISBN: 978–0–313–39622–9

16 15 14 13 12   1 2 3 4 5

This book is also available on the World Wide Web as an eBook.
Visit www.abc-clio.com for details.

Praeger
An Imprint of ABC-CLIO, LLC

ABC-CLIO, LLC
130 Cremona Drive, P.O. Box 1911
Santa Barbara, California 93116-1911

This book is printed on acid-free paper ∞

Manufactured in the United States of America

Contents

Introduction

Kelvin: the conscious effort to smile, nod, stand . . . performing millions of gestures that constitute life on earth . . . I studied these until they became reflexes.

—Kelvin in *Solaris*

George Timothy Clooney is arguably not just a fine actor but a major Hollywood player, acting as director, producer, and writer on projects that without his interest and creative input would never have been made. His influence within the industry has grown steadily over the last decade so that rather than merely featuring in polls of most handsome man, he now tops polls of powerful figures in Hollywood. At the same time, a growing number of films with which he has been involved have garnered a more positive critical response, resulting in Oscar nominations for Best Actor (*Michael Clayton*, *Up in the Air* and *The Descendants*), Best Original Screenplay (*Good Night, and Good Luck*), Best Adapted Screenplay (*The Ides of March*), Best Director (*Good Night, and Good Luck*) and a win as Best Supporting Actor (*Syriana*).

Reflecting the global interest he generates, there have been several overt biographies of Clooney, which differ range in range and detail. David Bassom's *George Clooney: An Illustrated Story* (1999) is a speedily produced, 80-page thumbnail sketch, while Jeff Hudson's *George Clooney: A Biography* (2003) and Nick Johnstone's *George Clooney: The Illustrated Biography* (2008) are more substantial but still fundamentally dealing with Clooney as a celebrity rather than a screen actor. Sam Keenleyside's *Bedside Manners: George Clooney and ER* (1998) is an information-based TV tie-in, and Tamra B. Orr's *George Clooney and the Crisis in Darfur* (2008) is clearly focused on Clooney's political activism beyond the screen. Even Kimberly J. Potts's *George Clooney: The Last Great Movie Star* (2007) offers a broad sweep of his celebrity lifestyle, high-profile romances, and political activism rather than a close analysis of his films. In terms of the background of the authors, Bassom is better known as a writer of companion books to the *Battlestar Galactica* and *Babylon 5* TV series; Hudson is a specialist on The Kinks; Keenleyside is a pop-culture critic and journalist; and Johnstone is a biographer—all of which are perfectly respectable professions but none of these writers are film specialists. The availability of Joseph Kanon's *The Good German* (2006), Tony Gilroy's shooting script for *Michael Clayton* (2007), and Clooney's own script for *Goodnight, and Good Luck* (2006), cowritten with Grant Heslov all show a substantial public appetite for reliving Clooney's more thoughtful and literary movies.

The missing piece of the jigsaw at the moment is analysis of Clooney's movies themselves, written by a film specialist, focusing on what we see on-screen rather than the cult of celebrity around it. This book will not be focusing on Clooney's private life, his latest girlfriends, or his presence in the news media, except where it relates directly to what appears on-screen. It is organized into generic sections as Clooney's work tends to fall within fairly specifically defined areas. A key element of the book is to consider how far he remains within generic expectations, when and how he pushes boundaries, and whether this succeeds. The development of an on-screen persona is not necessarily a simple sequential process. Movies may not be released in the order they were made, some will be screened (sometimes repeatedly) on television, and not everything will be seen by every viewer. Comments will focus on Clooney's starring roles but there is inevitably consideration of the films' broader strengths and weaknesses. Those films where Clooney also directs are given proportionately more space.

Overt plot summaries will be avoided; but since at the time of writing, Clooney has played a significant part in over 35 films and not every reader will have seen all of these, there will be some reference to narrative features in passing to help follow the points being made. At the time of writing, neither *The Descendants* nor *The Ides of March* had been released in Europe, so the book can make only limited comment on these films.

WHAT ARE STARS FOR?

It is tempting to think that there have always been movie stars as long as there have been films but this is not so. In the earliest days of the medium's development, particularly 1895–1905, films were extremely short, sometimes only a few seconds long, focused on one action, often comedic or spectacular, and figures were held in long-shot, making identification of individual actors difficult. In Edwin S. Porter's 11-minute *Great Train Robbery* (1903), although the narrative structure shows an evolving complexity, it was still possible for Gilbert M. "Broncho Billy" Anderson to play several roles (a passenger, a dancer, and a bandit). It was not until the close-up became more widespread, particularly through the films of D. W. Griffith, that individual actors could be seen clearly and were part of engaging narratives so that audiences would associate a role with a specific actor. Thus from Griffith's *Birth of a Nation* (1915) onward, and particularly after the end of World War I and the waning of the French film industry, the notion of the Hollywood movie star evolved, alongside other developments such as a realization by the studios of how stars could be used to promote films and how their interests were best served by putting stars under contract, meaning in turn that they (stars and studios) became associated with particular genres as it became the most profitable way to make films and increased the power and reach of Hollywood.

Film theorists have approached the issue in a number of different, but related ways. For Richard Dyer, star images are made up of four elements: features promoted by the film industry, the response of critics, the utterances and actions of stars themselves, and the reactions of audiences.[1] Susan Hayward states that stars are constructs, "representing something that actually isn't there" that we accept as real, which might equally be applied to the whole cinematic apparatus as well as the notion of fictional narratives.[2] Christine Gledhill suggests that stars are made up of three elements: a real person, a "reel" person (on-screen character), and a star "persona," which is a combination of the previous two. She argues that stars communicate with audiences primarily culturally, historically, and through bodily appearance, particularly with regard to female stars.[3] As idealized versions of our best selves, audiences do not always respond well to images of ageing, preferring the escapism of beauty and glamor. This has led to a scarcity of roles for older women, although perhaps with role models like Helen Mirren still finding work, attitudes are starting to change. Discussions of stars often use examples who are from the heyday of the studio era and nearly always female, like Marilyn Monroe, but the prime example chosen for this book is the most consistent leading man of the modern era: George Clooney.

Audiences come with expectations of stars. For Hayward, there are basically two different modes of acting. On the one hand, a star can play roles in line with his or her perceived personality, which might be termed "personification." Mid-career Arnold Schwarzenegger movies with his trademark catchphrase "I'll be back" establish a compact with the audience, who expect certain thrills (which can also be played with for comic effect). Alternatively, the actor might not play any element of his or her star persona but disappear into a role completely, which might be termed "impersonation." Actors who can (and who studios allow) to operate in this manner, such as Meryl Streep, are particularly rare. The demands of such acting are much greater and marketing is more challenging, so audiences do not always know exactly what to expect, leading in turn to mixed critical and commercial reactions. The tagline for Rob Epstein's *Howl* (2010) runs "James Franco *is* Allen Ginsberg." The idea that an actor is completely immersed in a role becomes the dominant marketing strategy for the film. Filmmakers will usually try to find a balance of recognizable features (allowing an audience to place a film in their own personal viewing experience) with limited surprise and innovation. Too much of the first element and you have just another formulaic movie; too much of the second and audiences will feel a star is miscast.

Star as a Reflection of Cultural Value

Stars clearly constitute points of identification in a movie, as either a reflection of our own concerns or an escapist fantasy that allows us to forget them. Stars are often at pains in interviews to stress just how normal and down-to-earth they are, while living in homes the size and value of which we can only dream about. They are a focus of wish fulfillment, as better versions of ourselves: wealthier, healthier, better-looking, and more successful. The link might be quite minor, for example with fans copying a particular stylistic look or fashion statement (like Jennifer Aniston's hair in the mid-1990s), or more substantial, for example as a full-time occupation as a look-alike. If the process of identification is too complete, we have an obsessive devotion to the object of adoration, we continually follow the life of the individual, and we imagine that there is a real emotional bond between star and fan, now dubbed a stalker.

Historically, male stars have been associated with particular genres, like Jimmy Cagney (gangster movie), John Wayne (western or war film), or Harrison Ford (action adventure), and act as a mirror for those qualities, which a culture and an era find attractive (put simply, boys want to be them; girls want to be with them). Such cultural values clearly change over time (Clark Gable might be seen as cool for smoking but Clooney would not today). Names are a key part of the fantasy world of stardom as distinct from everyday life. Clooney has chosen to keep his name, which was already connected to a certain level of stardom. His father, Nick Clooney, was a regional news anchor in Cincinnati and his aunt, Rosemary, was a major singing star in the 1950s. Clooney seems to have learned from such family connections about the fickle nature of fame and that it pays to take chances with projects that may not be possible once one's star power has waned.

Stars both reflect and generate shifting cultural values, and when stars cease to echo these, their resonance with an audience fades. Tom Cruise's Scientology and his eccentric behavior in interviews, and Mel Gibson's alleged problems with alcohol, domestic violence, and accusations of racism, threaten the pact that they have with viewers. If the excesses of a star's lifestyle (usually related to drink, drugs, or sex) appear to cross the bounds of what any given society deems to be acceptable, then offers of work start to dry up and products/studios start to distance themselves from a star. Ironically, if they were a rock star, such behavior might seem almost obligatory, but in the world of movies, the status of role model carries higher expectations about personal behavior.

Star as Managed Brand

Modern stardom is a branding exercise. Like Bob (Bill Murray) in *Lost in Translation* (Sofia Coppola, 2003), a movie star today might spend as much of his or her time endorsing products, like clothing lines, perfumes, or toys, as creating new films, so that names themselves literally become brands, like J-Lo or Beyoncé. Clooney, who abandoned plans for his own personal fragrance in 2010, appears in a series of Nespresso commercials (2006–present), discussed in chapter 9.

Part of the role of a star is to supply extrafilmic material for the circulation of comment about them. This includes not only interviews and photo shoots but also premieres and festivals, the latter of which are a particularly contrived affair. Cannes might well be a financial marketplace as film producers try to strike deals with distributors, but a large part of the media coverage is devoted to the appearance of stars. Like Tom Cruise's established act at charming the crowd at premieres, talking on cell phones borrowed from the crowd and happy to have his photo taken, so Clooney is also a regular at festivals, in Venice in particular.

In an age of media agents, PR consultants, and complex and sophisticated media campaigns, leaked stories, and off-the-record comments, the stories that swirl around stars are part of a carefully managed 24-hour media discourse. Negative publicity surrounding the conduct of the star can damage that brand, even at the level of unsubstantiated rumor or extremely loose connection, such as Clooney's appearance in a long list of potential witnesses in the trial of former Italian prime minister, Silvio Berlusconi. Friendly chats with David Letterman or Jay Leno are part of a media campaign, sometimes subtle, sometimes not, to promote a specific product. Questions are agreed to beforehand, avoiding no-go areas, which are often related to personal matters. Occasional mismatches occur and stars walk out of live interviews, but then this becomes the story itself, generating the magic substance being sought in the first place: publicity.

Stars also feed some of these perceptions. Clooney's activism for causes such as raising awareness over the situation in Darfur or natural disasters like the earthquake in Haiti, and their humanitarian consequences, illustrates his dilemma. If the media show an interest in him, he may as well use it as constructively as he can, but at the same time if he wants people to listen to what he says on serious extrafilmic issues, he must also accept that this will happen only as a result of publicity generated elsewhere.

Star as Deviant

In terms of sexuality, there used to be so-called "lavender" weddings, supported by studios, to cover up homosexuality, deemed by some to be immoral. Clooney's cultivation of a screen image akin to a modern-day Cary Grant also links him (in terms of era) with figures like Rock Hudson, who felt forced to construct such a veneer of heterosexuality to conceal his real sexual identity; and as a man, almost universally feted for his good looks, currently unmarried, Clooney is not an unnatural object of attention for gay viewers.

Clooney has clearly been angered at particular points in his career by actions of the paparazzi and popular press (both print and online). However, this is a difficult and reciprocal relationship as the media need stories to feed their insatiable desire for words and pictures, the more scandalous the better, and stars need publicity, preferably positive, but also privacy. One cannot live without the other. When the photographers held their cameras aloft in protest at the premiere for *The Peacemaker* in 1997 and refused to take Clooney's picture in response to his boycott of *Entertainment Tonight* and *Hard Copy*, after they had published unauthorized photos, it underlined his precarious position. As much as he may be right about media responsibility and integrity, there are always other stars to photograph. He might make a great movie, but if audiences do not hear about it or experience a barrage of negative publicity and choose not to see it, then his status as a star and an artist is diminished.

From a studio point of view, there is a financial incentive to maintain the role of stars as long as they act as a hook to draw audiences in. It remains difficult to secure a distribution deal without the presence of stars. At the moment, Clooney has secured funding for more personal projects like *Leatherheads* (2008) only if he stars in them. Danny Boyle's *Slumdog Millionaire* (2009), although sweeping the board at the 2010 Oscars, found only a last-minute distribution deal through Fox Searchlight, after potentially failing to find a backer, partly due to its lack of recognizable stars. However, there seem to be fewer films conceived as overt star vehicles, in part because there seems to be a decreasing pool of male actors who can open a film. There also seem to be few guarantees about finding a successful formula, except repeating one you have already found.

CHAPTER 1

From *E/R* to *ER* (Early Television Work)

I've done a lot of very bad television and I've been very bad in a lot of bad television.

—George Clooney[1]

While the shift from television to feature films is not unknown (Clint Eastwood's extended apprenticeship on *Rawhide*, for instance), lengthy TV careers usually represent a destination rather than a staging post in career terms. The number of contemporary actors who have made such a shift is extremely few with the exception of individuals like Guy Pearce from the Australian soap *Neighbours* (1986–89) to *Memento* (Christopher Nolan, 2001) to *The Time Machine* (Simon Wells, 2002) and back again to TV in *Mildred Pierce* (Todd Haynes, 2011) on HBO. In the following survey of Clooney's TV work, involving many failed pilots, dates in parentheses designate when he appeared in that show, not necessarily its full run.

Clooney's very first role on TV was in 1978 as an extra on the James Michener mini-series *Centennial*, which happened to be filming in Augusta, Kentucky, Clooney's hometown. A guest spot on the California-based crime-fighting series *Riptide* (1984), a bloodless version of *Miami Vice*, was Clooney's first on-screen speaking role, as one of a pair of kidnappers, eventually apprehended after a tussle and a roll down a flight of stairs.

E/R (CBS, 1984–85) was canceled after only a single season but gave Clooney a taste of regular employment on a serial sitcom. As Mark "Ace" Kolmar, his character worked as an orderly with paramedics in all 22 episodes, alongside his on-screen aunt, Nurse Joan Thor (Conchata

Ferrell, better known now as Berta in CBS's *Two and a Half Men*), and with Elliott Gould, with whom he would team up again 15 years later in the *Ocean's* franchise. Who could have guessed the direction Clooney's career would take a decade later in another drama based in a Chicago hospital?

Clooney appeared in single episodes of fledgling series, which ran for only a short time. *Street Hawk* (ABC, 1985) lasted only 12 episodes, featuring a superbike ridden by Jesse Mach (Rex Smith), a police public relations officer by day and a crime fighter by night, constituting a motorcycle version of *Knight Rider*. Clooney appears in episode 2, "A Second Self," as Kevin Stark, brother of a car thief killed in a pursuit, who tries to lure Jesse into a trap to exact revenge. Clooney's character dies (a rare early example), as dictated by the imperatives of the genre, in crossfire.

He had experience in single episodes of more established dramatic vehicles too. In an episode of *Murder, She Wrote*, entitled "No Laughing Matter" (1987), Clooney plays Kip, son of Mack Howard, one-half of a long-running comedy double act with Murray Gruen, now estranged due to a long-running feud. Kip seeks to marry Corrie (Beth Windsor), daughter of Murray in a *Romeo and Juliet*-style tale of family hostility. Clooney played Detective Bobby Hopkins in a 1987 episode of *The Golden Girls* ("To Catch a Neighbor"). He is one of a pair of cops who use the girls' house to watch their new neighbors, the McDowells, suspected of being jewel thieves. Clooney would probably be the first to admit that his acting here as "Bob Dishy" is hardly his best, accenting almost every word and trying to inject some drama into an episode whose writing falls below the standard of most others.

Clooney began to build experience in consecutive episodes (albeit in minor roles) in mainstream comedies. *Baby Talk* (ABC, 1991–92) was a direct TV spin-off from *Look Who's Talking* (Amy Heckerling, 1989). In the first season only, Clooney plays Joe, a construction worker and potential suitor of single-mother Maggie Campbell (Julia Duffy), whose advances are commented on by baby Mickey (via a Tony Danza voice-over). As carpenter George Burnett, in *The Facts of Life*, he was a regular cast member in season 7, starring in 17 episodes (NBC, 1985–86, recurring 1986–87) but did not even merit his own name. Originally a spin-off from *Diff'rent Strokes*, by the time Clooney joined the show it had evolved to include major changes of cast, and its focus had moved away from the privileged Eastland School with Mrs. Garrett (Charlotte Rae) as matriarchal headmistress to a gift shop called "Over Our Heads," built with Burnett's help after a fire at her previous shop.

Clooney's role in *Roseanne* (1988–91) is a little more significant in terms of the length of his appearance (11 episodes) and the enduring quality of the show. As the overbearing boss at a plastics factory, Booker Brooks, he also has a slightly more rounded character than in *The Facts of Life* or *E/R*. As Brooks he gets to date Jackie (Laurie Metcalf), don a moose costume, and work with John Goodman, who was also plotting a move into film. His presence is primarily visual and as a reverse-gender target of sexual harassment, so that we see him bending down to pick up a pen, provoking catcalls and getting his butt slapped by Jackie as she passes. The speed with which his character was dropped from the show, as it turned back toward the domestic and away from a work setting, reflects the brutality of network TV but also Clooney's own dispensable status at this time. It was during his time on *Roseanne* that he watched Metcalf go off for occasional film parts, an example of a gradual shift into film rather than a sudden risky jump, which could result in very public failure.

On *Sisters* (NBC, 1994–95) as Detective James Falconer, he gained the experience of a slightly broader drama show and was paired opposite Teddy (Sela Ward), who his character meets at an AA meeting at the beginning of season 4, marries by the end of it, only to be killed off by a car bomb in season 5. The show's dialogue rarely extended beyond the formulaic, but there were flashes of innovation, like a scene in which Falconer cannot give up his dangerous job. We also see a younger Teddy (Jill Novick) unable to commit to Mitch (Ed Marinaro), played out non-naturalistically on the same set at the same time, even with one line ("Why can't you do this for me?") spoken simultaneously by both male characters.

Bodies of Evidence (CBS, 1992–93) did not have a long run, but as Detective Ryan Walker in 16 episodes opposite Lee Horsley (better known as TV's Matt Houston), Clooney gained some experience of a formulaic cop show. He played a profiler helping Horsley's character, Ben Carroll, as part of an elite homicide unit. Though hardly *CSI*, it does show the shift of detective narratives toward more forensic-based story lines.

Sunset Beat (NBC, 1990) was a short-lived feature-length TV pilot, but it allowed Clooney to indulge in his passion for bikes with the wafer-thin premise of a group of LA policemen going undercover as bikers to solve crime led by Clooney's character, Chic Chesbro, who has seriously long hair and also plays lead guitar in a band called Private Prayer. The supposed bad guys try to blackmail LA authorities into handing over confiscated money by bizarre acts like poisoning elephants in the city zoo.

Explosions, stunts, and crude expositional dialogue all fight it out for attention. One scene will give a sufficient flavor: J.C., onetime mentor of Chesbro, is killed by being dropped from a helicopter onto the stage (using a very unconvincing dummy) while Chesbro is playing, and for a moment, the singer of the band, his girlfriend, almost starts to sing again.

Without Warning: Terror in the Towers (Alan J. Levi, 1993) was a TV movie of the 1993 attack on the World Trade Center. Clooney plays a young firefighter, spending quite a lot of the film in his hospital bed after being injured. The film uses lots of footage of the real attack but feels closer at times to a sensationalized reconstruction of the "When Insects Attack" subgenre than a piece of fictional drama. It focuses on the actions of heroic rescuers and pitiable victims, including a group of trapped schoolchildren, but does little to examine the possible causes of events.

Clooney's early TV career is dominated by comedy and roles as law enforcement officers, even blending the two in *The Golden Girls*. The significance of his TV career is that by the time his breakthrough role in *ER* appeared, he was older and no longer had the puppyish good looks of someone cast primarily for that reason. In a sense, he avoided roles in vacuous teen films by undergoing that apprenticeship on a succession of television roles. Cinematically, he made his first major features in his mid-30s, looking closer to 40. He has often mentioned, self-deprecatingly, his hair, and it is noticeable that in these TV roles, his hair is frequently the most memorable feature of any given scene. Whether it might be described as a mullet, the presence or absence of sideburns, or wayward strands that flop into his eyes, this distracting debate largely disappears when he starts his film career. There was comment at his cropped look on *ER* around the time of his filming from *Dusk Till Dawn*, but this signals a move away from matters of superficial fashion to that of utility and a look that is fit for purpose. In short, he grows up.

In terms of roads not taken, while trying to break into film Clooney auditioned for the role of sadistic Mr. Blonde/Vic Vega in *Reservoir Dogs* (1992), the part eventually going to Michael Madsen. He also tried out five times for the part of J.D. in Ridley Scott's *Thelma and Louise* (1991), a part ultimately taken by Brad Pitt. Before *The Descendants* (2011), Clooney was interested in the role of Jack in Alexander Payne's *Sideways* (2004), but Payne ultimately opted for the lesser-known Thomas Haden Church.

There are also rarely seen hidden gems like the 1996 promotional video, alongside Salma Hayek, for ZZ Top's "She's Just Killing Me" (also directed by Rodriguez), which appears on the soundtrack for *From Dusk Till Dawn*. More than a hastily cut promo for the film, in addition to a few fleeting shots from the film we see Clooney in black gloves on his motorbike approach a house, go in, and play a note or two on a piano, before Hayek appears in a striking red dress and gives him a bite on the neck. There are some strange shots of him removing his jacket (but keeping the gloves on) before he takes a few run-ups to a basketball hoop. There are a couple of signature turns and looks directly at the camera with his head still tilted. He also very briefly appears in a blond wig in Bree Sharp's video for "David Duchovny" (Will Shivers, 1999).

EARLY FILM ROLES

Grizzly II: The Predator (David Sheldon, no release date)

This production broke down due to lack of money (Canon Films went bankrupt), caused in part by an unconvincing bear creature, and remains unreleased. Despite the title, it has only a loose connection with *Grizzly* (William Girdler, 1976)—the main one being Sheldon, who codirected, cowrote, and coproduced the earlier film, and also Joan McCall, Sheldon's wife in real life, who has a part in both films (Allison Corwin and Carol Blevins)—and absolutely none with *Predator* (John McTiernan, 1987).

It did allow Clooney to work with Charlie Sheen and Laura Dern, but like *Return to Horror High*, Clooney's part was small (one of a group of campers) and was a similar early sacrifice to the monster of the title, attacked by a campfire within the film's opening 15 minutes.

Shot in Hungary, the film is a strange hybrid creature (a little like the brief glimpses of the bear) of monster movie and concert film (Predator is the name of the fictitious band whose concert is being recorded). There are glimpses of known faces, like Louise Fletcher (Nurse Ratched from Milos Forman's 1975 *One Flew over the Cuckoo's Nest*), John Rhys-Davis (who found fame via the *Indiana Jones* movies), British electro mime artist Barbie Wilde, all-girl band Toto Coelo, and unauthorized use of Michael Jackson songs on the soundtrack.

Thanks to the existence of video capture sites like YouTube, viewers can watch what exists of the film, including an incomplete climax involving the bear attacking the concert, being killed by an electric cable (reminiscent of Jeannot Szwarc's 1978 *Jaws II*), and being applauded by the fans who think this is part of the concert. It is certainly tempting to think that Clooney's early exit from the narrative was a wise move. The film regularly features in polls of contenders for the worst movie ever. Village People-style dancers, random explosions, and concert sections that look and sound like a camp version of an early Rick Springfield video—all this seems to genuinely excite the crowd who probably have never seen anything quite like this. One of the first bear attacks features a shot of a giant swinging paw, but the 20-foot grizzly of the title appears only in the partly-completed climax (as brief cutaways to a mascot-like creature). For the most part we have point-of-view shots from the monster and plenty of growling effects.

Clooney's cameo in a thriller about organ theft, *The Harvest* (David Marconi, 1993), is largely an opportunity to work with his cousin, Miguel Ferrer. It came back to haunt him as part of his dispute with *Hard Copy* magazine, who dug up this early work and gave it a prominence and significance that it did not deserve. Clooney appears briefly in one scene as a lip-synching transvestite, a role he has not been tempted to reprise. Unlike the protagonists of other contemporary camp cult hits *The Adventures of Priscilla Queen of the Desert* (Stephan Elliott, 1994) or *To Wong Foo, Thanks for Everything! Julie Newmar* (Beeban Kidron, 1995), Clooney's role here is barely a character.

Combat Academy (Neal Israel, 1986)

Percival: Can't we just act like adults for once? Who d'you think you are? Peter Pan?

The film is an overt generic mix with Neal Israel, writer of *Police Academy* (Hugh Wilson, 1984) and director and cowriter of *Bachelor Party* (1984), acting as director here and reflected in the derivative nature of the title and even the theme music. However, rather than the rapid-fire gags and cartoonish characters of its comic predecessors, here there is a strange attempt at naturalism. It is a comedy without gags and a drama without dramatically engaging characters. The two protagonists, Percival (Wallace Langham) and especially supposedly cooler, wise-cracking Max (Keith Gordon), remain annoying nerds throughout.

The opening montage of childish pranks in high school (exploding lockers and setting off sprinklers) sets the tone. Rather than learning any lesson, they essentially transfer this frat-house sensibility to Kirkland Military Academy, where a similar series of deeply annoying pranks follow, bringing them into conflict with General Woods (Robert Culp) and his son, Major Biff Woods (played by Clooney). Clooney's first appearance, leaping from a truck, shows him as looking incredibly young (he was in his mid-20s at time of shooting) and with a voice several octaves higher than he was to have in his subsequent film career. At the time, he seems too self-consciously slim to fill out a military uniform.

Whereas there are many films that deal with the reality of military training (Stanley Kubrick's 1987 *Full Metal Jacket*) or the stresses of life in a military academy (Harold Becker's 1981 *Taps*), or even take a comic route to the whole process like *Stripes* (Ivan Reitman, 1981), *Private Benjamin* (Howard Zieff, 1980), or *Volunteers* (Nicholas Meyer, 1985), *Combat Academy* falls between all these stools. The paintball exercises are ludicrous, and the supposedly climactic battle with a group of visiting Russian cadets and Max's homily about how we should all just get along and have fun is especially painful to watch. A military academy where nothing happens to a cadet who openly flouts all forms of discipline except having to do push-ups is hard to take seriously. The only character who fits the tone of Israel's earlier work, and who therefore seems completely out of place here, is a wacky science teacher, Colonel Long (Richard Moll), who addresses the Russian cadets at the airport with "Will you be my friend? I like your hat."

The appearance of comic actors from much better vehicles (John Ratzenberger, Cliff from *Cheers*, as Percival's father; or Jamie Farr, Klinger in *MASH*, as Colonel Frierick) cannot raise the quality of a very poor script. Whereas the character of Klinger was always trying to get thrown out of the army by his various poses of madness (an idea probably borrowed from Kurt Vonnegut's 1969 *Slaughterhouse Five*), here Max tries to be thrown out of military school by an endless series of pranks. Where the former shows the insanity of real war, the latter just underlines the immaturity of the protagonist himself.

The humorlessness of military life, dictating even how food should be eaten, is juxtaposed with extreme childishness, and the problem is that neither is particularly appealing. When conflict between Biff and Max reaches a climax over Biff's pushing a nonswimmer into the pool, there is a farcical fistfight between the two. Whereas in *O Brother, Where Art Thou?* (2000) Everett's challenge to love-rival Vernon results in a genuinely funny exchange (see chapter 4), here Max engages in some unbelievable acrobatics to avoid being hit, and after delivering a single punch, Biff just walks away without any explanation.

Clooney's character is given a tiny amount of depth with a subplot involving kleptomania, in which he steals watches apparently in an act of rebellion against his father, but we do not really have enough in the script to invest such conflicts with credibility. The last exchange between General Woods and Biff finally touches on some real emotion and shows the potential of Clooney's later work as he shouts "What's my name?" at his father, who always refers to him simply as "Major." However, the resonance of this exchange is undercut by a subsequent scene on the shooting range, where Biff bluntly admits to Max, "I miss my mom." Max reconciles father and son by putting Biff in charge of a winning group in the paintball exercise, but that is only a veneer over paper-thin characterization.

It is a rare example in Clooney's career where he looks credibly young enough to play a son and therefore have an on-screen relationship with a fictional father. Clooney does what he can with the lines and on-screen time that he has here, but unfortunately the film is too concerned with its agenda of pranks to pay much attention to developing credible relationships.

Return of the Killer Tomatoes (John De Bello, 1988)

Matt: It was the bravest thing I've ever seen a vegetable do.

Looking every inch a truly terrible piece of derivative, instantly forget-table awfulness, there is viewing pleasure to be had here, partly deriving from the notion of paracinema, films that offer a low-budget, exploitative reflection of mainstream film. Clooney, first seen with curly hair and a hat as he spins pizzas, is not the lead here but a supporting character, Matt Stevens, best friend of the hero, Chad Finletter (Anthony Starke).

The frame story of a fictional Channel 73 offering their $1 movie estab-lishes the film-within-a-film motif as well as the level of audience expect-ation. From the outset, there is a clear sense of fun, parodying transparent titles like "Big Breasted Girls Go to the Beach and Take Their Tops Off." Instead of seeking to hide its low-budget status, the film being shown flaunts its terrible model work (the picture of the spooky house used for a cutaway is held up later as an example of cost cutting). The derivative elements in the film are played for laughs rather than attempting to create shocks or suspense. The pods of Professor Gangreen (John Astin), like the teleportation pods in *The Fly* (Kurt Neumann, 1958, and David Cronenberg, 1986), alter matter but operate via a jukebox, and one of the early experiments produces Rambo-like soldiers, clones of which then act as guards throughout the film.

The film acts as a further subgenre of B-movie, most obviously in relation to films like *The Blob* (Irvin S. Yeaworth Jr., 1958). Panic about this "Red Menace" (the term is used twice) leads to mass panic, suppres-sion, and indoctrination (summarized in this film as backstory of the Tomato Wars from the original film). The notion of a Prohibition-style ban on tomatoes creates a black market and the need to improvise in cer-tain foodstuffs, such as pizza, now made with ingredients like strawberry jam instead of tomato sauce. Rather than simply absurd, the political parallels work quite well, so that the current generation is portrayed as naïve, having grown up without experience of tomatoes and therefore underestimating the threat they pose.

However, just as the film looks like it is descending into absurd B-movie cliché with unconvincing battles with giant tomatoes, the narrative is interrupted by a caller complaining about the cheap effect of intercutting footage from the first *Tomatoes* film, bringing us back to the world of the frame story. There are also some nice satirical touches like TV coverage of the Americas Cup yacht race seen in the background on a couple of occasions, and routinely intercutting excerpts from old black-and-white pirate movies with footage from races, hyping up anti-British sentiment.

In style, the film seems at times close to the episodic visual gags of *The Naked Gun* (David Zucker, 1988) with little attempt at naturalism. There are signs in the prison pointing to "Really Bad Guys" or "Former White House Aides," and later a yellow triangle sticker can be glimpsed in the truck in which Igor (Steve Lundquist) drives Tara (Karen Mistal) away, reading "Kidnap victim on board." A tight shot of the professor shows him screaming that he can "never get the eyes right" before pulling back to show him playing with a Mr. Potato Head toy. The most obvious break in naturalism occurs when the camera pans from actors to the director and crew off-frame right and an open debate follows about how little money there is left, with a stagehand holding up the painting of the haunted house used at the beginning. Matt, who is sitting being made up, stands and suggests product placement, only to face an objection from a representative from the Screen Actors Guild (with whom Clooney would tangle over *Leatherheads*).

Predating similar sequences in *Wayne's World* (Penelope Spheeris, 1992), we then start to see a series of ridiculously obvious product placements, including a dialogue scene gradually blocked out by a Corn Flakes box and a pause before a chase sequence when Matt and Chad discuss the relative merits of the quad bikes they are sitting on. There is a pan right to the director who tells them they now have enough money to finish the film, and the narrative restarts.

Self-reflexive generic gags pepper the narrative. Igor asks a passerby if there has been a chase scene yet, and when told no, he gets into his truck and drives it into some boxes. The later rescue plan for Tara, sketched out on a blackboard, could have been drawn by a five-year-old, and there is a neat visual gag as the professor spins a globe, shown in close-up, while talking of world domination. When the globe stops, it is still covered in splotches of color rather than specific countries. The climactic scene at the gas chamber is halted by a ringing telephone, not with a clichéd last-minute reprieve but with the host from the frame story giving the answer to the quiz for that day. The dramatic illusion is broken again as Chad addresses the camera directly to challenge whether we had noticed that everything set up in the first reel pays off in the last. Matt disagrees, only for the pizza we see him toss up in his first scene now landing back down on his head. The scene where Chad and Matt are shown putting on gloves and helmets, in a series of cutaway body shots, looks forward to the fetish-dominated opening of *Batman and Robin* (1997), and the final shot anticipates the end of *Michael Clayton* (2007), bluntly encouraging us to stay in our seats by the supposed mother of the director, telling us to sit and watch the work of her son as the credits roll.

Clooney's character is not the stereotypical brave hero. Holding onto Chad's jacket as they break into the professor's house, he is not strong enough to hold a window up; and rather than face his adversary in a climactic battle, he would prefer to stay behind in the lab and experiment with making beautiful women (the final shot suggests that perhaps he returns to this pursuit later). On the beach, he turns and thinks about delivering the final words to camera but then just runs off into the surf with his playmates. We can only guess whether part of Clooney might have been happier pursing this road less traveled. It seems to belong to another part of his life, represented in the film by the fake contest he masterminds to win a date with Rob Lowe. Clooney's image here is of the red-blooded hunk, happy just to be chasing girls.

Return to Horror High (Bill Froehlich, 1987)

Callie: Gonna be a star, Oliver?
Oliver: Gonna try.

The title suggests this is a sequel but it is not. Like *Tomatoes*, this is a low-budget horror film, with an element of self-awareness (reflected in the name of the location, Crippen High School). However, it is much more derivative than *Tomatoes*, and echoes do not seem to be used to parody cinematic precursors but act more like down-market versions of their better known counterparts. It has an unknown killer wearing a mask, long before Ghostface of the *Scream* series (Wes Craven, 1996), but there is little of the wit that makes the latter effective (at times). It uses a fairly standard horror trope, the film-within-a-film, as its narrative premise. But unlike *The Blair Witch Project* (Daniel Myrick and Eduardo

Sánchez, 1999), there is no suspense as to the contents of the film itself; it is merely an excuse for the cast to be predictably picked off, one by one. Musically, there are clear echoes of the sudden loud keyboard chords used by John Carpenter in *Halloween* (1978) and especially the piano in Brian De Palma's *Carrie* (1976), another school-based horror tale, but with little of the shock value evident in the earlier films.

The comment by token love interest Callie (Lori Lethin) about the film-within-the-film, that "there is nothing redeeming about this shit," may ring true; but the character of Oliver (Clooney) reflects a number of tensions in Clooney's own career around this time. Like Oliver, he had to decide whether to opt for the security of a reasonably well-paid career in TV with the possibility of long-term contracts and a regular income but also only limited exposure in global terms and generically predictable small-scale projects. Alternatively, he could risk that security for film projects, which might lead to the dream of a fully fledged film career but might entail a start in low-budget, poor-quality work. Oliver's description of the TV series he accepts ("It's an action-adventure with some humor. Kind of a rip-off of *Miami Vice* and *Moonlighting*.") sounds close to Clooney's roles in *Red Surf* or *Street Hawk*. When the producer intones that "Oliver's gone to a better place," it carries not only the unwitting sense of a literal death but also the metaphorical artistic death, represented by this kind of career. It was a fate Clooney himself only narrowly avoided.

Oliver, having walked out on his contract and dismissing the director's threats to sue, is punished in a sense by being the killer's first victim after only 13 minutes into the film. The film's generic confusion is clear as it attempts to create a frightening setting by having some inexplicable mist appear in a school corridor, before Oliver is grabbed by a hand in a yellow rubber glove and dragged into a nearby room. Oliver's bloodied face appears momentarily on the other side of the door, there is the thud of a blow, and he disappears from the film. This, however, is not the existential nightmare that Wes Craven creates in his school corridors in *Nightmare on Elm Street* (1984) with its oblique angles and sheep appearing for no apparent reason. Here we have some brooding percussion, but basically we are watching characters wander about in a poorly lit school, nothing more.

The film opens and repeatedly cuts back to a scene of carnage outside the school; although without clear fictional markers, this transition takes a while before it becomes clear. Even the exact distinction between past and present, fiction and reality, and naturalistic and the inexplicable are too easily mixed. We cut from a stumbling figure in rubber gloves to an inexplicable hand that grabs victims from a small sand pit (another nod to the end of De Palma's 1976 *Carrie*). The inconsistency and incoherence of this location, which later supposedly provides the opening for a network of tunnels, evokes other Froehlich-produced pictures like *Children of the Corn II* (David Price, 1992).[2]

Both *Tomatoes* and *Horror High* feel like substrata versions of more culturally accepted subgenres. *Tomatoes* works on its own terms, but in terms of *Horror High*, it is hard to know exactly what those subgenres are. It may have been granted some form of release (it has a theatrical trailer after all), but in terms of horror, there is little suspense created; in terms of a parody, it is only derivative rather than intelligent with its allusions; as a comedy, there is no sign that lines are meant to be funny; as an exploitation film, the portrayal of sex and violence is relatively restrained, and the character of Callie openly addresses the director during a scene to argue against the stereotypical role she is playing.

Red Surf (H. Gordon Boos, 1990)

Attila: Who the hell are you, the Godfather?

As Mark Remar, Clooney takes the lead in a film billed as action-adventure but that is closer to domestic drama in places, as he is faced with the needs of a pregnant girlfriend, Rebecca (Dedee Pfeiffer), and a loyal friend, Attila (Doug Savant). The film is a lone example of Clooney's character seen drinking heavily, swearing freely, and smoking drugs, though he is redeemed by an emotional bond with the heroine and particularly by his sacrificial death.

However, the level of transgression is limited. Clooney's character never carries a knife or a gun or perpetrates an act of violence on another. He does however tolerate violence performed around him, as scenes show gang leader Calavera (Rick Najera) living in a strangely decrepit house and throwing unfortunate spies to a pack of dogs. Drug dealing is certainly not to be condoned; but we see Clooney's character not as a hardened criminal, but rather joking around, playing practical jokes, and getting high instead of inflicting pain on others. Riding a Jet Ski at night to pick up his merchandise seems to be as rebellious as Remar gets. Putting a bandana on does not erase the dominant appearance of Clooney here with a goofy grin and a mop of curly hair. When Rebecca wants Remar to give up his current life, it seems more a life of partying than crime.

Whereas *Point Break* (Kathryn Bigelow, 1991) explores the notion of divided loyalties in a similar situation, it also includes credible surfing footage, something very lacking here as we cut from Remar standing on the shore to a clearly professional double out on a big wave. *Point Break*, though hardly a masterpiece, also articulates a sense of a relationship with the ocean, which rivals connections between humans. Remar's strongest connection is with narcotic substances rather than with the surf, friends, or romantic partners. Like his later ability to outrun a powerboat and a machine gun-toting pursuer with a small Jet Ski, narrative plausibility is sacrificed for attempted spectacle. However, maybe any film with Gene Simmons (as the surly Doc) explaining the workings of an AK-47 is not all bad, and certainly Tarantino liked *Red Surf*, which was one reason why he offered Clooney an audition for *Reservoir Dogs*.

Whereas *One Fine Day* (Michael Hoffman, 1996) is clearly a romantic drama, there is a useful contrast here with Clooney acting opposite a different Pfeiffer. This is a personal drama, a challenge to Remar to commit to a relationship and a family rather than the free-wheeling fun that he has with his male friends (echoing some of the conflicts Clooney has had in his own life). The film ends with a revenge attack on Calavera, and Attila adopting the position of hero substitute in going with Rebecca to Portland, an almost folkloric role of a best friend.

The Magic Bubble, aka *Unbecoming Age* (Alfredo Ringel and Deborah Ringel, 1992)

Julia: You remind me of someone.
Mac: Warren? Tom Cruise? Kevin Costner?
Julia: Charles when he was young.

The film is a rare example in Clooney's film career where, as Mac, he looks young enough to play the object of romantic attention for a clearly much older woman. Julia Cole (Diane Salinger) is an unhappy woman in a predictable marriage with unpleasant children who undergoes a miraculous transformation on her 40th birthday due to some mysterious magic bubbles, after which she starts to act in a more youthful and less inhibited fashion.

The motif of a magic role reversal or releasing of one's inner child can be seen in mainstream hits in the 1980s like *Big* (Penny Marshall, 1988), *Weird Science* (John Hughes, 1985), or even *Honey, I Shrunk the Kids* (Joe Johnston, 1989). The difference here is that the narrative is based around a very female sense of midlife crisis and wish fulfillment. There are some frankly embarrassing scenes involving Julia dancing

around the bedroom and hopping pretending to be a rabbit, few characters that rise above predictable cliché (insensitive husband and brattish
kid), and some clunky detail with the boom mike appearing in tennis
scenes and later during a dinner party. However, Julia's articulation of
the wish for age to be just a loose concept has some narrative interest,
particularly in Salinger's Susan Sarandon-style appearance, since it
is this aspect of her that sets her apart from Mac's usual choice of
girlfriends.

Clooney as Mac, despite his dominant presence on marketing material,
features in only five scenes; 27 minutes into the film, Clooney appears in
a supermarket checkout, and clearly finding Julia attractive, he poses as a
bagging boy, taking her groceries to her car as a means to flirt with her.
There is barely a line of dialogue spoken before he inexplicably drives
off in a classic car, clearly not the lowly worker she had taken him for.
The pair meets again by chance in an ice-cream parlor after Julia storms
out after a row with her husband, Charles (John Calvin). Here they sit
and chat for several hours. It is at this point that, perhaps jokingly, Mac
invites her to have an affair. However, Julia's refusal is important.
Clooney's star image is not that of a marriage wrecker. He is a figure of
temptation but one that is resisted. He remains a peripheral figure, whose
good looks and charm (and a mysterious, unexplained source of wealth)
cast him as more of a wish-fulfillment fantasy than a fully rounded character. His third appearance is in the supermarket again where he helps
her to buy beer. His appearance, sporting a baseball cap worn backward,
along with his floppy hair, seems symbolic of youth fantasy. He meets
her later on the street where he does not recognize her, as she has
reverted to her old appearance and habits to please her husband. Their
final meeting, on a hilltop, viewed by Charles from afar, feels almost like
the banishing of a dream. Indeed, after the initial bubble incident, the
magic catalyst is largely forgotten as Julia just acts increasingly as she
wishes.

The norms of marriage are protected as Charles blows the bubbles too
and discovers a sense of lost youth, and the Coles' marriage is reinvigo-
rated rather than abandoned. Charles responds to his son, Junior, now
renamed Willie to give him a greater sense of selfhood, and attends the
final symbolic baseball game as a supportive father. The symbolism is
fairly heavy-handed, like birthday candles that Julia cannot blow out.
More light romance than comedy but lacking the real punch of related
genre pieces like *Bull Durham* (Ron Shelton, 1988) or *Liar Liar* (Tom
Shadyac, 1997), it is a harmless enough piece of drama that is probably
about as revolutionary as its ambition.

ER (various directors, 1995–99)

Rachel: Monica, they are cute, they are doctors (spelling it out in the air for her slow friend), cute doctors, doctors who are cute!

Chandler: All right, what have we learned so far?
—*Friends*, episode 117, "The One with Two Parts, Part Two"

As pediatrician Dr. Doug Ross, Clooney managed to strike critical and commercial gold. It is perhaps easy to forget just how popular the show was, and particularly his appearances on it, in the mid- to late 1990s. His cameo in *Friends* (along with Noah Wyle) as one of two doctors double-dating Rachel (Jennifer Aniston) and Monica (Courtney Cox) reflects his notoriety at the time as well as his comic timing (memorably declaring "God bless the chick pea").

Through *ER*, he became a global phenomenon, the consequences of which still follow him to this day. In a positive sense, he was brought into the homes of millions of people in a role that was sympathetic and caring, rebellious in his dealings with authority but usually with the patients' interests at heart. First seen in the pilot, inebriated on St. Patrick's Day just hours before a working shift, Ross's drinking and womanizing (numbering over 14 sexual conquests across the first three seasons alone, including medical student Harper Tracy) added to the image of a loveable rogue, whose inability to commit to Nurse Carol Hathaway (Julianna Margulies) was the stuff of dreams for network producers hankering after a story line that would keep viewers coming back over repeated seasons. Finding romantic or matrimonial commitment difficult at the same time as apparently having a natural gift in caring for children—these character traits resurface in subsequent film roles. His role required not only learning mountains of medical terms, to be delivered at breakneck speed, as well as performing medical procedures in a credible way, but also regular close-ups of him looking down caringly, often with head tilted in a solicitous manner—an acting pose, which he has had to live down ever since.

With 25 episodes per season, it is not surprising that the dramatic quality of *ER* varies; but in terms of pace, it seems closer to the rhythm of film, avoiding sentimental cliché where possible and giving audiences some credit for filling in gaps by engaging with multiple narrative threads. Unlike other medical dramas, such as *Chicago Hope*, it focused much more precisely on the relationships between medical staff rather than on patients, whose traumas provide an input of narrative energy but who rarely survive, so to speak, more than an episode. Early on, Clooney's aunt, Rosemary, has a small part as a torch singer, Madame X, in "Going Home" (season 1, episode 3 and later in episode 11).

There is more than a touch of naiveté about the extent to which Clooney's character is prepared to bend or break rules on behalf of individual patients or the extent to which he emotionally invests in them, but this makes his role more compelling for audiences. In "Long Day's Journey" (season 1, episode 14), in a single shift he deals with an abused boy, a baby left by a suicide, and a worsening cystic fibrosis victim. In "The Birthday Party" (season 1, episode 17), he punches an abusive father, and in "And Baby Makes Two" (season 2, episode 5), his orders for tests on an HIV-positive boy are overruled by Mark Greene (Anthony Edwards), who as the financial and managerial line manager represents the institutional factors restraining Clooney's character.

There are a few particular stand-out episodes for his character. In "Hell and High Water" (season 2, episode 7), he saves a boy trapped in a drainage tunnel; most of the episode is focused on Doug as action hero, coming to the rescue of a vulnerable child, who like him is given to acts of recklessness. He makes mistakes (effectively killing a patient by mislabeling him in "Blizzard," season 1, episode 10), and his place in the ER is precarious financially, personally, and ethically as he continues to break rules, major and minor, on behalf of his patients. We are drip-fed a distant relationship between Doug and his father, who, it transpires, has many of the same less attractive character traits. However, in "The Healers" (season 2, episode 16) Doug is reminded by his father that he alone bears responsibility for his actions.

Clooney left the series in 1999, midway through season 5, his character unaware that Hathaway is carrying his twins. The pressure to close that narrative circle was so great that amid tremendous secrecy, Clooney filmed a small cameo for the episode "Such Sweet Sorrow" in 2000 where we see Hathaway joining him in Seattle. His character is kept alive by visual devices, like a photo at Carter's leaving party at the end of season 11 or a small reference in season 14 to their children, supposedly now in third grade. In the episode "Old Times" in season 15 in 2009, Clooney reprised his role, with he and Hathaway still married. They become involved in a plotline involving Carter who needs a kidney transplant, although they are unaware of the recipient of the organ. In a nicely understated scenario, the final line is given to Hathaway who talks of the kidney going to "some doctor in Chicago."

CONCLUSION

It is worth noting that the DVD cases for both *The Magic Bubble* and *Red Surf* feature images of Clooney that do not appear in the actual films.

For *The Magic Bubble*, an older Clooney with short hair appears, linked to the crop he had for *From Dusk Till Dawn*, and in *Red Surf*, although acknowledged in small print, the image is crudely doctored (quite literally) so that the smiling face of Dr. Doug Ross is pasted onto the leather jacket of Remar, the surfer drug dealer. You can even see faint traces of Ross's ER green uniform. This reflects how film marketing uses a form of retroactive rewriting of history, and that once a particular image of a star becomes dominant, it is pasted (sometimes literally) over previous work, overwriting or erasing it.

Sunset Beat and *Red Surf* feel almost like twins separated at birth. In both, Clooney plays a role given to lightweight rebellion, signaled by motorbike-riding leather jackets and big Michael Bolton-style hair (visible without the helmet). In both he has a vague backstory of a broken relationship, acts in a way designated as rebellious (by eating with his mouth open or putting his feet up on desks), and lives a lifestyle that constitutes an adolescent male fantasy, surrounded by bikes, guns, and potential action. Both films end with an explosion over water. In *Sunset Beat*, he survives to ride off with his buddies; in *Red Surf* he dies, but in an almost identical shot his partner takes his place and rides off with his girlfriend on a coastal road. Both are formulaic genre narratives, ensemble pieces in which Clooney is one of a group of men and relatively bloodless. In *Sunset Beat*, a kidnap victim has demands tattooed onto his chest rather than pieces being cut off his body. Also here, slightly reminiscent of *Rebel Without a Cause* (Nicholas Ray, 1955), we see Clooney at an observatory in a shoot-out scene; and at the close, framed by the rising sun, as troubled bad boy he scatters his friend's ashes from the balcony at the same location. However, unlike James Dean, it would take another decade before Clooney could credibly exude a sense of loss (see chapter 8).

Clooney's early film work shows him trying out different roles: drug-dealing villain faced with the imminence of young fatherhood (*Red Surf*), a son in conflict with a father (*Combat Academy*), and object of an older woman's fantasy (*The Magic Bubble*). The roles show him toying with rule-breaking, criminal, or immoral acts and evolving from peripheral parts with single names (Mac and Biff) to more central roles with two names (Mark Remar). Loquacious wise-cracking charm, a winning smile, and (by his own admission) good hair—these features are present too. But perhaps more importantly, these early efforts show roads not taken, such as *Red Surf*'s R rating, presumably for the portrayal of drug use, rare in Clooney's film work and an experiment with more violent content in a crime genre. We also see him trying out a range of potential genres—horror, crime, action, family drama—but often with a pervasive light touch. The horror films are more parodies than outright attempts at scaring audiences, the moral dilemma in *The Magic Bubble* carries little dramatic weight, and as a criminal in *Red Surf*, it seems like Clooney's character cannot really bring himself to commit to the brutality required by life as a drug dealer.

In terms of *ER*, Clooney honored a five-year contract at a time when he could have earned more (as coworkers argued to improve their terms) or walked away to concentrate solely on a film career. Long working days and the juggling of schedules were very challenging as he dovetailed *ER* with shooting *Batman and Robin*. However, by sticking with *ER* he showed himself to be a trustworthy, hardworking actor and one who realized that it gave him the chance to improve his craft, work on emotionally intense story lines with a high-quality ensemble cast, and network with directors who would play a part in his subsequent film career, such as Tarantino (like "Motherhood," season 1, episode 24) and Mimi Leder (like "Day One," season 1, episode 2). He brought to his studio work the same kind of joker persona that he would show on film sets, easing tension and making difficult schedules more bearable. Generally speaking, other actors have only positive comments to make about working around him, which would be a real asset when he later worked on more stressful films or took the opportunity to direct himself.

CHAPTER 2

Romantic Hero (What Women Want)

I'm a handsome man, conventionally-proportioned, but with flair. Old tailors love me. They tell me I remind them of men from forty years ago, slim but sturdy, on the small side but broad.

—Ryan Bingham in Walter Kirn's *Up in the Air*[1]

ONE FINE DAY (MICHAEL HOFFMAN, 1996)

Jack: Guess what? I'm not like every other man you know.

One Fine Day follows Jack Taylor (George Clooney) and Melanie Parks (Michelle Pfeiffer) across a supposedly average day in New York, trying to juggle the stresses of demanding jobs, journalist and architect respectively, with the difficulties of looking after Jack's son, Sammy (Alex D. Linz), and Melanie's daughter, Maggie (Mae Whitman).

Conventionally, romantic comedy works by juxtaposing unfamiliar elements, bringing characters together who might not usually meet. The problem here is that the script spends much of its energy in keeping the protagonists apart. The film is an exercise in crosscutting to the point where all we see is frenzied attempts to meet deadlines that have no dramatic weight. The "will they, won't they" is strung out for the length of the entire film, by which time we may feel that the pressure of generic predictability weighs far too heavily.

The fractured nature of the narrative means that the two leads maintain the presence of the other by talking about them to a third party (Jack to his boss and Melanie to her mother). The means by which the pair are kept separated but supposedly in the minds of one another (and the viewer) become increasingly contrived, not just swapping children at points but also (accidentally) mobile phones so that they have to take and pass on messages for one another, literally dipping into the lives of the other for a day. Jack's carrying of the goldfish bowl becomes a physical representation of the burden of looking after children, and although the fish are eaten by a cat later, he cares enough to get some more and take them around to Melanie's flat (although by that stage the fish are a thinly veiled justification for seeing her). In the run-up to their first meeting at the locked door of the school, they are placed increasingly closer to the point where they almost inhabit the same scene as she bobs down to tie Sammy's laces and he walks behind her, out of shot with Maggie. The pair tries to use each other's children as sources of information to see how serious the other person is about potential emotional involvement.

The character of Jack is straining after an Everyman significance, which it struggles to carry off convincingly. When he claims "I'm sick of resent-ful . . . fish, who think that you owe them but who won't trust you for a second to do anything for them," the potential seriousness of his role as a spokesperson for modern man is undermined by his position on a couch, his choice of metaphor, and the fact that we are looking at George Clooney, twice voted the world's sexiest man. Lines of dialogue like Melanie's "That's a totally ex-husband thing to do" countered by Jack's "Well, you would know because that's a totally ex-wife reaction," clearly echo one another but never reach the wit or even fun in language taken by Walter Burns (Cary Grant) and Hildy Johnson (Rosalind Russell) in *His Girl Friday* (Howard Hawks, 1940) or other screwball comedies, which this film dimly resembles.

Initially, Sammy and Maggie echo their parents' animosity, pulling faces at each other in the taxi, but predictably over the course of the film they act as catalysts to bring them together. It is the search for Maggie, who wanders off after a kitten, and Sammy's soccer game that bring into sharp focus Jack's qualities as a parent, particularly in contrast with Melanie's largely absent ex-partner. At the denouement, the seal of approval for the implied future relationship of Jack and Melanie comes from the children coming into the room, where the adults are eventually at ease with one another sufficiently to fall asleep on the couch together.

The sense of a divided screen is present in the vertical wipes used as transition devices and the shot composition, like in the first taxi ride, where the symmetrical two-shot clearly juxtaposes the two in enforced proximity. Actual split-screens are used for phone scenes as the deadline pressure on both Jack and Melanie increases. As they separate after the drop-in center episode, the camera remains on a street scene and the pair walk out of shot, only to return four times, suggesting the difficulty they now have in walking away from each other but also the need they both feel to have the final word.

The choice of basing the narrative around a single day is potentially interesting but simply put, not enough happens, literally or emotionally. This is very much an ordinary day for Melanie and Jack. She has an important presentation; he has a big story—but we get the impression that this is the nature of their professional lives. The film ultimately follows the agenda of the protagonists, i.e., work related rather than personal, and is the less interesting for it. Both are under some pressure (to win over an important client or to source a big corruption story) but the same might equally happen the following day or next week.

The film attempts to undermine cynicism, to emphasize that these two characters really do not know each other and judge their opposite gender harshly. Melanie does not necessarily hate all men, and Jack can find time in his life for children. The problem is that a lot of Melanie's distrust lacks any real basis in the film. We see Jack playing, and happy to do so, with his child, improvising a *Hunchback of Notre Dame* scenario in the scaffolding in his flat. As ex-partner Kristen leaves for her honeymoon near the opening, she gives Jack and Maggie a look of wistful envy, suggesting this is a glimpse of the husband and father that Jack could have been (with her). He is happy to live among boxes, toast marshmallows, and indulge in games of hide and seek. Later, he even retrieves his willful daughter as she hides under a table; without losing his temper and despite an urgent deadline, he patiently negotiates a deal with the child to have a cat.

Maybe he seems happy to accept the fun elements of fatherhood rather than the longer-term aspects of paternal responsibility (Kristen calls him a "good-time father") but he seems far closer to the children in action as well as spirit than Melanie, who finds play difficult and spends her time scolding and giving lists of dos and don'ts. She is the one who loses her temper with Sammy in the design studio (for the boy playing), and although provoked, Jack does not. His version of play, involving an element of risk, seen in Sammy's accident with the marble, allowing the children to eat burgers for breakfast, and carrying Maggie on his shoulders, is portrayed as more healthy than Melanie's control freakishness. Like Sally in *When Harry Met Sally* (Rob Reiner, 1989), Melanie's fussiness is also expressed about food (this time for her child), but here we are not encouraged to laugh at this behavior as endearing, and her precise directions to the taxi driver just seem annoying. By her own admission she is "horrible" to Jack all day, while he responsibly looked after her son and she managed to lose his daughter.

If the sexual politics of romantic comedies such as *Sleepless in Seattle* (Nora Ephron, 1993) or *While You Were Sleeping* (Jon Turteltaub, 1995) overtly raise the question "Where have all the good men gone?" *One Fine Day* attempts to suggest that they are still here, just unrecognized and misjudged. However, the assumption that Jack puts his career before his children is refuted by Jack's action on screen. The film touches lightly on what it is to be a father, suggesting it is more connected to what you do rather than what you are: Melanie laughs at the drop-in puppet show until she sees it is created by Jack. However, if the film is seriously trying to exact a promise from Melanie as typical of hard-nosed women that "I can't do everything on my own," it seems to be quite strained as if Jack is desperately needing a form of vindication, i.e., that men still have a role in society, even if no one is quite sure what that is.

At the climactic press conference, as we have learned so little of Jack's corruption story, it does not seem to matter to the viewer whether he succeeds in proving his point or not. The key witness he has been searching for suddenly appears in a taxi and virtually throws her story at him. The stakes are purely personal in his meeting Melanie at an agreed point in place and time. It is his demonstration of his credentials as a reliable father that matters here. In *Notting Hill* (Roger Michell, 1999), a climactic press conference actually features one of the two protagonists, Anna Scott (Julia Roberts), lending the event a sense of genuine emotional jeopardy, which seems lacking here. Melanie's outburst in defense of Jack, "at least he's honest," seems more motivated to delay the press conference than to express a moment of realization of Jack's worth.

In the hectic nature of the narrative, particularly in the number of scenes that show the pair walking through crowded New York streets, it is tempting to see the film as actually dramatizing its very opposite: that here we have two adults for whom children are primarily an encumbrance to be dragged around and palmed off on any available child care. The guilt of using inadequate child care, particularly with reference to the drop-in center, eats away at Melanie. However, she is still someone who is in a position to buy a solution to most of her problems, from taxi rides to last-minute alterations to her broken building model. Ultimately, the film puts forward the fairly conservative notion, that bringing up children with two parents is better than one, but more for the prosaic factor of time sharing than any suggestion of a broader experience of gender and sexuality, and that a modern definition of parental paradise is a half-decent babysitter.

The film cemented Clooney's status as a romantic lead (his name, along with Pfeiffer's is enough to open this picture) but it also developed his on-screen persona, drawing on the child-friendly associations of Doug Ross from *ER*. He is likeable and charming, while also a little childish and shy of long-term adult commitment (with a backstory of a failed relationship). Ironically, a central problem for Clooney in any romantic narrative is that he looks like George Clooney. The idea that someone who looks like him would have serious difficulty attracting female attention stretches audience credibility and sympathy. Even here, his face is known, plastered on adverts for his column on buses, and certainly Melanie's mother is very susceptible to his charm. The central premise of the film is implicit in the slogan accompanying his picture ("You don't know Jack"). Melanie is forced to accept this, while Jack already sees that she is not as strong and independent as she likes to appear. Most romantic comedies work on the basis of having misconceptions to undermine, but here he seems to read her quite accurately from the outset.

As an exposé of modern parenthood, it does not take us much beyond cliché, including the parental nightmare of losing a child (although here it is not Melanie's own). She is more distraught at the prospect of being exposed as an irresponsible parent in the eyes of Jack. The breakdown of the previous relationships of the protagonists seems vindicated: Sammy's father appears at the soccer game only in order to let the child down about spending time with him, and Kristen's initial appearance apparently dumping Maggie on Jack for the duration of her honeymoon does seem inconsiderate.

The puddle scene, signaled as a supposed emotional climax by the swelling score, is mawkish in the extreme, and Van Morrison's following "Have I Told You Lately" (1989) bleeds over shots of Jack sheltering Sammy from the rain, demonstrating his paternal protectiveness with Melanie lost in thought at a window of her apartment. The notion of dreaming of the object of your affection (represented by the music) and his or her sudden appearance on the doorstep all seems quite clichéd and designed more for narrative closure than emotional credibility.

Even in the final scene further obstacles are contrived, delaying further their eventual but chaste consummation. Their first kiss is interrupted by Jack's wisecracks about her dropping a bomb in his mouth like in *Jaws*; then the children need to be removed from the scene with the bribe of a video (Victor Fleming's 1939 *The Wizard of Oz* with its central mantra, "There's no place like home"); then Melanie goes to freshen up; and lastly by the time she returns, Jack has fallen asleep. It feels more like a coy squeamishness in dealing with the sexual stage of the relationship, rather than the perpetuation of a romantic atmosphere. The action of the camera pulling back and out of the building, craning up past other apartments might suggest the same scenario is being played out in other homes, but rather than the sense of typicality, there is also the feeling that this particular narrative has gone as far as it can credibly go. To introduce a sexual element here would take the plot in more serious and difficult territory (with certification, at least) and the film shies away from this.

As a romantic comedy, both elements are actually fairly scarce, the latter in particular. The funniest line in the whole film is probably Melanie's "If you don't want your balls juggled, don't throw them in my face," but this feels more like an overwrought metaphor than knowing innuendo. The situation comedy of the pair improvising some superhero costumes has Jack's nice line, as he asks in awe "Where d'you get a bag like that?" but again this operates largely at the level of stereotype about the contents of women's handbags. Jack's use of deliberately provocative language on the phone in the taxi while sitting next to Melanie has some wit (he is speaking to his editor and yet asks "Are you wearing panties?") as does his later warning to Sammy to "put the gun down," but this does not really develop far beyond light banter. It seems more indicative of a light and easy charm that Jack regularly indulges in and, judging from the reaction of Melanie's mother, usually seems to work. The beauty parlor scene is interesting for its inclusion of a bullish receptionist who is openly oblivious to his superficial charms. When Jack asks for details of clients, she bluntly tells him that she has five sons and "when they make eyes at me like that, I make them a pot roast." When presented with someone impervious to his charm, Jack is rendered fairly powerless (although with some luck, as the woman is called away, he gets to see the names on the register anyway). Melanie suspects he "can make women smile," but this is more a cause of suspicion than engagement for her.

Like the scene in *The Full Monty* (Peter Cattaneo, 1997) in which a garden gnome is waved up at a window during an interview, Melanie struggles to concentrate during a meeting as Jack fools around outside with the children. Play is foolish and distracting but ultimately that is the point. The problem is that in the film, if he represents fun and she personifies responsibility, he is always going to be more dramatically engaging.

INTOLERABLE CRUELTY (THE COEN BROTHERS, 2003)

Miles: So, you propose that in spite of demonstrable infidelity on your part, your unoffending wife should be tossed out on her ear?

Rex: Well . . . (brightening) Is that possible?

Miles: It's a challenge.

Clooney's second collaboration with the Coen brothers sees him move toward the screwball comedy, in particular the tension between marriage and capital, money and love. As Andrew Sarris defined the screwball comedy, here we have "a sex comedy without the sex."[2] The cliché of a character discovering an adulterous coupling in a house would usually climax with a sex scene but we are denied this. Handheld camerawork takes us into the house but, sharing the point of view of Donovan Donaly (Geoffrey Rush), we only glimpse a fleeting figure, a rumpled bed, and an apparently innocent spouse with an implausible explanation. Manic visual gags predominate with Donaly firing his gun blindly at his departing wife speeding away in his car and then trying to take pictures of his wounded backside, having been symbolically stabbed with his trident-like Daytime Television Lifetime Achievement Award. The most we see between Miles (George Clooney) and Marilyn (Catherine Zeta-Jones) is a chaste kiss and plenty of flirting in the elevator, at dinner, and at legal meetings in front of lawyers. Deviant sex lives are described verbally in court, Rex's eccentric indiscretions are interrupted by Petch (the eccentrically named Cedric the Entertainer) bursting in with a camera (and later by a heart attack), and Miles's attempt at becoming tactile in the elevator is prevented by Marilyn's poodle biting his hand.

However, although there are surface features of the screwball, we have little of its emotional heart. There is certainly wit and banter (in place of the sex) effectively written with lots of memorable lines by the Coens. The first meeting with Marilyn features rapid, playful sparring, not between flirting couples but between their lawyers, Miles and Freddy (Richard Jenkins). Marilyn might look the part of a smart but undervalued individual, determined to prove her worth in a male world. However, the way that Marilyn plans to gain independence is not through her own intellect and ability but through her beauty and how it can ensnare men into marriage. She does not seem to crave respect for her own achievements, just the empty material benefits of a life lazing by a pool, typified by her friend, Sarah (Julia Duffy).

In terms of screwball types, there is a rich woman who attracts an emasculated hero, the latter part played particularly effectively by Clooney, accurately described by Freddy later as "a buffoon, too successful, bored, complacent and on [his] way down." The fixation with his teeth provides a neat counterpoint to Clooney's previous part in a Coen brothers' movie, Everett in O Brother, with his obsession with Dapper Dan hair pomade. He is first seen here as a body part, via an ultraviolet close-up on his teeth—as he waits for Marilyn at dinner, he checks out his reflection in the back of a spoon, his face ludicrously distorted. He declares "Maybe I'm reckless," but that is the very last thing he is. In court, he struts up to Marilyn in the witness stand and gives her a lingering stare, before executing a ludicrously dramatic and calculated turn at her claim that she loved Rex (Edward Herrmann) at first sight.

Costume designer Mary Zophres put Clooney in exactly the same cut of suit as worn by Cary Grant in *Indiscreet* (Stanley Donen, 1958). While this is effective at first, over time Miles is not an easy character to relate to. The idea that an individual who looks like George Clooney would be paranoid about his appearance might be possible, but audiences might feel it is a tad self-indulgent. Massey's performance in his own office, striking a pose even before speaking, is a practice for the preening and grandstanding of the courtroom (essentially just another form of theater). It is hard to know at what point this is just a professional act and at what point there really is any substance to his character. Even in the marriage ceremony between Miles and Marilyn, the listing of Miles's company after his name makes this feel more like a business merger than an emotional attachment. The final section of the film with Miles's resolution to hire (and then cancel) the services of an unlikely assassin shifts the tone into the absurd. Miles's and Wrigley's exaggerated gait through Marilyn's house, and particularly their backing into each other and spraying each other in the face, feels more akin to the slapstick of *Scooby-Doo*.

The figure of the senior partner, Herb Myerson (Tom Aldredge), who invites Miles into the inner sanctum of his office where he is surrounded by medical machines, is a physical manifestation of mortal transience, signaled by the choral singing, which Miles seeks to deny. The reality, that this is the best future he can aspire to, visibly shakes him but only temporarily. Although he later has a nightmare in which Herb's face is translated into a vampiric figure via lightning flash-cuts, there is no moment of realization at the inequalities of the law. Clearly we are a long way from social realism, but the idea that a top law firm would ever employ the services of a cartoonish figure like Wheezy Jo (Irwin Keyes) rather than the cold killers of *Michael Clayton* seems unbelievable, even in the context of a black comedy.

Wrigley (Paul Adelstein) represents Miles's less charismatic double, what Miles might be without his good looks and charm. Wrigley is a company man, musing "Who needs a home when you've got a colostomy bag?" Wrigley is the norm, not articulate enough to speak in open court, against which Miles measures himself, assuming there is a great distance between them when they are really two sides of the same coin. Wrigley's nerdish recitation of company policy ("Only love is in mind when the Massey is signed"), or his opening advice that Miles is just experiencing a midlife crisis and should get a car, may be uninspired but this is only a less visually appealing version of Miles's own nature. Wrigley's excessive outpouring of emotion at Marilyn's wedding may embarrass Miles but it is at least genuine—the kind of feeling that Miles cannot find in his own life. Wrigley also provides the function of a side-kick, but this really develops quite late on in the film, the two sharing a flat after the collapse of Miles's marriage.

Marilyn is extremely hard to like or indeed really to know. She betrays everyone, so why she should be trusted at the end seems unclear, and unlike most screwball comedies, there is little sense that she really learns anything. By the close, she appears just as calculating as ever. She has already conned Miles into marriage once, and apparently little changes late in the plot to suggest a rapid conversion from this position (perhaps indeed a hardening of resolve would be more credible since he pays some-one to kill her). Like the bombers in *Fail Safe* (see chapter 7), the fact that he subsequently tried to call the plan off does not deny the motive behind the plan in the first place. The role played by Zeta-Jones here seems strongly reminiscent of her performance in *Splitting Heirs* (Robert Young, 1993), where she exudes glacial charm, cynically marries for money, and spends her time lounging by a pool. She stands next to Miles in silence in the elevator, not because they are inhibited but because they really have nothing to say to each other.

More problematically, she looks the part but there is little on-screen chemistry between the pair. When Miles grabs her away from Howard (Billy Bob Thornton) for a second and kisses her, she seems to be trans-ported into a state of ecstasy one moment and then coolly walks off the next. Later, after dinner, they both realize that having achieved their main goals, their lives remain empty and neither feels hungry. Her coquettishness never really thaws (except supposedly right at the end as they kiss across the table that first separated them). She declares that divorce is a "passport to wealth, independence, and freedom," but we see her having little idea of what to do with this freedom or that either of her husbands oppressed her particularly. She leaves Miles, coldly tell-ing him that he will "always be my favorite husband," but then she seems sad and almost tearful on the plane. In terms of character development, we have little sense other than the expectations of genre and the need for some form of narrative closure as to why there is a sudden change of heart on her part. Miles tells us (twice) that he finds her "fascinating" (once even with something akin to a raffish growl), but this is asserted rather than shown dramatically or explained.

The number of quotable lines, perhaps, suggests a script that is too diffuse to be convincing (with a long history, the Coens picking up a story from Robert Ramsey and Matthew Stone) and that might have felt cutting edge a decade or so ago, but debates about prenuptial contracts (or prenups as they are termed in the film) feel dated. Often the best lines come from minor characters, such as the woman testifying against her husband on the grounds that he used the vacuum cleaner for a sex toy, thereby depriving her of a cleaner for a considerable time, or about matters in passing, such as Miles's sarcastic order for a "ham sandwich on stale rye bread, lots of mayo, go easy on the ham," which is taken down without reaction from the waitress. However, the exaggerated dialogue (such as Miles's climactic summing up of the Baron as "the silly man"), visual gags (like the magazine *Living without Intestines* that he reads while waiting to see Myerson), or farcical actions like his tennis practice, barely moving his racket as the machine fires balls right at him, all seem almost placed to be used as trailer material.

Rather than exploring any complex notion of motivation, Miles's resolution to "find her Norgay" (the individual who helped her to achieve greatness) only leads to the camp comedy of Baron von Espy (Jonathan Hadary) and some cheap anti-French jokes. Miles's advice to Wrigley in the pursuit of wisdom, which seems echoed in the script more widely, is to "start with the people with funny names." Ellen Cheshire and John Ashbrook make much of what they see as the rampant homophobia in the film, and certainly there are a large number of thinly veiled references to same-sex relationships.[3] However, this does not really coalesce into anything approaching a coherent ideology but is closer to the anally fixated comic sensibility of a Richard Pryor or Eddie Murphy stand-up routine. Where the comic elements of *O Brother* resonate with depth, *Intolerable Cruelty* seems happy to operate at a much more blunt level, in terms of its use of stereotypical characters and sexualized dialogue (such as Miles declaring "Darling, you're exposed" after Marilyn rips up the prenup).

Miles's supposed great change is signaled by departing from his prepared speech and then symbolically ripping it up, but even this is taken as a stunt leading to applause, which we clearly see Miles enjoying. He may declare that he is "naked, vulnerable, and in love," but he does not seem capable of real depth of feeling, only stating "Love is good" in a self-conscious echo of Gordon Gekko's "Greed is good" from *Wall Street* (Oliver Stone, 1987). His resolution to be a better man is undercut by his comic inability to describe precisely where he might do good works (practicing in "East Los Angeles or one of those other . . . "), finishing with a dismissive wave. This is not a portrayal of genuine emotion but a parody of it, with a sentimental piano score, the audience rising to its feet through which Miles passes to increasing adulation, and eventually Wrigley (his alter ego) declaring in tears, "I love you, man."

Certain elements of screwball are certainly present: an emasculated hero (in Clooney's absurd running style in racing to the elevator to talk to her), a sexually aggressive female seeking a closer form of equality in the battle of the sexes, and some snappy banter. However, there are several missing elements, which hamstring the emotional power of the narrative. Classic screwball heroines are defined in relation to their work, or at least want recognition in relation to it. Marilyn's relation to work is to seek to avoid it altogether by freeloading from rich husbands. In this, she is a reflection of changing social values, but it is questionable what proportion of the female audience would really want to aspire to her vacuous lifestyle here. Also conventionally, there is an element of reversal in that hero and heroine learn something from each other. It could be argued that Miles learns the value of true love over cynicism, but Marilyn seems unworthy of his adulation, weakening his status further, and as her motivation remains questionable right up to the end, what she might learn is open to question. Unlike in O *Brother*, where the generosity of spirit is emphasized, here it is emotional mean-spiritedness that prevails. By choosing to close on the TV show, which may be intended as a parody but probably exists somewhere, it is Petch's slogan and the notion of marriage as material for cheap television that endures.

LEATHERHEADS (GEORGE CLOONEY, 2008)

For Clooney's second directing experience, he gathered around him personnel with whom he had worked before, most particularly Thomas Sigel as cinematographer, Grant Heslov as producer (as well as playing minor part, Saul Keller), and Stephen Mirrione as editor. Clooney plays Jimmy "Dodge" Connelly, based very loosely on the career of Johnny "Blood" McNally of the Green Bay Packers, and the situation of Carter Rutherford (John Krasinski) is reminiscent of George Halas, coach of the Chicago Bears and his signing of halfback Harold "Red" Grange from the University of Illinois. Critical reaction to *Leatherheads* is typically lukewarm, which in retrospect is a little unfair. If there are weaknesses in the film, they lie in its underlying structure rather than its execution.

Like the preceding films in this chapter, *Leatherheads* is related to screwball comedy, particularly the way it displaces explicit portrayal of sexual matters into highly charged dialogue, as seen in the verbal sparring between Lexie Littleton (Renée Zellweger) and Dodge, in their first meeting in the hotel foyer and later in the train cabin, mistakenly taken by them both. The film provides the opportunity for Clooney to indulge in his passions for motorbikes and sports and plays to his strengths in terms of comic timing and romantic entanglements requiring charm from the hero. His age, perhaps a growing impediment to gaining leading roles, becomes an asset in screwball, where the quintessential screwball actors, like Clarke Gable, were at least a decade older than the average leading man today.

There are some similarities with *A League of Their Own* (Penny Marshall, 1992) in the portrayal of a fledgling professional sport in the early part of the twentieth century. There is a social element as we see the itinerant and fragile nature of the team, which travels to games only for them to be canceled when teams go into liquidation. Teams are rapidly built and dissolved, which is particularly hard on individuals who, according to Dodge, "are not exactly the cream of America's workforce." A montage of working locations (a factory, a mine, and a field) stands for the lives that the team have escaped from and to which they must return if Dodge cannot conjure up a deal to make professional football turn a profit.

Part of the empathy that we might feel for Dodge is that with hindsight we know that he is right, whatever the wisdom prevailing at the time. C. C. Frazier (Jonathan Pryce, based on the real C. C. Pyle), symptomatic of the evolution of a new species, the sports agent, is seen as exploitative (taking a 25% cut from Dodge), unprincipled (threatening the *Chicago Tribune* with legal action, using a false witness), and opportunistic (he leaves the narrative, declaring "There's always baseball," before being seen framed among the corrupt New York Yankees team in the closing snapshots). A deleted scene would have shown C.C., like brutal boss Bob Brown in *A Perfect Storm* (Wolfgang Peterson, 2000), shrewdly but callously dividing up the take, leaving the individual players with very little to show for their work (see chapter 3). Corporate sponsorship is also waking up to the commercial opportunities in sport with Carter's face even appearing on the huge clock, next to the sports field.

In terms of staging sporting action, Clooney's camera often gives us a tight shot on the ball carrier, increasing the sense of speed and avoiding the need to choreograph complicated plays (as well as suggesting the chaos of the opening game in a field). Individual plays and final scores are important but there is little sense of a play-by-play drama. Commentators are present but we hear their words only in the final game with Chicago. Shots of Carter tend to be reverse tracking shots as he runs at the camera and then forward tracking shots like a defender who cannot catch him (similar patterns are used in *Forrest Gump*, Robert Zemeckis, 1994). Shots of Clooney in particular tend to be tight so as not to emphasize his relatively diminutive size. The idea that his character could earn a living in his mid-40s in a fairly brutal sport, without obvious size or speed, is something the film does not dwell on, but the fact that Clooney had to cast extras who would not dwarf him, and order extras not to hit the director during plays, does tend to suggest a slight awkwardness here.

A Changing World

There is a strong parallel here between the increasing regulation of football with restrictions on those aspects of life that represent fun (players smoking while warning up or Dodge drinking and fighting until dawn the day of a big game, for example). Alcohol is ubiquitous, from Dodge taking a swig from a hip flask at the end of the game to Lexie getting drunk alone at the bar in a speakeasy to the whole notion of Prohibition (the ineffectiveness of which is stressed as Dodge greets the mayor). Dodge on his classic bike (a 1918 Indian replica custom-built for Clooney by specialist Eddie Paul), with goggles but no helmet, personifying the pleasure of biking, feels like a 1920s version of *Easy Rider* (Dennis Hopper, 1969) and also anticipates similar shots of friend Brad Pitt in *The Curious Case of Benjamin Button* (David Fincher, 2009). This is not allowed to be too inflated, however, as the following shot shows Dodge pumping up a flat tire as a car passes him. The exterior shots have a crisp autumnal brightness, creating a fondly nostalgic view of an era on the verge of professionalism and the loss of something in the process.

Along with provision of better equipment, Carter summarizes the ethos of the new era, "All that matters is that we win," reflected in the booing of the big crowd at the climactic game.

The final game is played cleanly but is described as a "muddy snoozefest" by the commentator. The challenge here is to make a game that is described as "boring" not seem so for viewers of the film, a challenge it does not entirely meet. The two teams, indistinguishable in the mud, are not playing for a title, a trophy, or money, and there is no sense that the heroes are really pitted against one another (although this is part of the hype around the game). There is little sense of a spectacle here (possibly bearing out C.C.'s earlier skepticism), and Dodge's gag of swapping sides is funny in its absurdity but it is fairly unbelievable that no one in the crowd, aside from Lexie, would notice.

The ragtime-style piano of Randy Newman (who appears briefly himself as the pianist in the bar fight) sets the mood and tone, but there is perhaps a greater focus on evoking a bygone era (two-piece phones, the *Ladies Home Journal*, custom-made motorbikes, advertising boards) than the dramatic structure of the narrative. The scene where the Bulldogs are sent off on tour allows shots of old cars to race alongside a steam train (which we see later several times passing through the frame obliquely) despite the fact that the situation scarcely merits such grand gestures. A tracking shot (possibly from a truck or another bike) shows us Dodge riding around looking for his team, motivating views of the car lot and stadium at Ennis Park. The sequence of Lexie and Carter in the waiting room frames them nicely against a window so we can admire the train in the background, but it seems designed to draw attention to art and production design, rather than convey anything about the characters. Similarly, it seems odd that Carter and Dodge are shown walking past the back of the hotel and onto a piece of conveniently well-lit railway line to settle their dispute in a fistfight. Exactly what they are fighting over is also unclear: Carter insults Lexie but he is the one who challenges Dodge.

The visual style of the film reflects the times in which it is set, 1925, just prior to talkies, with a blend of conventional shot/reverse-shot exchanges and other features more evocative of the silent era and films like *Brown of Harvard* (Jack Conway, 1926) and Harold Lloyd playing football in *The Freshman* (Fred C. Newmeyer, 1925). The long shots of the stadium, the men running, a hero raised aloft as a hero, huge crowds, and the sepia tinting feel oddly reminiscent of Fritz Lang's *Metropolis* (1927) in matters of scale and chronology, even if not its aspect as a political parable. Clooney's acting in the football scenes is exaggerated in the style of silent-era performance, cartoonishly girding his loins before running at a defender, and a cut as he runs straight into the camera before we cut to the defender, who picks him up with his legs still flailing. He is framed in close-up, pinned in a headlock as other players dive on top. In a later game, he is seen tackled from behind, signaled by a melodramatic throwing up of his arms as he runs at the camera. The new giant player they sign from high school predictably responds to being told to hit anyone who comes near the ball carrier by punching two opposition players and then the referee. In context, such acting style is appropriate and sometimes effective. The problem comes in dialogue-based scenes, where such exaggeration seems melodramatic to contemporary audiences.

The chase through the back of the speakeasy draws explicitly on silent-era traditions as we have the slapstick of slamming a door in the face of chasing Keystone cop-style policemen and then a change of identity by the jump cut to the theft of their uniform. The bird's-eye-view down the stairwell juxtaposed with a piano-led score leads into the visual gag of appearing at an open window just above a man contemplating suicide. We have the low-angle point of view of the crowd below, looking up as Dodge persuades Lexie to jump, and creates a diversion with a "Hey look, there's two more" as their pursuers reach the open window. The later shot of them peeking out from behind an on-street display makes them look as if they are actually inside a shop window, and the following kiss, the only one we see in the whole film, is framed almost in silhouette, back-lit by this same display.

Screwball

Clooney opts to set his narrative in the past but the audience is still viewing it in the present and are not necessarily trained in reading a genre, which is rarely attempted, deceptively complex, and requires wit and intelligence in both writing and performance. The first meeting of Lexie and Dodge is highly choreographed. He first spies her in a raised seating area some distance away but is immediately struck by her appearance, possibly by the vibrant red dress she is wearing. The emphasis is very much on his reaction to her, who as far as we can tell remains oblivious to him at this stage, as we zoom in to his rapt face, giving a slight tilt of the head, a bit like some kind of strange courtship dance between birds. We shift between high angles of him and low angles of her as he moves around a pillar to get a clearer view and his curiosity is sufficient to motivate a closer shot. Dodge goes up the stairs, past the man (Leonard) who is being humiliated by Lexie, and sits across from her, picking up a magazine, which he then tries to hide behind. Lexie and Dodge appear to indulge in that staple of screwball, flirtatious banter but with a twenty-first-century slant as Dodge states that he is in love with Leonard and feigns injury at how cruelly she cast him aside. This breaks Lexie's reserve and she laughs despite herself, admitting "You're a lot of fun"; but even though both are sitting forward and have shaken hands and exchanged formal introductions and friendly smiles, he pushes her sense of propriety too far in asking her out. She chides him—"Just because we had a laugh, doesn't mean you know me"—but although apologizing, he repeats his assertion that he does know her true nature.

However, there is little evidence that this is actually true. Her excuse (that she is waiting for her boyfriend) is actually not true; she is waiting for an interview with Carter. He takes her for a tease ("the kind of cocktail that comes on like sugar but gives you a kick in the head") but actually the only one she teases is him. She does not appear to flirt with

Carter to get her story; instead she takes her time befriending him but makes no promises of anything in return. A deleted scene, in which Dodge disagrees with Carter that C.C. will not be able to seduce a stranger on the train, shows that his confidence in his knowledge of women is misplaced as he loses the bet. Although screwball conventions dictate that insults should be read as displaced compliments, her comment that being "the slickest operator in Duluth is kinda like being the world's tallest midget" has some edge to it.

The farcical situation comedy of Lexie and Dodge winding up in the same cabin is the kind of more intimate experience in which, as in typical screwball, potential lovers are thrown together by circumstances and is an excuse for further high-speed banter, largely picking up the conversation from the foyer, possibly signaling a thawing of the frostiness between them. This is an explicit allusion to Frank Capra's *It Happened One Night* (1934) where hero and heroine (Clark Gable and Claudette Colbert) are separated only by a blanket over a rope. The thin borderline here is represented by the curtains on their individual sleeping berths, producing a version of a split-screen effect as both Lexie and Dodge can be framed within the same shot. Dodge is the more powerful position here, having established his territory, and can look down on her discomfort with some pleasure. Her "You wanna play dirty?" is batted away with "Maybe later. I'm a little tired right now."

In general, some of the banter feels like slightly warmed-over Oscar Wilde (Leonard's "I didn't come over here to be insulted" is answered by Lexie's "Where do you usually go?"), and Dodge's admission "Well, you got me on that one" (in relation to being too old for Lexie) is delivered out of the side of Clooney's mouth, almost like a Groucho Marx impression.

The banter is picked up in the speakeasy, where Zellweger's persona is reminiscent of Bridget Jones. Her tipsy dismissal of his date, dubbed "Miss Nipplewidth," initiates some witty exchanges about the girl's age and IQ (reckoned to be 21 in both cases) and her suitability for Congress. His resorting to cliché (opining "You're only as young as the woman you feel") is undercut by her more sarcastic "How quiet it must be at the Algonquin with you here in Duluth." What appears to make the difference here is his persistence, his winning smile, and the offer of their first physical contact through the socially acceptable means of dance. The song being played (Ledisi Young's version of "The Man I Love") suggests that Lexie has been thinking about him but we have little corroboration of this. She feels comfortable enough with him to tell him about Carter's confession, but screwball contrives to disrupt intimacy, and the dissolve, showing them moving closer, is broken up by the police raid. Similarly, her answer to Dodge's implied proposal is interrupted in an extremely contrived fashion by a phone call from Carter.

The characterization of Lexie has several of the surface features of a screwball heroine but little of its depth. Shown first in close-up as elevator doors open, in a red hat with a prominent feather, she is positioned as stylish and unconventional; but on being called into her editor's office, the sassiness that she shows, perching uninvited on the desk opposite an unknown guest (a senior officer in uniform), seems cheeky to the point of impertinence. That said, she is bored with predictable stories featuring handsome heroes, whether soldiers or football stars. As an intelligent journalist, she is operating in a predominantly male environment, but despite realizing that a marriage proposal from Dodge represents the admission that she "can't make it in a big man's world," she appears to accept this.

There is a slight reversal of conventional gender roles, in Dodge's admission of feelings for her ("I'm nuts about you") and her assertiveness in interrupting his speech by initiating a kiss. Her presence in the press box causes comment, but in the climactic game it is her tendency to swear that seems to provoke more reaction in a traditionally all-male preserve. At the end, she is the one who picks him up on a bike but the inversion seems only half-hearted. The position of pillion seems unnatural for him, as he flips off when the bike moves away, she needs his help to restart the bike, and we dissolve to a shot of Dodge steering.

There is a certain level of sexual coyness (Carter walks Lexie to her cabin and later Dodge walks her back to the hotel) and we are told (twice) that Lexie has great legs (a fact she herself declares) but neither see them nor see their effects on anyone else. The appearance of Dodge with red lipstick prominently on his face is the kind of cross-dressing element impossible in black-and-white, but it is really just a comedic ploy, undercutting his protestations of innocence. However, again, matters of a more intimate nature are interrupted, again by physical comedy as Carter puts his arm too close to a nearby candle and his sleeve catches fire (visible as Carter raises his flaming arm into the frame).

Despite Lexie's protestations to the contrary, she is used as the bait in a honey trap to make Carter open up and tell the truth about the war. Carter declares to Dodge that he will confess everything, but Dodge advises him against this, noting "We like our heroes." While a fair point about American society's thirst for positive role models, this rather ignores what it means for Lexie, supposedly the love of Dodge's life, as it condemns her to remain a discredited journalist. In a sense then, Dodge wins Lexie by default. The banter in their first meeting ends with Lexie assuring him "I'll live" to which he adds "Alone." The specter of spinsterhood for a 31-year-old unmarried woman may play a part in her decision by the end to allow Dodge to be a little more familiar.

Overheard dialogue is a further part of screwball, but apart from the humor of Dodge walking out of shot and then popping back, his reaction to hearing Lexie's plan is a little strange. He confesses while they are in the cabin that he knows what he she is up to but does not warn Carter, a fellow sportsman, apparently a reasonably decent fellow and hardly deserving of Lexie's scheming. Dodge's silence is a character action (or inaction) based on the functional needs of structure rather than arising credibly from a character's motivation.

Carter is likeable enough but remains more of a handsome, privileged type than an individual. Without more edge to his character (he recounts his war story with a sense of bemusement) or arrogance (perhaps justifiably so given his talent), it is hard to have any strong feelings as a viewer about him, which makes his rivalry with Dodge problematic. We are told from early on, rather than shown, that Carter's reputation is built on a lie, undermining the possibility of a dramatic revelation. He confesses his wartime tale but Lexie rewards him only by betraying his trust and printing the story (although to have refused would have cost her job and also appear to cave in to pressure from the unscrupulous C.C.). Carter seems closer in age to Lexie, and as a future Harvard law graduate, socially and financially is clearly a much better prospect. When Dodge looks across at Carter and Lexie chatting easily at a nearby table as he negotiates with C.C. or looks back at the pair as they sit behind him on the train, there is interest on Dodge's part but also an implicit recognition that this match seems entirely natural. A deleted scene in the dining car would have shown Carter describing his rather bloodless regime and all the things he cannot eat and declaring at the end that he is "no fun at all," but we feel its loss in giving us more direction about his role in the film. He does not create the lie about his wartime record (even if he bears some responsibility for perpetuating it). He does not, as Dodge does, try to push his interest in Lexie beyond what she will accept, walking her to her cabin door like a perfect gentleman. The one thing Carter cannot do is knock insults back and forth. Another line deleted from the dining car scene is Lexie's answer to Dodge's question of what C.C. has that he does not. Slowly she lists "money, power, influence" but then after a pause continues, "taste, charisma . . . intellect," prompting a spluttering Carter to admit, thumping the table, "You are a loaded pistol." More cynically, Dodge observes that she is more "like a fox in a henhouse."

Clooney might look like a Clark Gable figure (although short of six feet) but he does not have the character of a screwball male. His social and sporting position is eroded (the curfew is arranged on the train as he sleeps, and his calls for a night on the town leave him looking lost and alone, the only one not following the fashion for an ostentatious fur coat) but this is not enough to place him in the role of emasculated hero. In the chase sequence he acts as the dominant hero, thinking up the blocking of the door, the swapping of clothes, and the gag of leaping from the building.

As a screwball hero, there is a problem in the vagueness of Dodge's background. As his name suggests, he is evasive when asked at the employment office how he has survived for the last 20 years. He speaks with the eloquence of an educated man, at least in comparison to his fellow players (he draws their attention to "tried and tested methods for diverting the defense from the ball carrier") but exactly where this comes from or what he did in the war, we can only guess. As Dodge corrects a questioner who asks if he went to college, "Colle*ges*" might be seen as a slight echo of Clooney's own faltering experience with education. A deleted scene in the dining car features him saying that he was shot and taken out early but we have no corroboration for this. In other genres this might not matter, but screwball is closely related to matters of social status and education (in the sense of learning a moral lesson). Lexie rejects Leonard's advances as clumsy and predictable and yet she ultimately accepts Dodge, although he shows no perceptible character change from first meeting to last. The only aspect of Dodge that is constantly emphasized is his age (by players, at the employment office, in a row with Lexie and Carter, and by a soldier as a provocation before the fight). In the row in the hotel foyer, the question of age surfaces, with Dodge asserting that Lexie (31) is too old for Carter (24) with Lexie retorting that Dodge (admitting to be at least 45) is too old for her.

However, in screwball terms, it is unclear what he and Lexie have to learn from one another. Neither are brought to question serious aspects about their characters or beliefs, neither have to sacrifice anything (Dodge's time as a player is up anyway and Lexie's journalistic integrity is exonerated), and rather than being attracted by her aptitudes, Dodge is drawn to Lexie from some distance in the hotel foyer, simply by looks alone. Likewise, although there is certainly some wit in Dodge's dialogue and a lack of stuffiness, it is not clear what suddenly makes her feel sufficiently drawn to him to ride off, literally, into the sunset with him. He is handsome but he is so when they first meet.

In 1925, Lexie might observe to Leonard that there are "no rules," but when Dodge talks of marriage as a next step for her, she does not question, as might be logical for an intelligent woman in this position, just how Dodge proposes to support her. The "What will become of us?" exchange feels like the epilogue of a Victorian novel, but the list of possibilities, some more frivolous than others (marriage, children, a car, or a spell in jail for tax-related offences) all seem equally possible. In 2008, narratives can hold all these as open choices. However, the final collection of photos includes a slow zoom out from their wedding picture, suggesting narrative closure under pressure of generic expectation. Here is perhaps the crux of the problem. Classic screwball expects a character arc, perhaps a particularly sharp one. Disparate characters are thrown together, learn something about each other, and are changed by the collision with their opposites. Neither Dodge nor Lexie, nor indeed Carter, really changes. What does is wider society, and it is this aspect of the narrative that is more convincing than the characterization.

Leatherheads is based on a script by sports journalists Rick Reilly and Duncan Brantley from 1993 and had additional uncredited input from Stephen Schiff and Steven Soderbergh. Clooney claimed that all but two scenes bear his hand as writer and that therefore he should get a credit: a position rejected by the Writer's Guild of America. Consequently, Clooney resigned his position as a voting member of the Writer's Guild of America but is still a Financial Core Member. The film has a strongly personal element for Clooney and received its world premiere in his hometown of Maysville, Kentucky. However, the lack of detailed DVD extras beyond some deleted scenes, without titles or explanations, feels like this is a project that Clooney put time and energy into, and there seems some residual bitterness about the way he feels he was treated in not being given sufficient (or indeed any) credit for the work he did on the script.

UP IN THE AIR (JASON REITMAN, 2009)

Craig: Do you want to be in the boat?
Ryan: Yeah, alone.

The opening credits may be intended to reflect a collection of vintage postcards, and Reitman talks on the DVD commentary about trying to avoid identification with a specific era, but the movement of segmented lines and text across quintessential images of the United States also evokes Hitchcock's *North by Northwest* (1959) and links the protagonist of Reitman's film, Ryan Bingham (George Clooney), with that of Roger Thornhill (Cary Grant) in the earlier film. It is however only a light nod, as generically, although both are concerned with the identity of the protagonist, the two are very different, underlined by the following voice-over explanation of Ryan in which he clearly explains "Who the fuck am I?" He is a character who almost operates above the realm of mortal men, dropping down to deliver his bad news and then returning to his rarified life of executive travel.

The use of nonactors in the montage segments where we cut between individuals being fired gives those scenes real resonance, at a time when millions of Americans are experiencing similar pain. It would have been very hard with scripted lines to match the sense of reality or range of emotional reactions in which a visit to Chuck E. Cheese becomes an unattainable luxury. Reitman carefully prepared those involved so that they could be fired on camera and the improvised reactions be captured on film. A later section of nonactors, with some figures appearing again, shows responses to the question of how they manage to carry on, which provides a sense of balance, potential hope, and dignity to their situation. By mixing nonactors with professionals, Reitman gains a strong blend of the dramatic with almost a documentary sense. Regular collaborator J. K. Simmons plays Bob, a father seeking the approval of his kids (adding improvised lines about his family with pictures of his actual children) who is won over by Ryan's appeal not to give up on his dream of becoming a chef (as well as gaining more status for Ryan as someone who makes the process more palatable and who prepares well).

Walter Kirn's 2001 novel of the same name begins with a scene in which Ryan befriends a stranger in an adjacent seat, and this is where he explains his whole philosophy. Reitman filmed a version of this, ending with the powerful shot of the other man just about to say goodbye as they walk through departures but abruptly cut off visually by a partition. It is an effective sequence, but by cutting it we see more of Ryan explaining his philosophy himself, and his extraordinariness is emphasized rather than sharing the common experience of a liberating conversation with a stranger. Most of us will have traveled on planes; very few of us do so in the manner or volume of Ryan. Reitman's script massively expands the role of Alex who represents only a casual sexual exchange in the book. Kirn's snappy dialogue with a typical fellow male passenger, complete with restaurant tips, is transposed into flirtatious context in the banter with Alex (even with specific terms like the sexually ambiguous question to Alex, "Can you push?").

The book is much more unremittingly from Ryan's point of view, including references to his crumbling health, and it becomes clear in Kirn's narrative that his character is undergoing some kind of breakdown,

almost akin to the schizoid Patrick Bateman in Bret Easton Ellis's
American Psycho (1991) or Tyler Durden in Chuck Palahniuk's *Fight
Club* (1996). Ryan claims to be a victim of identity theft but it becomes
clear that this is not true. He denies being in places where he has been
sighted, he carries around a piece of luggage claiming it belongs to someone else (but that is revealed to contain his possessions), and most telling,
his grand philosophy, entitled "The Garage" (rebranded as the backpack
theory in the film), along with the lucrative book deal, collapses when
it transpires it was copied, wittingly or not, from someone he met a few
years ago. Like Palahniuk's novel and David Fincher's 1999 film version,
there is even mention of a drop in cabin pressure as reality crashes in on
the protagonist.[4] The novel is perhaps more overtly existential, with
Ryan describing his life in what he terms "Airworld" and describing himself as "a sort of mutation, a new species."[5] Reitman filmed a sequence
with Clooney walking through a number of typical sets, dressed in a
spacesuit, but ultimately felt that the point about him being disconnected
and living in his own world could be made without resorting to such existential devices, breaking the predominant mode of naturalism in the film.

   Kirn's Ryan is a less empathetic character, clearly reliant on prescrip-
tion drugs, constantly plotting ways to extort money or air miles from
his employer, using random vocabulary from self-improvement tapes,
and expending effort avoiding Linda, a well-meaning girlfriend.
Reitman shifts her dialogue ("We miss you, Ryan") and that of another
girlfriend Wendy ("You're awfully isolated, the way you live") both to
his elder sister, Kara, making his connective failures familial rather than
romantic.[6] In the novel, Alex has to remind him that she was someone
he coached through the loss of a job three years ago. For Kirn, Ryan's
mention of aircraft lights as his wingtip passes over is part of a mental
breakdown rather than Reitman's use of the phrase in the film, where it
feels like the elegiac bestowing of a blessing on the people below him
and represents a character more at peace with himself.[7] The novel has
Ryan spending time with Julie, his younger sister, as she gets cold feet
about her impending wedding. Reitman shifts this to an uncertain bride-
groom, and through the more rounded figure of Natalie forces his version
of Ryan to adopt an actively positive view of marriage. Reitman's script
takes occasional phrases from the book, like the poetic description of
Ryan's role as "ferrying wounded souls across the river of dread," but generally uses it as implicit backstory.[8]

   In Kirn's novel there is a description of Ryan's realization that what he
had thought of as far away was actually now within reach and that "the
world was really one place."[9] In a brave move, Reitman filmed but

ultimately cut this speech, involving a near-death experience from Ryan's youth and being airlifted from an accident by helicopter. It appears to be a key piece of backstory, motivating everything Ryan does, but Reitman manages to convey this in visual terms, especially by compressing Kirn's opening line ("to know me you have to fly with me") with his "To know me is to fly with me" montage. This is the most stylized sequence in the film and close to parody with whooshing sound effects as Ryan dexterously whirls his small case on and off the security conveyer belt and passes through security with choreographed ease. It feels like a trailer in itself, condensing Ryan's whole lifestyle into his well-practiced time-saving routines at airports. There is almost a balletic sense here, and it could be said that through the course of the film, Ryan learns to dance with another (Alex) rather than just move to his own particular rhythm. This is literally so at the party they crash together, but in a wider sense he has to accommodate another individual in his life, which, as he says, is all about moving.

The character of Natalie Keener (Anna Kendrick) is not overtly present in the novel but is possibly inspired by Lisa, a minor character, new to Ryan's firm, who is small, dark-haired, and an expert in a form of management consultancy that can be carried out electronically. Reitman's character is reflected in her name as an ambitious, driven individual who attacks her keyboard (typing "with purpose" as she calls it) and who favors new technology as a way to make the firing process more efficient. Her buttoned-down nature is made literal in her costume, a business suit, which she wears in every scene in which she appears. Such attention to detail is also reflected in the fact that Clooney's character wears only what might be realistically packed in the kind of small suitcase that he carries in the movie.

Reitman's film is based on the triangular relationship of Ryan, Alex (Vera Farmiga), and Natalie, but Ryan is very much at the apex of that triangle. The two female parts, though interesting in themselves, matter only insofar as they relate to Ryan, who occupies almost every scene on screen. The triangle constitutes an alternative family, with both women representing a challenge to Ryan's hermetically sealed lifestyle. Alex, as a romantic diversion, is a quasi-wife, and Natalie is a daughter figure (stating on the phone that Ryan is not a potential figure of attraction, especially since "He's old"). She is a challenge in a different sphere, his career, looking to supersede the previous generation.

The initial meeting of Alex and Ryan, swapping views about loyalty cards, may seem a little like two nerdy kids in a playground transposed to a more glamorous setting. Alex initially may seem one-dimensional, describing herself as an overt reflection of his desires ("think of me as yourself, only with a vagina"), but in his discovery of such an apparent ideal, Ryan fails to notice that she is compartmentalizing her life, just as he does his, and she admits to having done a little research on him. The revelation of a husband and family, a whole secret other life, should hardly come as a surprise. In her longest speech to Natalie about what is important in seeking a husband or long-term partner, she mentions family. When the question "How do you sleep at night?" is thrown at him at the outset, an implicit answer is that he does not have a family or children to whom he has to explain himself. By contrast, Natalie finds that she cannot do the job easily in person (with Ryan) or via a screen to the weeping Mr. Samuels (Steve Eastin), a real individual. Given to forming romantic bonds and without Ryan's emotional hardness, she is upset by the firing process.

Although Ryan denies his connections to other people, he does have them, and it is through Alex that his backstory, so to speak, is teased out. He shows her his old school, with photos of himself as a college athlete (with real shots of the young Clooney) and iconic spots around the school site. Ryan has developed to the point where he can reveal these connections, thereby making himself vulnerable, and the smile that he and Alex exchange at the basketball practice might suggest that they are on the way to forming a more permanent relationship. Clooney's improvised calling "I'm lonely" after Alex leaves him underlines the fragility of his emotional state. Inexperienced in involved relationships, he leaps straight to the nesting stage, buying and furnishing an apartment in Omaha in an elaborate sequence, ultimately cut from the finished film, only for Alex to fail to show up, prompting his uninvited appearance at her house.

The opening of the film underlines the heartlessness of Western capitalism in Ryan's delivering of unwelcome news. If viewers are affected by Clooney's charm, the pill is sweetened but his character remains fairly dark. He makes promises he knows he will not keep, stating to fired employee Steve (Zach Galifianakis) "This is just the beginning," knowing full well he will never see him again. Ryan is avoiding responsibility, most obviously in his family and personal life but also professionally. He flies in, delivers devastating news, and flies out again. When the possibility arises that an employee has committed suicide, he is brutally dismissive of following up on what people do after being laid off ("No good can come of that"). The appearance of Natalie and Alex force him to start to take some responsibility, to edge out into the world of risk taking, and although he is still living a nomadic lifestyle at the end, he has been shaken out of his comfort zone. Reflected in the question that he mishears ("Would you like the can, sir?"), his inescapable mortality lies just beneath his pampered existence.

There are cinematic precursors to such a role. In *Pretty Woman* (Garry Marshall, 1990), Edward Lewis (Richard Gere) flies around the United States buying up companies and breaking them up to be resold at a greater profit. Both films, although part romantic comedy, have at their core a good-looking hero delivering unpalatable news about the fate of companies and individuals at the hands of a ruthless economic market. Like Ryan, Edward also is avoiding commitment by a life of wealth and privilege, which is challenged when he meets a woman (Vivian, played by Julia Roberts) who makes him reappraise his views. Like Clooney, Gere is an actor whose performances have been criticized as being based on facial twitches and good looks alone (also subject to sporadic gossip about his sexuality) and who inspires fierce loyalty and dislike in equal measure.

We hear only the opening rhetoric of Ryan's backpack speech. It seems like an inversion of E. M. Forster's mantra, "Only connect," but without explaining how. Away from the gradually increasing scale and glamor of the lighting and stylized shots of Ryan's conference speeches, the blunt truth of his philosophy is less beguiling. He explains to his older sister, Kara (Amy Morton), that "I tell people how to avoid commitment," prompting a bemused reaction: "What kind of fucked-up message is that?" When Natalie confronts Ryan, while taking one of the photos for his sister, she describes him as a 12-year-old, and there is arguably something emotionally retarded about a man in his 40s who has never made a home for himself.

There are new aspects to Clooney's persona on display here. We see Clooney dancing, smiling, and joining in the lyrics of a rap performance (without the substance abuse needed by his character in *The Men Who Stare at Goats*). For some, the juxtaposition of an older couple (he and Alex) in among a group in their 20s might jar a little but their presence could also be seen as empowering. Rather than trying to be something they are not, Alex and Ryan are a mature couple, unwilling to give up youthful fun. They drop in and out of the hotel group, crashing the party in the hotel and on the boat but not participating in the karaoke. Like the character of Bob (Bill Murray) in *Lost in Translation*, a middle-aged man is shaken out of his routines, in part by partying with a crowd of people a generation younger than himself. Murray communicates a clearer sense of real joy (exacting a promise of a tape of some new music), but Clooney's character here is neither being laughed at as out of place nor adopting a position of patronizing superiority. In both films, the embracing of human contact is seen as a healthy development for an individual who leads an isolated life of global travel. Also, by choosing to use MC Young playing himself as a rapper, with his best known 1989 hit "Bust a Move," the position of Alex and Ryan are in a sense strengthened, as they are familiar with the song, an old-school classic (and can sing along).

What perhaps is most noticeable is the mature range in Clooney's performance here. He can be the smiling, charming cad with Alex but also the brooding, empty face of loss, like on the subway, trying to understand what kind of a relationship he has or can ever have with her. His expectation of praise (in producing the photos for his sister or offering to walk her down the aisle) is converted in a moment into a suppressed sense of loss and disappointment. Natalie is the more obviously emotional character, with her feelings barely kept in check, but Clooney's character has a more nuanced depth, which is often dismissed simply as charm. In scenes where he is alone on-screen, there is no need for such performance for a third party, and here he brings the somber and almost elegiac tone of *Solaris* (Steven Soderbergh, 2003) and *Michael Clayton* (Tony Gilroy, 2007).

It is a film that deals with overtly philosophical issues, particularly around the need for and value of human connectivity. As Jim (Danny McBride) bluntly expresses it, when having last-minute doubts about marrying Ryan's younger sister, Julie (Melanie Lynskey), "What is the point?" Reitman raises the notion of what is worth keeping in life, to what values and people should we be paying most attention. Linked to this is the notion of loyalty: most obviously in Ryan's card, showing loyalty to a particular airline (as the airport posters remind us), but Ryan is forced to evaluate to whom or what should he be loyal. Surrounded by people in his working environment, Ryan is essentially alone, living out his backpack theory as well as selling it as a motivational speaker. However, like Miles Massey's planned lecture on divorce in *Intolerable Cruelty*, the hero's speaking engagement becomes impossible when the life of the speaker shows the flaws in the central idea.

Natalie's use of the blend "Glocal" reflects the film's tension between the macro and micro, between the big and small scale. Ryan's job of laying people off ultimately leads to his own status as dispensable, and his dismissal of marriage as a concept contributes to Jim's doubts; but then he must, in the style of a debate, argue against his own position in order to understand a contrary point of view (foreshadowed by Natalie's attempt to sell Ryan the idea of marriage on the shuttle). The sacking of Bob, which Ryan takes over as Natalie's strategy falters, includes lines about the process being a "wake-up call" and a "rebirth," which also reflect his own development. He is forced to rethink his whole view of human nature and whether indeed we are like sharks (isolated, predatory, and essentially nomadic) or better suited by nature to the monogamous bonds represented by swans.

The breakdown of Natalie's relationship and her subsequent outbreak of hysterics in an airport hotel lobby may seem a little out of place with the emotional tone of the film, but her brutal dumping by text reflects an emotional version of the work that she and Ryan are engaged in. However, she seems just a little too easily damaged for a 23-year-old here. The subsequent exchange between the three about expectations and coupledom includes some interesting and funny lines; but again, Natalie, expecting a child and a partner with a Grand Cherokee, sounds like someone much younger than her age might suggest. It feels as if the script almost wants to identify her as a teen, a clear generation apart from Alex and Ryan, at home with new technology, having a psychology degree, and full of naïve hopes about romance and marriage ("I followed a boy"). Natalie's catalog of romantic hopes and dreams is juxtaposed with Alex's briefer and more realistic checklist. Although not intended to destroy Natalie's worldview, Natalie's reaction is comic as she is not ready to give up on her dreams too quickly ("Wow, that was depressing").

However, the film, via the reaction of Alex and Ryan, does not judge her harshly. In fact, the very opposite is true, as they take a parental and protective view of her. This makes Alex more likeable to audiences, who otherwise might have seen the two women as rivals, so that the advice Alex passes on to Natalie seems heartfelt rather than world-weary and cynical. Likewise, Ryan takes Natalie literally under his wing, giving her a hug in the middle of the lobby, supporting her in the journey to try out her new software, and even arguing on her behalf with his boss that she should be allowed to continue when a sacking by video conference turns messy, and giving her a supportive reference, helping her to get a new job.

Although we have a protagonist who lives in or around anonymous airports, who leads a life of little emotional connection, broken only by casual sex, this is not the world of J. G. Ballard. The film has a much warmer heartbeat. As Ryan eventually declares, "Life's better with company." The posed pictures that Ryan takes with the *Amelie*-style cutout (a request for Ryan to pick up some salmon in the novel) seem kitschy, but the truth is, although Ryan can afford to travel to exotic places, he goes no nearer to them than his sister does. Indeed, at times the film feels close to a Wes Anderson movie, particularly in the wedding section, where we are encouraged to laugh with, rather than at, the unpretentiousness of small-town weddings. Like Anderson, Reitman likes to work with particular actors in supporting roles (like Ryan's boss, Craig, played by Jason Bateman) and key technical roles, like the use of design company Shadowplay for the opening credits. There is a similar inclusion of the quirky and small scale, the notion of a surrogate family, and most obviously, perhaps, the work of musical supervisor Randall Poster. Like Anderson, Reitman writes and directs and builds up a store of preferred music while he writes. There even feels like a small nod to Max in *Rushmore* (1998) in Jim sitting on a tiny chair, both representing individuals struggling to accept grown-up responsibilities. However, Clooney, who worked with Anderson on *Fantastic Mr. Fox* the same year as *Up in the Air* was released, is given more leeway to improvise by Reitman, such as the flirtatious scene with Alex about their attempts to join the Mile High Club.

Very few shots draw attention to themselves as self-conscious art. Technology and artistry are largely subordinated to the needs of the story. As Ryan's life starts to come under more pressure, extras in the background were given instructions to move around more and dressed a little less smartly. Shots of chairs all piled together or rooms empty but for dozens of phones on the floor provide powerful images of an economy in decline, and time and energy are devoted to providing fake snow for the school scenes or Ryan's appearance at Alex's house, just to keep the sense of seasonal continuity. The extremely complicated but unobtrusive matching of eye lines in the scene between Natalie, Ryan, and Craig, where they play out fictional firing scenarios, creates a vibrant and dramatic scene and conveys the balance of power shifting from Natalie back to Ryan, who then ultimately scores a hollow victory by humiliating her.

The film dramatizes how unattainable the American Dream is for millions who may be laid off through no fault of their own, what priorities individuals set for themselves, and how they decide that they are a success. By the close of the film, Ryan has achieved his aim of a specific number of air miles, has gained an exclusive card (only the seventh person to do so), and gets to meet the iconic pilot, Maynard Finch (Sam Elliott), whose mustachioed face we have seen on airport posters. Now however, Ryan literally has nothing to say as he realizes the insubstantial nature of that dream. When the captain expresses wonder at how he has found the time to do this, the waste of Ryan's life spent denying the kind of human connections that he now comes to understand is driven home. However, Reitman refuses easy sentiment. Ryan arrives too late in the lives of his family to be welcomed unquestioningly with open arms. He cannot suddenly take the role of father of the bride, and his pictures occupy only one of many on the board. In his absence, his family has made other connections.

Reitman also refuses the easy ending of some kind of bond with one of the female leads, which might have made Clooney's character less problematic to mainstream audiences but would have required a distortion of what we have learned about Alex and Natalie up to this point. This even extends to Ryan himself, after Alex describes him as merely "a parenthesis." Her character has not fundamentally changed: she is still a strong, independent individual, using sex as a form of escapism, very much in the way historically men might have done. However, Ryan's character has changed and such a compartmentalized life is no longer enough for him. The film explores the importance of a sense of home and belonging, and Ryan symbolically lets go of his luggage in slow motion; but in his weary close-up, looking up at the destination board, there is little sense he really knows where he is headed. As the title suggests, he is still literally up in the air, in a state of limbo. He is still a global citizen, and as his backpack philosophy states, all he can do is keep moving.

Reitman delivers a witty script that carries its subtext lightly (Kirn himself appears as a cameo next to Clooney in the meeting scene), at the same time giving Clooney the space and time to deliver one of his strongest acting performances. There is a blend of Clooney's physical charms (we see his torso twice: first in the first seduction scene, using his concierge key, and later after the conference party), his self-deprecating wit (his sudden look in a mirror behind him on hearing Natalie describe him as old would not be out of place in his commercials), and a more cynical world-weariness (in the setup gag to Natalie in which he describes the "moment when you look into somebody's eyes and you can feel them staring into your soul and the whole world goes quiet just for a second?" only to add that he does not feel that). However, Reitman allows Ryan only a handful of such flip comments, which would push the film more in the direction of romantic comedy and which, though raising a laugh at that precise moment, would feel like a cheap shot and erode sympathy for Ryan, especially when aimed at Natalie who believes in such romantic ideals.

Exact responsibility for precise parts of the script remains a little ambiguous. Reitman initially claimed sole credit but the Writer's Guild of America awarded shared credit with Sheldon Turner, who wrote an earlier draft (apparently unknown to Reitman at the time). Reitman began work on the project before *Thank You for Smoking* (2005) and *Juno* (2007), initially conceiving the narrative as more of an overt comedy, but following the global financial crisis altered the tone significantly, giving some elements almost a documentary feel. Reitman persuaded his father, fellow director Ivan Reitman, to gain the rights to Kirn's novel, and with his father as producer, Ted and Nicholas Griffin were commissioned to produce a script, which was then worked on further by Reitman (Jason).

It is the first time that Clooney's name alone stands at the top of the billing, and along with *The American* (Anton Corbijn, 2010), it represents a further step in Clooney's stature within the industry. He still makes (and possibly prefers) ensemble pieces, but he is now able to carry a film narrative that sits very much on his shoulders.

CONCLUSION

Despite a cinematic image based largely on the notion of the romantic hero, it is striking how rarely Clooney post-1996 has actually played such a role. Only in *One Fine Day* (and as a small-scale echo in *The Magic Bubble*) does he act as a clear repository for female desirability, uncomplicated with generic subtext (like his work with the Coen brothers) or matters of his own input as writer or director (like *Leatherheads*). In many other films, such as the *Ocean's* series, his on-screen charm is key to his character's success, but this is nearly always within a more generically complex narrative than a simple romance. The romantic pairings in all four films discussed in this chapter are passable but they all lack the intensity and frisson generated between Clooney and Lopez in *Out of Sight* (see chapter 5).

Intolerable Cruelty feels like an attempt to bring screwball up-to-date in its content, but this is always going to be difficult as this is a subgenre with specific historical roots and based on subtlety of wordplay and characterization. Unlike the generous tone of most classic screwball comedies, characters tend to operate in their own egocentric universes. Where such factors are taken into account (*O Brother* and, to a lesser extent, Clooney's own *Leatherheads*) the result seems more generically harmonious and viewers are encouraged to laugh with characters, rather than at them.

CHAPTER 3

Action Hero (What Men Want)

BATMAN AND ROBIN (JOEL SCHUMACHER, 1997)

Remember everyone, this is a cartoon.

—Joel Schumacher[1]

I think we might have killed the franchise.

—George Clooney[2]

This is the sequel *to Batman Forever* (1995), also directed by Schumacher and scripted by Akiva Goldsman, and represents an effort by Warner Brothers to widen the profitability of the *Batman* franchise with more family-friendly content. However, this is also accompanied by a tendency toward lightweight plotting, garish colors, and the kind of melodramatic overacting associated with the long-running TV series *Batman* (ABC, 1966–68), and further from Tim Burton's darker conception of Gotham in the first two films, *Batman* (1989) and *Batman Returns* (1992).

Perhaps it sounds perverse to criticize the film for being cartoonish, since that is the nature of its origins, but it is hard to find human qualities in the narrative with which to identify. In terms of generic expectations, it does not really deliver. There are fight sequences, but they are long, drawn-out affairs and several seem to achieve little beyond the destruction of scenery; and the sudden high-angle wide shots in such scenes feel like the style of the 1960s TV series with the obligatory "Pow!" signs appearing on screen. The visual styling is what predominates, and the upgrading of the Batmobile feels more like visiting a motor show than a movie theater. As an action movie, it lacks set-piece spectacular stunt work, the dialogue lacks witty Bond-like one-liners (an increasing part of the franchise), and there is no on-screen chemistry between Batman and his villainous adversary Freeze (Arnold Schwarzenegger) or romantic tension with Poison Ivy (Uma Thurman).

The cartoonish visual style also contributes to a lack of narrative development. The plot seems to go from one set-piece so-called action scene to another with very little action on display or narrative jeopardy at stake. The film as a whole is very episodic with the sense that several of the scenes could happen in almost any order. We see a series of large interior spaces—Gotham Art Gallery, the Observatory (twice), and the Costume Ball to auction the diamonds—and yet they each look exactly like what they are: large film sets. The scene as Poison Ivy reclaims an old Turkish bath as her new base has a particularly pointless fight scene, which lasts only a few seconds, with Bane (Jeep Swenson) ejecting a group of curiously painted thugs (accompanied by a sound effect like an old-fashioned swanee whistle, more redolent of musical hall than contemporary cinema). Poison Ivy's sidekick, Bane, looks like a WWF fighter in a gimp mask (not perhaps surprising since Swenson is a wrestler) who can only roar and throw people around. His sole piece of audible dialogue ("Bomb") could be quite funny, like his final fate as a literally shrunken figure, lying on the ground if it was meant ironically. A strangely similar scene in O Brother, where Delmar sees Pete's clothes lying on a rock, yields comedy but here this is not possible as we never see Bane having any kind of emotional life.

Fight sequences are overtly choreographed with Batman and Robin (Chris O'Donnell) performing parallel kicks and backflips, and assailants attacking helpfully one at a time and all dressed in identical costume, identifying them as baddies, giving so-called action sequences the appearance of rehearsals. In the fight with the "hockey team from hell," Batman's attackers look like extras from Starlight Express, and the wire work with Batman and Freeze seems cumbersome and unbelievable as they seem able to jump out of trouble at any point. It is the same weakness in The Matrix (the Wachowski brothers, 1999), where Neo can apparently fly off at will, logically making the fight scenes redundant. The key difference is that viewers do not mind this as those fights are spectacular; here, they are just ponderous. The action sequences use a camera positioning almost permanently on an oblique tilt, and unlike Burton's Gotham, here the cityscape and all the major landmarks (such as Arkham Asylum) look like models.

The stunts, such as Robin climbing up Freeze's escape capsule, the jump from Arkham Asylum, or the final fall from the Observatory, all follow the laws of gravity or probability extremely selectively. That in itself does not stop films from working, but one has to believe that in the universe of the film such things are possible. Even where there is narrative jeopardy, suspense seems willingly avoided. We cut bizarrely and without explanation from a shot of Robin holding Barbara by a boot, dangling perilously off a bridge after being thrown from her bike, to the Wayne mansion with no explanation of how the pair escaped.

Batman himself represents the sometimes dull force of good and moral behavior and needs charismatic adversaries to fight against. The Batman movies have benefited from memorable performances from Jack Nicholson (the Joker), Danny DeVito (the Penguin), or even Jim Carrey (the Riddler), whose casting plays to their acting strengths as well as their physical appearance. However, in *Batman and Robin*, from the first name appearing on the opening credits, the towering presence of Schwarzenegger dwarfs other areas of production, in terms of his personal salary ($25 million), his dialogue, peppered with often unfunny one-liners, and the logistics of the hours of makeup that his character needed every day. His dialogue consists of little more than predictable gags and puns ("The ice-man cometh"), and after zapping an underling with his ice-gun, as he was trying to watch a copy of his wedding video, he declares, "I hate it when people talk during the movie."

In theory, the plot twist of a good character, a scientist, turned bad through grief at the loss of his wife ought to make Freeze more nuanced, especially since this obviously sets up a link with Bruce Wayne's butler, Alfred (Michael Gough), who is also suffering from the same disease. However, Freeze's method of threat, covering Gotham in ice, reflects a character dominated by stasis rather than the literal ability to be chilling. From the opening with the Warner Brothers logo freezing, the film atrophies too. The visual conception of Freeze seems confused, shifting between two distinct looks: a neutered *Terminator*-style outfit with *Last Action Hero* cigar and cumbersome freezing gun or a bizarre dressing gown. Even extreme close-ups of his eyes tearing up, and later him actually crying, fail to humanize him. His henchmen are all interchangeable stock characters and are forced to do his eccentric bidding (singing "Frosty the Snowman").

Schumacher, who is openly gay, might be criticized for adding unnecessary homosexual innuendo in the dialogue (Poison Ivy's offer to Batman to retrieve his stolen diamond is expressed more colloquially: "I'll help you grab your rocks"). The lack of engaging characters and action means that the audience's attention is more likely to be drawn to the superficial campiness of the whole production, and with the greater prominence of Robin as Batman's sidekick, it is perhaps inevitable that a gay subtext (never far beneath the surface of the superhero franchise) seems more obvious.

The very first sight we have of the superhero duo is in a montage of suiting-up with a series of paired close-ups of gauntlets, leg protectors, chest, and codpieces. They seem a compilation of rubberized body parts (including prominent butt shots) rather than living beings, and the fact that each shot has a little motorized zoom, immediately followed by a parallel shot of the other man, creates a sense of almost dressing up in fetish wear for their partner. The final toe-to-head shot explicitly conveys a voyeuristic point of view of two fit men in rubber suits. In this context, such sequences feel more like part of a love story, reflected in the title, especially since the pair expend as much emotional energy on bickering with each other as they do on fighting crime. It is true that Batgirl is similarly attired in a further montage sequence much later but she has much less time on-screen. The increasingly phallic Batmobile, the close-ups of Clooney's crotch and butt, the additions of nipples to the batsuit, enlarged codpieces for both Batman and Robin, and even the gadgets (not huge in variety but at least 10 times a Batclip was fired from a belt to save one or both men), all suggest a certain amount of displacement activity.

Even Freeze rejects the attentions of a scantily clad black girl, and Poison Ivy jokingly describes Freeze's wife, held in suspended animation, as "frigid." Barbara (Alicia Silverstone) is first seen dressed in schoolgirl uniform, which seems more evocative of clichéd erotica than strictly likely in context. The camera tilts down, inhabiting Robin's point of view as we are invited to look at Barbara's legs, but this is closer to a sibling situation and the relationship remains chaste through the film. Robin kisses Poison Ivy but only with special film over his lips to expose her duplicity and attempt to kill him: clearly women cannot be trusted. Uma Thurman's Mae West-style delivery promises steamy content, but beyond the skintight outfits the film delivers very little erotic charge. Her answer to Robin's request for a sign with "slippery when wet" seems as predictable in tone as Freeze's one-liners, and the fight between Batgirl and Poison Ivy seems more like a camp burlesque show.

Some of the background of the Batman franchise certainly supports a gay reading: A lone male hero, sharing a house with his companion, Robin, lives a secret double life. He does not seem interested in the approaches of women like Vicki Vale (Kim Basinger) in *Batman*, Catwoman (Michelle Pfeiffer) in *Batman Returns*, Dr. Chase Meridian (Nicole Kidman) in *Batman Forever*, and Julie Madison (Elle McPherson) here, who even proposes to Batman but he ignores her (supposedly for her safety). At the unveiling of the new Gotham telescope, he jokes with the paparazzi, "Just don't point it at my bedroom." Like the pose of togetherness for the cameras (Julie claims they are "recklessly in love" although we do not see this), there is something false about this performance of heterosexual normality as Bruce ducks the marriage question. Later at dinner, Julie is the one who obliquely proposes but Bruce bats (!) this away with "I'm not the marrying kind," adding "There are things about me that you wouldn't understand." He kisses Julie but calls her Ivy and momentarily projects the other woman's face onto the girl in front of him. As in the later function where Poison Ivy gains the keys from Commissioner Gordon (Pat Hingle) to activate the Batsignal, Bruce's attention seems distracted, looking away from Julie at his side at something he cannot place, giving him the look of a heterosexual hero not fully at ease with himself.

The scene with Alfred, in which Bruce declares "I love you, old man" before kissing him and receiving the same expression of love in return, which could emphasize Alfred as a surrogate father, would not usually attract much attention; but without the emotional depth in the film as a whole to support such statements, this sequence only adds to the suggestion of a suppressed sexuality. Add in the fetish leatherwear, the cave that might double for a metaphorical "closet," dialogue like Robin's line to Batman "You have some real problems with women, you know that?" and that the only attraction that the male characters have for any female on screen is due to the pheromones that Poison Ivy blows onto the faces of her helpless male victims, and it is not hard to see why a gay subtext might suggest itself.

Clooney's decision to be in an episode of *South Park* this same year (1997) and more precisely to take the part of Sparky, Big Gay Al's dog, suggests not just a liking for the show but also a delight in playing with his media image. Rather than taking the kind of celebrity role associated with shows like *The Simpsons*, to associate himself with a show still in its infancy and particularly in a subservient role as a barking dog reflects decisions he has made on more substantial cinematic projects. A couple of years later, he voiced Doctor Gouache in *South Park: Bigger, Longer & Uncut* (Trey Parker), parodying his *ER* persona through a series of ridiculously wrong diagnoses. He is not afraid to try edgier projects, especially those that allow him to subvert audience expectations. The skit he filmed with the cast of *Modern Family* shown at the 2010 Emmy Award ceremony still shows a willingness not to take gossip about himself too seriously, with the final shot of him in bed with Jesse Tyler Ferguson and Eric Stonestreet, leading to the line "I've gotta get a film," delivered in an exaggeratedly low pitch to accentuate his heterosexual credentials.

A bigger problem for *Batman and Robin* is not so much a denial of a gay subtext as the fact that the character of Robin is at best superfluous and at worst annoying and egotistical in a narrative that suffers from too many peripheral characters distracting us from the hero. Here we have light-weight villains and an insubstantial helper, who adds little to the plot. The comic-strip Robin was added to attract a wider demographic (chil-dren), and there is the sense here too that a family audience (rather than a gay one) is being targeted but ironically by means of an unattractive fig-ure, representing moaning teenagers.

Clooney's acting style when on camera as Bruce Wayne is dominated by the same facial and body positioning: looking down, starting to speak, stopping and looking up with his head still tilted down, as when he is explaining to Robin (and us) about Freeze's backstory. In scenes opposite Alfred, he is often framed in slightly low angle, like a doctor looking down at a patient, and there is still quite a bit of *ER* posture and emo-tional range here (Clooney was working on the two projects at the same time). Even when he is later explaining to Robin about Alfred's condi-tion, there are the same half-smiles, which seem inappropriate here, and when asked how he knows about this, he simply states "I can tell." Walking outside with Alfred, Clooney walks with his hands clasped in front of him with the solemn, reserved demeanor of someone attending a funeral. This may reflect the serious nature of Alfred's condition but it is sequences like this that make Wayne hard to engage with. Even though his name is in the title, the character of Batman (or his alter ego as Bruce Wayne) does not dominate the screen, either in time or in manner when he is present. This is not Clooney's fault: the part is just not fleshed out enough to engage and sustain audience sympathy.

He wears black at all times—a turtleneck sweater, a tuxedo to the opening of the observatory, and even at the climax when Alfred faces death, he is in a hooded sweatshirt. However, the script does not allow us to see anything of a Hamlet-style darker psychology behind such cloth-ing choices. The only broadening of his emotional life we are given is in relation to Robin's expressions of frustration and some heavy-handed sen-timents about notions of family (letting Robin make his own mistakes and allowing Barbara to stay—"after all, she's family"). In this, Clooney is basically acting as a surrogate father to his nearest characters. He is showing a protective, slightly world-weary approach to them, and like a parent with a rebellious teen must bring his young charge (Robin) back into the family fold with some controlled risk taking and sharing of responsibility.

Batman's disabling of Robin's bike, preventing him from making a dan-gerous jump in pursuit of Freeze, feels like a parent concerned by (and possibly overreacting to) his offspring undertaking unnecessarily dangerous risks. The subsequent dialogue between the two reads like a parent laying down house rules, which the youngster must follow "if you want to stay in this house and on the team." However, the positive elements of Clooney's character are dissipated by the petulance in Robin, storming off not once but twice, declaring "I'm going solo," and later marching off again after calling Batman jealous over Poison Ivy.

Batman momentarily doubts whether he is being "pig-headed" about this and asks Alfred's advice, but the older man can provide only some strangely high-flown rhetoric ("What is Batman if not an effort to master the chaos that sweeps our world?" and later "Not all heroes wear masks"). The cartoonish context of the film as a whole renders such philosophizing fairly ridiculous. Like Robin, his female parallel, Barbara, also looks like she needs some paternal protection as we see her taking bets with groups of bikers and groups of gangs, dressed like Droog-wannabes from Kubrick's *A Clockwork Orange* (1971).

Clooney's character has three visionary flashbacks of himself as a boy being looked after by Alfred (he looks off-camera and we cut to a dissolve of Alfred picking him up when he falls, a later bedtime story, and a final projected vision on a window, where he is putting flowers on his parents' grave). These intrusive snapshots of the only family life he has known do not sit well with Barbara's description of freeing her uncle from "this dismal life of servitude." Although Wayne asks Alfred later whether he regrets working all his life for the Wayne family, the loyal butler denies this. There is, nonetheless, the residue of a baronial manner here. Wayne is a multimillionaire and perhaps his acts of philanthropy reflect guilt about how he derives his wealth. However, the occasional arresting shot (like the snapshot of the Riddler's costume in the Criminal Property Locker at Arkham Asylum) does not make up for the emotional neutrality of the film as a whole. When Batman, Robin, and Batgirl put their hands together at the end, it feels less like the beginning of a Three Musketeer-style adventure and more like the conclusion of a business meeting.

The fact that in this the fourth incarnation of the series, we have the third different actor playing the part reflects the anonymity of the role of Batman. Unlike the Bond franchise, where individual actors can bring some new elements to the role, it is much more difficult with the dramatic realization of Batman. With 90 percent of the body covered by a rubber suit, it is the costume and the gadgets that dominate (the latter a similar distraction with Bond sometimes). There is a limit to how much emotion you can exude from lips and cheekbones alone. Clooney does have an edge here however with a distinctive voice, reflected in his TV commercials (see chapter 9).

Batman and Robin signals a shift away from a more adversarial focus on Batman and a single villain to a diversification of subsidiary roles, with two goodies (Robin and Batgirl) and two baddies (Freeze, Poison Ivy, and even a further sidekick, the feral Bane), the effect of which is a loss of narrative focus and of a greater sense of the serial over the climactic event. If Batman vanquishes one opponent, another will appear a few minutes later.

Critically, the film fared poorly, and certainly given the hopes of the studio it was not the blockbuster it might have been. Perhaps denigrating one's own work and playing up its camp qualities is the best that Clooney can do. Certainly, compared to other films considered in this book, although it made more money than almost any of them, in terms of quality, even on its own generic terms, it represents a low point in Clooney's career that he did well to escape from. Reports of the death of the Batman franchise were premature, but it did not really recover until eight years later with Christopher Nolan's *Batman Begins* (2005) and especially *The Dark Knight* (2008). However, it did show Clooney what being part of a franchise could mean for his career. A more successful reception of the film might have meant making the difficult choice of whether to stay in a role that was lucrative but limiting as an actor. As it was, the decision to move on to other projects was not hard to take.

THE PEACEMAKER (MIMI LEDER, 1997)

Devoe: In the field, this is how it works: the good guys, that's us, we chase the bad guys. And they don't wear black hats. They are, however, all alike.

The film has a strong Bond-like feel in its action sequences, criminality filling the void of post–Cold War politics and minimal concern with character motivation. Villains are either rogue Russian generals, like Kodoroff (Alexander Baluyev), or dissident Europeans, like Dusan Gavrich (Marcel Iures), whose political motivation is more hazy than their emotional reaction to personal losses in war. Despite mentions of Sarajevo or Bosnia, there is no attempt to educate viewers about European politics: it is strictly an otherland of political infighting and double-dealing.

The opening Bond-style prologue, showing the theft of the nuclear device, blends *Harry Potter*-like anachronisms in the steam train with the gratuitous spectacle of shadowy figures jumping from one train to another. Several other Bond films also dramatize the attempt to steal nuclear weapons, like *Thunderball* (Terence Young, 1965), particularly in a destabilized former Soviet Union through the course of the 1990s. The pairing of Dr. Julia Kelly (Nicole Kidman) and Lt. Col. Thomas Devoe (George Clooney) adds to this impression of a Bond-like universe. Initially, Kelly appears to have some elements of strength in her character, like her civilian rank, her title, the ability to speak Russian, and her political knowledge. However, as soon as she shares the same screen space as Devoe, her character visibly wilts, becoming instantly deferential to his assertive manner and forceful personality. Kelly's breaking into Russian in Vienna feels like Major Anya Amasova (Barbara Bach) in *The Spy Who Loved Me* (Lewis Gilbert, 1977), asserting at every opportunity the equality of women, but here she is still excluded from the nods and winks exchanged between Devoe and Dimitri (Armin Mueller-Stahl).

Kelly's presentation is instantly derailed by Devoe's fairly rude interruption, which reduces her to a breathless nervousness. There is a sense of playful one-upmanship about his reading of the photos on display, which at least suggests insensitivity in undermining Kelly's position. If a more romantic relationship were to develop in the film, it would have to accommodate such awkward scenes and may be one reason why it does not happen. He apologizes with "my enthusiasm sometimes gets the better of me," but it is delivered with a smirk and by then the damage to her on-screen credibility is already done. Rotating camera movement around the characters in the offices does not conceal that their lives are essentially static; i.e., Kelly's area of expertise is at some distance from the action.

Theoretically, he is her "military liaison," i.e., subordinate to her in political and management terms but given relatively free rein in the theater of combat. The problem is that after this first presentation, the relationship is not playful or combative: Devoe takes charge and Kelly defers. On the phone and in person in her office, Kelly tries to assert authority, issuing commands, but she seems weak and hesitant in dialogue with Devoe. At the mention of a suspect's name, he takes charge, literally grabbing the phone, and from this point, he is the one driving the investigation forward. Even though she is the one who has the ear of the president, we almost forget her superior position, until Devoe has to wait for clearance from her before launching the helicopter raid into Russian airspace. There seems little real steel in her character.

On the plane ride they share, there are several instances of Clooney looking down and half smiling, as if at some private thought or joke. For some viewers, such gestures suggest sweetness and an inner life; for others, this may convey alienating smugness. Clooney's subsequent films represent a struggle to escape the trap of such gestures, to embrace a wider emotional life of his characters and deny viewers the potential reading of his character as patronizing.

Devoe's first appearance in the film, after 22 minutes, presents him as a rule breaker, defending his arrest for a brawl, possible involvement with a prostitute, and inappropriate use of taxpayers' money in negotiating with an arms dealer. He seems to be a character that has to apologize or at least explain his actions fairly regularly as he does so effectively. The lone hero, unorthodox but effective, again aligns him with the early and late Bond narratives. His military rank, lieutenant colonel, and the fact that he is in the Special Forces, may explain his arrogant self-confidence but makes him quite difficult to work with as he assumes command of any situation of which he is a part.

In the sequence in Schumacher's palatial Viennese offices, he enters the lair of the enemy with a *Mission Impossible*-style deadline, as a computer identifies (with unbelievable slowness) his face from a CCTV picture. This device appears in films like *No Way Out* (Roger Donaldson, 1987), which also uses a male lead as a high-ranking American officer, Lieutenant Commander Tom Farrell (Kevin Costner), unmasking corruption, but here it seems quite contrived and more a prompt for Devoe to show his physicality in smashing Schumacher's face in a table. As soon as violence occurs, Kelly becomes a stereotypical screaming victim who must be protected, although her reaction of terror is genuine because he has not told her his plan of action. Her skills are more refined, hacking into the computers; his methods are blunter, pulling a gun on the man and literally twisting his arm to extract information.

He takes the wheel, driving the narrative as well as their car. The car chase evokes films like *Goldeneye* (Martin Campbell, 1995), which also features a car chase in the narrow streets of a European city, St. Petersburg, and shots of cars racing parallel to one another. It also looks forward to more recent films aspiring to the Bond mantle, such as *The Bourne Identity* (Doug Liman, 2002), which has a lengthy car chase in Paris between a single hero and apparently insurmountable opponents. The close shots of German automotive engineering, Mercedes and BMWs, and the frenzied pursuit down narrow streets evoke the headlong speed of *Taxi* (Gérard Pirès, 1998) in Marseille but especially *Ronin* (John Frankenheimer, 1998), also placing American stars (playing character with backgrounds in Special Forces) alongside European minor characters but decidedly European in location with car chases in Nice and Paris. *Ronin* also uses no musical accompaniment to these scenes, except at the end of its final chase, and some actors (including Clooney) perform their own driving or are at least visible in the car; i.e., stunt work was kept to a minimum.

The car chase, prompted by the shooting of Dimitri (shown in in slow motion), uses fairly standard means to generate suspense, cutting between low-angle shots within the car and cameras placed in low positions on the front and back of the Mercedes to give the impression of headlong speed. Devoe has Kelly move to the front, supposedly for her safety, but it also allows Leder to frame both lead characters in an overhead two-shot. Slow motion is used for spectacular collisions, as when Devoe deliberately reverses back into one of the pursuing cars. The appearance of several identical black BMWs with their windows blacked out creates strong Bond-like associations, making the antagonists to the hero easily identifiable and equally expendable (all hanging out of the windows, waving pistols). Devoe's car is not customized with the usual Bond gadgetry, but we are told by Dimitri that it is an embassy car, complete with bulletproof windows and armor plating, which presumably partly explains its indestructible nature. The chase reaches a climax in a public place but the reversing between two pursing cars seems excessively choreographed to be believable. Likewise, Devoe's last-minute maneuver, supposedly causing his pursuers to crash into each other and skid into a restaurant, seems closer to the cartoonish stunts of The Dukes of Hazzard (created by Gy Waldron, 1979–85).

In the brutal physicality of Devoe's hand-to-hand combat and his driving (reversing into a crippled car four times), blending quick thinking with a preparedness for destruction (shooting through a bullet hole in his windshield, subsequently hiding down a side street in a brief hiatus in the chase, and firing his pistol in the air to cause panic in the square), his character feels close to the conception of a more muscular and brutal Bond. The forward and reverse tracking shots that follow Devoe as he walks up to the crushed car in which his friend's killer is still alive, and fires twice into his chest at point-blank range, is both an act of revenge but also quite savage. This is a throwback to a conception of Bond, closer to Ian Fleming's original character and seen in Sean Connery's first appearance as Bond in Dr. No (Terence Young, 1962), in which he calmly shoots Professor Dent (Anthony Dawson) from a sitting position, and in Daniel Craig's shooting of Dryden (Malcolm Sinclair) in Casino Royale (Martin Campbell, 2006).

The shot of the explosion behind Kelly and Devoe as they move away is an action movie cliché, featured in trailers for most Bond films, in other action movies such as Clear and Present Danger (Phillip Noyce, 1994) and even bookends the prologue sequence in From Dusk Till Dawn as the liquor store blows up. The opening of the following scene, linked by a slow dissolve, shows Devoe with his head in his hands, suggesting no triumphalism. They escaped with their lives and the information they wanted but at the cost of the life of a dear friend. Kelly's shocked reaction reminds us that her environment is far from the brutality of military operations, and the admission "I've never watched anybody die" prepares us for her grief at the losses in the helicopter raid. However, the coldness of her delivery might also imply some judgment on Devoe and whether he really needed to kill the final man. Devoe's next appearance, landing from a helicopter in uniform, underlines the different world in which he operates and serves to make any kind of romantic link with Kelly's character nigh impossible and something the film does not pursue, beyond his dropping a comforting hand on her shoulder.

The character of Dusan Gavrich (Marcel Iures) appears only some 38 minutes into the film, and his status as an embittered man is only really explained in the final chase sequence in New York. Having his character appear so late makes sustained engagement with him difficult. Gavrich's claim, "I'm a Serb, a Croat, and a Muslim," hints at the complexity of the issues here but also shows how the film is content to bundle troubling notions together. The murky politics of the West arming both sides in the Bosnian war is not really explored. In taking the role of the murdered diplomat, Gavrich appears to be taking the moral high ground, and yet as it seems he was behind the crime his status is compromised. The speeches that he makes at the end in the church seem unconvincing as we do not really see sufficient justification for his action. The re-creation of the sniper attack is effective but it makes his revenge personal, and yet his action is global in its implications. Even despite Kelly's shrieked comment that Gavrich wants his death to "mean something," the practical reality is that he could have exploded it from his hotel rather than the UN building and achieved the same effect.

In the action genre, character development and particularly romantic entanglements only impede the main generic imperative: forward narrative motion. Therefore such elements are most often seen as weak spots, interludes in the action for audiences to catch their breath before the next piece of spectacle. Perhaps such delays are important but they are functional rather than emotionally engaging in themselves.

As soon as the SWAT raid misses Gavrich at his hotel and the bomb is switched to a backpack, the film moves into more dynamic territory. Elevators just missing one another or handheld cameras tracking the progress of movement of a raid up to a room are familiar elements of the action/thriller genre, and filming in New York is commonplace enough, but the frenetic passage through crowded streets on an apparently ordinary day is less common. *Die Hard with a Vengeance* (John McTiernan, 1995) takes the crosstown shortcut to ridiculous wish fulfillment levels, with Zeus (Samuel L. Jackson) driving through Central Park, but here we have the handheld camera in forward and reverse tracking mode, creating the growing panic of Gavrich. We start to inhabit his point of view for a few shots, and slow motion conveys his growing sense of unreality, including a glimpse of himself and his wife with a child. Flashbulb transitions, more rapid cutting, slight wisps of smoke, and some shots at ankle height all create a sense of disorientation so that the explanation of his motivation, even this late in the film, is quite powerful. The practical difficulty of keeping a containment perimeter secure in a huge city and the moral dilemma of snipers unable to take a clear shot without civilian casualties are touched on but really only function as obstacles for Devoe (poring over a map on the hood of a car, instinctively taking charge) to overcome.

The game of cat and mouse is complicated by the appearance of an accomplice, rescuing Gavrich from arrest. Here Devoe starts to act unconventionally, running across the roofs of cars, appearing in the blurred background, in the same shot as Gavrich for the first time, reflecting the two narrative threads, the hunters and the hunted, finally coming together. Cornered in an alley, Gavrich looks trapped but miraculously his accomplice reappears. Devoe, apparently reacting to Gavrich's look, spins around and shoots his new adversary. However, the choreography of the scene is unconvincing. Whereas a similar scene in David Fincher's *Seven* (1995) works through obscured or distorted vision in shadowy light, here everything is clearly visible. There is no reason why Devoe and Kelly survive simply by rolling beneath a helpfully placed step. The gunman could have just stopped and shot them. In *Seven*, it is the killer's deliberate choice not to shoot the hero, which is revealed as important only at the close of that narrative; here, it just seems unbelievable.

Devoe's threat as a marksman is underlined as he shoots Gavrich once but allows him to escape to a nearby church. Kelly is the one who hears the choir, reflecting her observant nature, but in the church itself, Devoe (and by implication Clooney himself) displays protective and nurturing qualities in securing a child who is hiding under a pew. He represents masculine force but not in an indiscriminate manner.

Gavrich dies, but by committing suicide he shifts the narrative into its final frenetic phase, in the unlikely defusing of a bomb: a Bond favorite from *Goldfinger* (Guy Hamilton, 1964) to *Octopussy* (John Glen, 1983), the latter also using a planned nuclear explosion to involve Western powers, albeit in a disarmament race. It seems a throwback to notions of crazed villains plotting world domination, and even with the adjustment here of Gavrich's political motivation, derived ultimately from the personal, it seems no more convincing. There is a small nod to plausibility in having the making safe extend only to removing the nuclear element of the bomb and allowing Kelly a final piece of dramatic status by using her knowledge, but even though she does the thinking and the actual defusing, Devoe notes the time with plenty of tilting action of his head. The demands of spectacle (breaking glass plus and explosion), the triumph of good over evil (as Gavrich dies), and the saving of the heroine by the hero (if not in bomb disposal, at least in protecting her from the force of the blast) all seem close to generic cliché. As convention dictates, he hugs and she cries before being dragged off by rescuers dressed in protective suits. This action as he calls her name might be seen as a microcosm for the action genre, in which personal and especially romantic relationships are hustled out of the narrative by the generic concerns with narrative action.

The final pool scene, reprising the opening but now with Devoe's shoes coming into shot, marks the close of the narrative but leaves the relationship between the two fairly open. The film has not allowed space for it to develop, so although the final shot of Devoe standing at one end of the pool, declaring "I'll wait" while Kelly finishes her 10 lengths, might be seen romantically, his rather ham-fisted way of asking her out for a drink suggests we have actually learned fairly little about these two characters during the film itself.

Clooney is a credible action hero who is battling terrorists rather than vampires and acts on behalf of others more than himself, helping to save the world (or a sizeable part of New York), looking dashing in a military uniform, and (by implication at least) getting the girl. The film includes iconic shots like him standing astride a crate of explosives as a truck falls away and explodes. However, despite a few interesting shots (like the man trapped in the elevator with a SWAT team, shielding the eyes of his poodle from the impending violence), there is not enough here that breaks out from generic expectations to make the film particularly memorable. It is highly episodic, meaning that it is possible to drop in at almost any point in the narrative and pick up the thread of the action. This is in part because of the simplicity of the through line, find the bomb, but also it feels almost designed for dividing into bite-sized pieces on television. Goran Visnjic, who would go on to work on ER, appears as a border guard in The Peacemaker, albeit not sharing screen space with Clooney himself.

THE PERFECT STORM (WOLFGANG PETERSEN, 2000)

"What was the final moment? What was the final, final thing?"

—Chris Cotter in Sebastian Junger's *The Perfect Storm*[3]

Twenty years earlier, Wolfgang Petersen directed a seminal piece of suspenseful television drama, *Das Boot* (1981), involving a tight-knit, all-male community at sea who were doomed to face a watery grave. While generically *The Perfect Storm* might be classed with other disaster movies and open to the criticism of being special effects-driven, it also examines the more philosophical issue of how men face the prospect of almost certain death and in this perhaps represents a small element of the human condition: how does one exist in the knowledge of one's impending mortality? The opening subtitle establishes time and place precisely (Gloucester, Massachusetts, Fall, 1991). We are in a specific fishing community and focus on one particular sword boat, the *Andrea Gail*, and its crew, particularly its captain, Billy Tyne (George Clooney).

There is a slight touch of Ernest Hemingway's *The Old Man and the Sea* (1952) in the intrusion of external circumstances to scupper the fishing exploits of an intrepid hero. Here it is not a single shark that eats the catch but a huge haul of fish that must be partly abandoned due to a convergence of storms. The film opens with a series of dissolves over the names of dead on the wall at City Hall. The prominence of 1918 might suggest the First World War, but further shots underline that the losses stretch back much further. The final dedication refers to the 10,000 Gloucestermen who have died since 1623.

What is something of a delicate topic, given the outcome of the narrative, is the element of blame, if any, that should attach itself to Billy Tyne. Clearly, his living family were concerned that his memory not be besmirched; but in the context of the film, the idea that an experienced fisherman would not know the risk that he was running, especially given the technical support open to him (via detailed radio and TV weather reports), and the simple fact that he is alone in proposing going out, not just to Sable Island but beyond, to the Flemish Cap: all this raises questions about the judgment of the captain. In the film, this is portrayed as strength of character and a stubborn unwillingness to accept their fate, with which he draws the rest of the crew along, but it might equally be seen as an example of hubris and poor judgment. According to Sebastian Junger, whose dramatized account of real events formed the basis for the film, the real Billy Tyne "truly loved to fish" and the script does capture some of that sense of passion as well as raising the question whether that can cloud judgment at times.[4] On the other hand, the confluence of storms is exceptional, Tyne is experienced and has ridden out rough seas before, and at bottom, he needs the fish. There is the strong sense throughout of the need to be respectful to the memory of those who died not just in this disaster but of the many, many others who have given their lives from this small, tight-knit community.

Like Herman Melville's *Moby Dick* (1851), the careful husbandry required by fishing is underlined and a respect for such traditions is engendered by dissolves, of iconic images of fish being landed and nets and boats both being cared for. Petersen portrays boats returning to harbor as the source of communal joy, craning up to show friends and family rushing to greet those returning, already elevating the fishermen to the status of returning heroes. The centrality of this action and where it takes place, within sight of the Crow's Nest, sets up the key dynamic of the film: leave taking and returning (or not). The film touches on how communities live in the face of repeated separation and possibly death. The dissolves used as the two boats, the *Andrea Gail* and its rival the *Hannah Boden*, steam into harbor, along with James Horner's swelling theme, establish a strong elegiac tone, which pervades almost all of the film, except the action sequences. The theme returns as the crew walk out to the ship a couple of days later, like heroes going off to war but with a strongly elegiac feel, since audiences probably know the true story that the film is based on and therefore realize they are watching the actions of dead men. Petersen uses the number and nature of the greeters to establish the lives of his main characters. Chris runs to Bobby Shatford (Mark Wahlberg) and jumps into his arms, Murph (John C. Reilly) stands awkwardly looking around without obvious family, and Tyne is the last to leave the boat, foreshadowing his eventual demise.

Clooney's character, Tyne, is established as respectful of the lives of others, taking exception to the bluntness of owner Bob Brown (Michael Ironside) who only makes jibes about Tyne's poor catch rather than showing respect to a fellow seaman who died on board the *Hannah Boden* while at sea and whose body is unloaded at the quayside. The presence of Brown is important to establish the different pressures Tyne is under: economic (his catch is small and potential profit is drastically eroded by deductions), professional (if he does not improve, Brown will offer his boat to another), personal (his rival, Linda, has outperformed him), and almost spiritual (his sense of self-belief that he will find fish, reflected in the decision of Douglas Kosco (Joseph D. Reitman) not to go with him, which Tyne takes as a loss of faith in him personally).

In appearance, Clooney is rough-shaven throughout, typically sporting a green baseball cap. Apart from the brief scene in the bar and approaching Sully (William Fichter) about a job, we do not see him outside a work-related situation. Even in the bar, he is coming off the phone from arranging another trip out and delivering the news to Murph and Bobby, and in speaking to Sully, the harsh economic realities of the community dependent on fishing help to explain character choices (Sully is working for free for a friend).

There is a flirtatious element in Tyne's exchanges with Chris Cotter (Diane Lane), on his side at least ("not only is she pretty, she's smart"), but she hates him, less for who he is but for taking Bobby away. For his part he remains civil, taking his leave at the bar with a "Ma'am" to Chris and Murph's ex-wife. Here is also a tiny gesture of tipping his chin up, often used as a greeting, but here not directed at any particular character and denoting a moment of thought. There is an oscillation between a manner that is polite and one that is more blunt: he sets out the proposition of heading out again but adds, "Join me, don't join me," claiming he will go with or without them and their replacements are only a phone call away. Since they do not call his bluff we do not know how real this threat was, but there is an uncompromising side to Tyne's character, which is perhaps an integral part of surviving at sea but on land can make him seem a little brusque, possibly explaining his failed marriage.

Tyne is seen certainly as driven but not incompetent. Linda pays tributes to his knowledge of charts, and he seems to believe his later assertion to Bobby that he is doing what he "was made to do." Later as he settles into his captain's chair, cap pulled over his face, this seems possible. The low angle of him stepping out onto the bridge and the reverse angle of him looking down at the men waiting expectantly suggest that (at this point) they are happy to serve under him and how he relishes the position. On board, he is the one who makes decisive action, breaking up the fight between Sully and Murph, shooting the shark, resuscitating Murph when he is back on board, and stitching his hand.

The work, especially the laying out of nets, is hard and dangerous, including operating at night with little sleep, while being sprayed with freezing cold water. Top shots of real fisherman landing fish are intercut relatively seamlessly with closer shots of the main actors in low-angle close-up apparently landing them. We see the extremely cramped living conditions on board, Sully's view that, although fit to do the job, he does not "see the romance in it," and the fact that even without accidents, men die on board as the life is so hard. Murph's son wants to be with his dad but he definitely does not want to be a fisherman. The old man at the bar who notes ruefully that he was out on the Flemish Cap in '62 is a physical representation of the potential future of the crew, if they live that long. There is even some related genuine suffering among the film crew (in front of and behind the camera) in being blasted with wind machines, sprayed with powerful hoses, and rocked by some fairly vicious wave machines in Warner Brothers' immense Soundstage 16 (Wahlberg in particular was often seasick).

The prime reason few ambiguities attach themselves to Clooney's character is the sentiment that drives the film. Few others question the actions of the captain, except at the beginning when Chris resents Tyne's suggestion about going to sea at all, rather than precisely where, and the two exchanges in the boathouse with Bobby Shatford (Mark Wahlberg) are both cast as a father and son with Bobby in no position to question the actions of his senior as well as superior officer. The first of the two scenes, in which Bobby declares that he loves the sea but cannot stand being more than two feet away from the woman he loves, prompts a laconic replay from Tyne: "Then you've got a problem, son." Here, Tyne praises him and calls him "a natural," casting him as a form of successor. The second, in the growing storm, sees Tyne as an angry father, calling Bobby "nothing but a punk." We see tears of frustration welling up in Tyne's eyes as he hears the crew shouting to each other to motivate each other, clearly dispirited. However, there is also an element of paranoia in his verbal assault on Bobby, assuming the men are talking about "how I lost it" and telling Bobby, whom he had praised earlier, "don't fuck with me." There does not seem to be much between these two extremes of indulgence and abuse. The mini-mutiny that takes place when the men state that they want to go home provokes a scathing response from Tyne, and it seems that clichés are enough to win them back ("separating the men from the boys" and "this is the moment of truth"). By the time that Linda Greenlaw (Mary Elizabeth Mastrantonio) screams her warning into the radio that he is "headed straight for the monster," the script is closer to the poetry of *Moby Dick* than rational argument.

As the storms converge, it seems that Tyne becomes almost unhinged as he yells at the waves as much as his fellow crew members and there is a sense of a Lear-like loss of sanity. This can be seen as an admirable obstinacy, an unwillingness to accept what fate has thrown at them, or an irresponsible loss of sanity, that he literally leads the men needlessly to their deaths. There is a fatalistic streak to Tyne's character ("I want to catch some fish, it's what I do"), which lends his role a sense of driven determination, but for Clooney it also deprives him of much depth to play with. The commercial pressures are clear from the outset, but it seems that even were this not the case, Tyne would still rather be at sea than on dry land. Rather than an exploration of a fully rounded psychological entity, it feels more like a lament for decisions based on tradition and feeling. There is inevitability about the narrative in which rationalism is passed over in favor of superstition (the crew sees a rogue wave, a low haul, and the shark attack, as signs of bad luck, as if their voyage is cursed).

In the script, credited to Bill Wittliff but with an uncredited rewrite from veteran Bo Goldman, Tyne does not smash the radio like Quint in *Jaws* (Steven Spielberg, 1975). On the contrary, he keeps trying to communicate and even goes to extreme lengths, hanging from a mast with the blowtorch trying to reattach an antenna. However, Tyne acts as a focus for the elegiac sentiments that underpin the film. His longest speech is the lyrical description of heading out to sea, which he delivers to Linda to explain his love of the job and returns as a voice-over at the end as his requiem. It is present too in the virtually omnipresent orchestral score of James Horner, which casts a grand, elegiac tone over the film, from its opening images to any wider shot at sea. Horner, responsible for over 100 film scores, such as James Cameron's *Titanic* (1997) and *Avatar* (2009), represents the Hollywood mainstream in terms of composing.

Without a radio, Tyne claims that "we're back in the nineteenth century." However, he is no Ahab. He asks the crew if they want to carry on and shows them the fax showing the storm fronts. They give in relatively easily, although once out at sea, perhaps they have little real choice. We pan around their faces but the option to wait it out or "to say to hell with it and drive right through it" is hardly equal in dramatic terms. It feels like a speech before battle, equating to surrendering or fighting on. At the same time the film tries to give Tyne the aura of a slightly darker figure, choosing to step back into the shadows of his boat rather than swim to the surface. It draws on the cliché of the captain unwilling to leave his ship, but there is more the sense of a marine version of agoraphobia, possibly an inability to function outside a familiar environment, which are also overtones of the "go-it-alone" hero of detective fiction as he declares, "I don't like partners, business partners that is."

The heroics of the Coast Guard rescue almost seem like a subplot. The yacht sequences especially, whether based on fact or not, feel like additions to show Tyne in a more positive light. Tyne has a professional reason to do what he does and, despite his ultimate demise, is seen as an expert seaman. The yacht is engaged in a foolhardy pleasure cruise, arguably taking rescue crews away from their ability to reach the *Andrea Gail*. On board, the film becomes quite episodic, as we shift from one obstacle to another (releasing a flying "anchor" that threatens to smash the wheelhouse or turning the boat around) usually followed by an element of euphoric whooping, which seems progressively empty. A beatific moment of hope is signaled by a glimpse of the sun at a moment of calm but Tyne realizes, unlike Bobby, that they are not going to escape. He plows on, up an almost vertical wave (the iconic poster shot for the film) before the ship is flipped over and sinks.

It is debatable how historically accurate the film can be, since there were no survivors, no wreckage was found beyond a few pieces of deck gear, and the data on the nearest buoy went off the scale. In the foreword to the 1997 nonfiction account of the same name, Junger explicitly rules out fictionalizing his material, feeling "that risked diminishing the facts of whatever facts I was able to determine."[5] It is debatable, however, how far the book follows this resolution with extended passages written in the present tense, effectively guessing what is happening at any given time. The film is really an exercise in dramatized conjecture but with the one element that Junger rejected making up: dialogue. Incidents that Junger records over an entire career, like being pulled overboard, a shark landing on deck, or the wheelhouse windows being blown out, are condensed in the film, all happening on a single trip.[6] Junger recounts tales of captains who have stayed with their boats and conjectures Tyne "heading straight into the mouth of meteorological hell" (language that the script appropriates, recasts, and puts in the mouth of Linda).[7]

It is clearly to the film's advantage if it can emphasize the support of the local community in its making, and certainly featurettes on the film's extras include sequences with local people as extras, meeting the cast, and generally expressing positive views about their alter egos. Clooney and Wahlberg in particular went to some lengths to charm (or at least not antagonize) the community with Wahlberg staying in Bobby Shatford's actual room in the real Crow's Nest in Gloucester.

In the case of Tyne, the film plays up a flirtatious relationship with Linda (the pair jokingly call each other captain, exchanging lingering stares, and this scene evokes his extended description of sailing out of harbor), whom the real man barely knew, and Petersen's narrative also exaggerates the poor haul of fish he brings in at the beginning. The vindication of Tyne's professionalism (his subsequent large haul of fish) may be a matter of wishful thinking as the ship was never recovered, although Clooney asserts on the extras that Tyne "was a good fisherman." Perhaps then, as with any fictional scenario supposedly based on real events, it makes sense not to be too pedantic about authenticity. Although time and place are clear from the subtitle at the outset, and despite using the names of real people, the film is not claiming to be a documentary.

A major part of the appeal is the special effects of models and the spec-tacle of environmental catastrophe (films portraying extreme weather proliferated through the 1990s, like Jan de Bont's 1996 *Twister*), but despite the shots of giant waves and the helicopter rescues, it is the human drama that takes center stage. The incident in which Murph is dragged off the back of the boat gains in power by his disappearance being unnoticed by the others as they scrabble to pick up light sticks that Sully had dropped. The camera tracks up to Sully to provide a more powerful contrast with the reverse angle as Sully looks up to berate Murph and we have a shot of the empty space where he had been standing. It is space, absence rather than presence, that is significant. Death at sea can be sud-den and unannounced. The reconciliation between Sully and Murph is effective in its portrayal of male emotional illiteracy. Even Murph, the one who seems the man most able to express emotions to others in the whole film, still cannot bring himself to apologize. Sully draws on cliché ("You'd have done the same for me") but he is aware of its emptiness ("Isn't that what I'm supposed to say?"). The distance between the two men, placed on the edges of the frame, right outside the T-frame, makes it clear that this is unlikely.

The film is partly a celebration of the human spirit but also strangely of forces beyond human control, implicitly a sign of divine power. When Tyne sees they are doomed, he personifies the storm ("She's not going to let us out") and earlier exhorted the men to pray. Whether Tyne repre-sents hubris inviting punishment, or the grandeur of human resistance in the face of insurmountable odds, depends on how engaging viewers find his character. The crew each accept their fate stoically, perhaps Murph most of all, selflessly noting that "it's gonna be hard on my little boy." However, even here sentimentality creeps in with Bobby, hardly the most articulate member of the crew, expressing the simple but poetic farewell to Christine, "It's only love," which (even more sentimentally) she some-how hears in her dreams and then shares with Ethel, Bobby's mother (Junger records both women testifying that they really had such dreams). If we are swept up in the emotion of the moment, particularly by the score, this might work; if not, it might seem a desperate (if understand-able) way to derive meaning from something which denies human understanding.

The film's general attitude to its subject is one of respect. Irene cares enough for Michael to see him off at the dockside, Sully responds to a fel-low human being (Murph) to save his life, and Murph shows magnanim-ity toward his ex-wife's new partner. The final scene is the church service to the men, and the film as a whole is clearly a testament to their memory.

Their full names remind us of how wider society views them, but the final words are Tyne's impassioned speech about moving out of harbor, giving the ending the veneer of an upbeat ending as well as reflecting the notions of the men's souls setting forth on a spiritual journey. Throughout, there is a wish not to alienate the Gloucester community, but all this admirable behavior is a little too close to lionization to make the film dramatically credible and engaging as a whole.

CONCLUSION

It has been 10 years now since Clooney starred in an overtly action-driven picture. *The American*, although trailed as an action film, is far more of an exploration of an individual's soul. Part of this shift is probably due to a wish to produce a body of work more thoughtful and dialogue based in nature and partly due to the simple mechanics of age. It becomes more difficult, as Sean Connery and Roger Moore found, to be accepted as the credible hero of an action narrative into one's 50s. There is a personal element too in the toll that such films take on the human body. After injuring himself quite seriously on *Syriana*, Clooney may well think long and hard about accepting such roles in the future, possibly one reason behind his dropping out of a remake of *The Man from Uncle*.

CHAPTER 4

A Mixture of Several Genres

Genre is one of the key concepts by which viewers make sense of what they watch. It is one of the key factors that we use to help decide whether we even choose to watch a film at all. To the experience of any given film we each bring a host of assumptions about kinds of locations, situations, dialogue, and forms of resolution that we expect. If the filmmaker disrupts those expectations too sharply, we may react with confusion, boredom, or even anger. If generic boundaries are not pushed at all, a film may seem wholly predictable and forgettable. It is a notable feature of Clooney's career that since 1997, he has chosen to be involved with films that stretch generic boundaries, sometimes significantly further than critics and general audiences expect, and in particular to blend existing genres.

FROM DUSK TILL DAWN (ROBERT RODRIGUEZ, 1996)

Seth Gecko: Do you think this is what I am?

The difficulties for some viewers perhaps lie in the genres, which the film attempts to mix (gangster, western, and horror). The film is really a celebration of exploitation cinema, and reviewers unfamiliar with this often criticize the film by unwittingly listing the typical components of this subgenre: a blend of big-star names with an unapologetically lurid portrayal of sex, violence, and special effects.

The opening sequence ends before the titles roll with Seth Gecko (George Clooney) berating his brother, Richie (Quentin Tarantino), about the meaning of the term "low-profile": "It is not taking girls hostage. It is not shooting police. It is not setting fire to a building." With a less brutal scene before this, such dialogue might find its natural home in a comedy or buddy movie. The theatricality of the opening scene in the store is underlined as Rodriguez's camera pans from the ranger as he briefly exits the scene to reveal the Gecko brothers in hiding, bringing them forward into shot and then pushing them back out again. It feels like a more decorous theatrical form of art with which Richie has no patience, unable to wait for his cue but stepping onto the "stage" of the action and acting preemptively, shooting the ranger with little apparent justification.

The progression of the main section of the narrative, once the characters are holed up at the club, slides into more familiar monster movie territory, anticipated by the red, George Romero-style titles at the beginning. The presence of special effects expert and horror director Tom Savini in the cast, and a narrative that quickly descends into a series of battles to the death with supernatural creatures, shift the film into low-budget horror.

From the outset, we are not in a fictional landscape dominated by realism. Richie holds up his hand with a hole blown in it, not to howl in pain but to look through it at Seth in wonder. The same shot had already been used in *Terminator II* (James Cameron, 1991) and would reappear in the TV movie of Stephen King's *Thinner* (Tom Holland, 1996). If this were not enough, as the car drives out of shot Rodriguez gives us a privileged view through the body of the car to the female hostage being held within, perhaps influenced by Michel Gondry's 1993 video for Björk's *Human Behavior*, which featured a similar shot of the singer being eaten by a bear but remaining visible in its stomach. The fact that Cheech Marin plays not only a border guard (with a badge reading "Oscar Marin," the name of his real father) but also the parts of Chet Pussy and Carlos suggests that there is less a focus on fully rounded psychological characters than on action. Similarly, Texas Ranger Earl McGraw (Michael Parks) is killed in this film but reappears playing the same character in volume 1 of Tarantino's *Kill Bill* (2003), *Deathproof* (2007), and *Planet Terror* (2007).

There is tongue-in-cheek character naming with Kelly Houge as a newscaster played by Kelly Preston (known for her modeling work at the time). The naming of the Fuller family (Jacob, Kate, and Scott) is a conscious reference to Sam Fuller, seminal director of pulp fiction cinema. The naming of Sex Machine is a gag for the director playing him (Tom Savini) and that he will become a blood-seeking "machine" like the other vampires in the film. Casting includes figures chosen more for their physical appearance or notoriety in other spheres rather than acting talent, like Frost (former NFL defensive back Fred Williamson). Rodriguez, known for his ultra-low-budget breakthrough hit *El Mariachi* in 1992 at the Sundance Festival, also appears in the band in the club and edited the film too.

However, the most interesting aspect of the film falls not so much in the vampire element but in the film's first 20 minutes. In this we have George Clooney, Dr. Ross of *ER*, being rude and disrespectful to an old motel keeper, subsequently punching another old man, a pastor no less, and threatening to shoot him in the face in front of his daughter. Clooney's character swears aggressively at his captives, and from the very opening sequence and the information given to us via a TV bulletin, he and his brother seem prepared to kill others in order to escape. He is a bad-mouthed, ruthless killer. He is prepared to indulge in homophobic and racist abuse, asking Jacob (Harvey Keitel) and Scott (Ernest Liu) if they are "a couple of fags," and assumes Scott is Japanese before Richie corrects him that Chinese is more likely.

There is an interesting paradox here. Seth promises that he will release them unharmed if they help them get through the border to Mexico. Jacob must have faith in the word of another and Seth must decide if he will keep "his word" (given earlier to the unfortunate female hostage left in Richie's care). Issues of faith and belief run under the relationships here, not just in the obvious sense of a pastor who cannot bring himself to preach any longer after the tragic death of his wife. This is also reflected in the language of the script with Seth declaring that giving up a percentage of ill-gotten gains to the local crime gangs is "scripture . . . So it is written, so shall it be done." He operates under different conventions of morality than Jacob, but the need for some form of order and rules permeates both criminal and religious codes of belief.

Clooney makes a visually striking villain here, dressed in black, with cropped hair and a snake-like tattoo rising up his neck. He is shot several times in the opening section from extreme low angle (from the back of the car as he unloads food at the motel and later holding a gun to Scott and Jacob in their room). Kate (Juliette Lewis) describes him as a "creepy guy" when their bus first almost collides into him, but his salute with a beer bottle and his usual smoldering look do not really convey "creepy," suggesting Kate is using such terminology to deny her own attraction to him. Verbally, he alternates between being bullying and charming, encouraging Scott and Kate after they have followed orders, like a personal coach.

Ten years before David Cronenberg's brutal opening in *A History of Violence* (2006), we have two apparently amoral robbers, prepared to kill to get what they want from small-town motels. Agent Robert Newman describes the film as "being about a couple of serial killers," but while this may reflect the disturbed side of Richie, it misrepresents the character of Seth Gecko.[1] Particularly important, Seth is defined in opposition to his brother Richie, to whom his sibling loyalty overcomes any qualms he might have about Richie's deeply disturbed and sick attitude to women. Richie is the real evil here. His sly, predatory glances at any nearby female are clear from the outset, and his delusional fantasies in which Kate invites him to perform an intimate act on her, which, Rodriguez's close-up subjective shot of her makes subsequently clear occurred only in his head, mark him as the dangerous sex offender.

The episode in the motel defines the distinction between the nature of Richie and Seth. Left alone with a hostage, Richie retires to a back room to watch TV and pats the bed next to him, indicating that his petrified woman should join him. When Seth returns, it is only some minutes into his conversation that he freezes with a choice of burgers in hand and no hostage to give it to. Rodriguez's camera pans to an empty seat and Richie explains in a casual offhand manner, pointing at the bedroom, "She's in there." In stepping into the doorway, Seth occupies this position, just looking, trying to make sense of what he is seeing, for over 35 seconds without a cut. There is no conventional reverse shot, giving us a privileged view of action, but we share with Seth a series of very fast flash-cuts as key images are seared onto his consciousness (a bloodied phone, blood sprayed on furniture, and perhaps most shocking, a blood-covered body with a head covered with a pillow, marked with the scorch marks of several pistol blasts). A category error is occurring in Seth's mind. A hostage has been altered into an abject dehumanized corpse, a map of Richie's perversions, with a key clue in the tape that was on his hands now used to bind those of the woman. It is only after Seth turns away that Rodriguez allows us a partial view of the room, the central grue-some sight blocked by Seth's body (as if he is shielding us from our own worst impulses in looking).

He asks a question, essentially rhetorical in nature ("What is wrong with you?"), and the answer, which he himself provides himself, almost reads as a definition of the Clooney on-screen persona and brand: "I'm a professional fucking thief. I don't kill people that I don't have to and I don't rape women." He may have played occasional amoral characters like Jack in *The American* but outright, unredeemable evil of the sort represented by Richie here has not appeared in his résumé. Even in the opening scene, he shoots the storekeeper because he threatens them with a gun, not like Richie's random shooting of the ranger (claiming the victims were trying to signal to one another). Seth struggles to assert some kind of order on events, even a sense of a code of honor among thieves, forcing Richie to admit by brute-force grabbing hold of his lapels that what he (Richie) is doing "is not how it's done."

In the store, in the motel, and in the bar, Seth is the one with the patter, the one who makes the threats, who defines the situation. Rodriguez gives us a stylized medium close-up of Clooney, holding a gun in a threatening pose in a low angle, exuding threatening cool in all three locations with the gun blurred in the extreme foreground. Such a role seems credible for Clooney from early on in his film career, even though he was far from first choice for the part and was cast only once John Travolta, Steve Buscemi, Michael Madsen, Tim Roth, and Christopher Walken all passed. However, there is some wilful blindness in his character here as clearly Seth does know "what is wrong with" Richie whose promise under compulsion not to do it again has the sense of a schoolboy promising not to be naughty. This is very much a sibling bond based on inequalities. Seth as the elder, more responsible brother makes the sensible plans (getting to Mexico, meeting a contact, and lying low in El Rey), looking after his brother like a nurse, buying food, redressing the wound, and telling him to put his "bit" in while they drive to stop him grinding his teeth. Most obviously, Seth uses hostages to gain some advantage rather than just killing them. Richie whines childishly and complains about having to give a percentage of their loot to a local gang but Seth accepts the situation more realistically. Where Richie is impulsive, vicious, and sadistic, Seth is calm and brutal only for a purpose (interrupting Richie's later complaining in the van, for example, by knocking him out rather than letting him give them away). The fact that Seth is not Richie is a clear point in his favor, but the fact that he so easily forgives him is not.

Richie's lust for Kate is signaled by a whooshing, rumbling sound effect when he projects his fantasy onto her (a similar distorted, rushing sound is used later to convey the vampire's desire for his bloody hand), and Rodriguez gives us his distorted subjective point of view with a wide-angle lens as he picks up the car keys at her feet. In the van, we cut between a series of dissolves of Richie looking and (apparently nonsexual) parts of Kate's body, especially her feet. Rodriquez's use of Jimmie Vaughan's "Dengue Woman Blues" (1996) in the score here with lyrics like "You've got me all crazy" is a disturbing assumption of a sex attacker's point of view, not only literally but also seeing complicity on the part of the desired individual.

Tarantino rejected the offer of directing the picture so that he could concentrate more fully on his own performance. Originally, Tarantino's script had all the Fullers and Geckos survive but slimmed this down to a representative member of each group. Although he had written other scripts, and in the chronology of his subsequent career *From Dusk Till Dawn* seems to come after his breakthrough successes of *Reservoir Dogs* (1992) and *Pulp Fiction* (1994), this was actually Tarantino's first official, paid writing job, with early drafts dating back to 1991. The initial stand-off with the family is reminiscent of *Reservoir Dogs* with male, aggressive robbers, dressed largely in black suits, pointing handguns at targets in quite a choreographed, stylized manner at angles from one another and Seth even turning his pistol sideways for no reason other than to look cool. Later, in the club the camera circles Seth and Richie, back-to-back as they attempt to hold off the vampires, and as in the opening sequence with Vince (John Travolta) and Jules (Samuel L. Jackson) in *Pulp Fiction*, they are framed in a two-shot, firing their pistols at the same time to shoot down Chet. The lengthy quotation from Ezekiel 25:17, climaxing with a threat to "raise vengeance," which eventually finds its natural home in Jules's speech delivered before killing people, was in early drafts of the script here.

Mexico represents freedom from U.S. law and, at a personal level, freedom from moral prohibition. The club, the unsubtly named Titty Twister, is a liminal state, a place where the normal rules of life no longer apply, making it a suitable place for the appearance of the supernatural. Chet's monologue on the steps of the club, listing the various types of sexual service on offer, also reflects the sense of carnival and excess that operates here. As the film's title suggests, its borderline status is also related to chronology during the hours of darkness, literally from dusk till dawn—according to folklore, the period when vampires may operate.

There is a further generic twist in the club, as the out-of-tune piano of a western is replaced by the diegetic music from the band and particularly the act of Satanico Pandemonium (Salma Hayek, overcoming her phobia of snakes), so named after a 1975 Mexican horror film, which Tarantino saw while working in a video store. A large saloon brawl becomes a fight to the death with female vampires, and Seth shoots down the chandelier in an updating of a Zorro-style stunt, so that the structure stakes Satanico. The same iconic setting of scantily clad dancing women, a snake, and the foot-in-mouth act appears in Ramstein's video for "Engel" ("Angel") (Zoran Bihac, 1997).

As a vampire narrative, it hardly stretches the conventions of the genre, beyond the film's opening. The use of masks, animatronics, and computer-generated imagery represents the state of special effects technology in the mid-1990s for a relatively low-budget movie (although it had crept up to $17 million by the time of its release). The action even halts after the initial outburst of violence so that Seth can organize a regrouping and a gathering of knowledge about vampires (mostly derived from films), possibly also for audience members unfamiliar with the genre. It is confirmed that they (vampires, not viewers) can be repelled with crucifixes, even makeshift ones, that they need to be staked through the heart, and to kill them you need garlic, sunlight, or silver (although they are not entirely sure about the latter point). The entities include some that have very little connection with vampires. The creature that almost pins Seth and that is dispatched by Kate is more an indication of the special effects genesis of the script. The film, given an extensive rewrite by Tarantino, was based on an original idea by John Esposito and Robert Kurtzman, whose background in special effects meant that first drafts of the script were really just contrivances for plenty of gore and makeup. Esposito created similar monster scenes in *Graveyard Shift* (Ralph Singleton, 1990), where a potential allegory of an industrial machine literally eating its workers morphs into a random creature attacking humans in tunnels.[2]

Like the buddy movie dialogue at the end of the opening sequence, in the middle of the film there is a moment of philosophical reflection, which sits uneasily with the trashy generic markers around it. After the pastor has punched Seth after taunts about his faith, Seth asserts that despite having no religious faith himself, if the creatures outside represent pure evil, then there must also be a heaven. It is unclear at this point whether he is just trying to rationalize what he has seen with his own eyes or trying to act as a catalyst in reigniting the pastor's faith, so that this can be used as a weapon, in blessing holy water for example.

The film seems to drift further into cliché with Sex Machine starting to recount a lengthy Vietnam anecdote (ironically the sort actually experienced by Savini personally), but Rodriguez takes advantage of the empty dialogue to take the volume down and cut back to Savini, who has been bitten, and the voices that he is starting to hear. With almost a comic touch, we see the physical signs of transformation in his hand that he tries to hide behind him. This is continued in the shot in which Savini's anecdote continues, but as he faces the camera (and the other characters) a pair of gnarled, vampiric hands slowly appears on his shoulder. The impossible gradually invades a realistic shot. There is a playful element in the dialogue, not just in Satanico's resolution to make Seth her slave dog and call him "Spot" but in Seth's rejection of slavery with the quip (improvised by Clooney himself) "No thanks, I've already had a wife."

The film has overtones of the work of John Carpenter, not just in linking ethnicity with a sexually deviant social underbelly as in *Big Trouble in Little China* (1986) but more explicitly in his later *Vampires* (1998), where we also see a modern-day narrative set in the American West with vampires, apparently unkillable unless staked, bursting into flames on contact with sunlight, especially seen breaking in shafts of light through a building at daybreak. There are even minor Carpenter tropes like the use of jump-cut dissolves as Seth stakes his first vampire with maximum effort, unseen just out of shot. As with Carpenter, the jump cuts seem to suggest a reduction of time and yet the slow dissolves act in the opposite direction, producing a curious effect, mixing compression and elongation of time within the same sequence.

By the end, the club has been destroyed, but since we do not see the source of the vampires their complete destruction is impossible to ascertain. The pastor, Scott, Richie, and countless others have been killed, but Kate and Seth survive, the money is intact, and Seth gets to meet his contact. Kate seems to inherit the motor home and a new sense of independence, driving off alone. The very final shot, pulling back to reveal the back of the club, which seems half landfill site and half Mayan temple, suggests that the club may not be a solely modern manifestation of evil but its crude style also makes it more of a nod to the kind of grindhouse cinema to which Tarantino seems drawn.

There is a bond of sorts between Kate and Seth, who have lost both a brother and perhaps their innocence about things supernatural. As he lets her go with a wad of cash, Seth's final piece of dialogue underlines the difference between himself and his late brother: "I may be a bastard but I'm not a fucking bastard." Exactly what Kate is euphemistically offering, when she asks if he wants "some company," is a little ambiguous but the George Clooney persona is not ready to be linked with associations of exploitative sexuality. Although operating in a very different genre, both here and in *One Fine Day*, his on-screen character keeps his word and comes to represent the values of reliability and paternal protectiveness. In both roles, there is also a quick-thinking, resourceful element, whether it is using a security guard to speak Spanish over the phone to help reach a key interviewee in the earlier film or improvising makeshift crucifixes here.

O BROTHER, WHERE ART THOU? (THE COEN BROTHERS, 2000)

Pete: That don't make no sense.
McGill: It's a fool looks for logic in the human heart.

The parallels between Ulysses Everett McGill (George Clooney), Pete Hogwallop (John Turturro), and Delmar O'Donnell (Tim Blake

Nelson) as they escape from prison and Homer's *The Odyssey* are clear from the outset with the text appearing on screen ("O muse"), the first line of Homer's epic poem. However, in an irony suitable to the quirky nature of the film, it was nominated for an Oscar for both Best Original Screenplay and Best Adapted Screenplay. The classic tale is evoked in several names, like the central character, Ulysses, as well as the Reform Party's candidate for governor, Homer Stokes (Wayne Duvall), the incumbent governor, Menelaus "Pappy" O'Daniel (Charles Durning), and McGill's ex-wife Penelope (Holly Hunter). Even Big Dan Teague (John Goodman), with his eye patch, alludes to the monstrous Cyclops. Like Homer's *Odyssey*, the narrative opens with an escape from imprisonment and climaxes as Ulysses returns to Ithaca (here in Mississippi), disguised as an old man (he dons a terrible false beard at the final concert) to prevent his love from marrying a rival.

The nameless blind man whom they meet on the flatcar and who delivers a number of ominous pronouncements (that they will travel a long way, find a fortune but not the one they seek, and see a cow on the roof of a house before ultimately finding salvation) is clearly an Oracle figure, close to Homer's Tiresias, who returns at the end, similarly unexplained and slightly detached from the narrative that occurs around him. The odd notion of a blind driver does not seem to occur to the trio of escapees, but it is picked up in the character of Mr. Lund (Stephen Root), the radio host and record producer (except his loss of sight does not really grant any increased wisdom since McGill is able to fool him into paying more for nonexistent musicians). As McGill, Pete, and Delmar are sitting by a campfire, they (and the viewer) gradually become aware of movement behind them. White-robed figures, men and women, walk slowly past, singing in what McGill describes as "some kind of a . . . congregation." The power of song and movement acts hypnotically on the trio who follow the figures to their destination, suggested by the lyrics: the river. The camera cranes up to take in the river scene of communal baptism.

Perhaps the most obvious allusion is the scene with the siren-like women, whose voices are heard by Pete as the trio are driving along in a stolen car. We follow Pete as he bursts through foliage and share his sight line as he is struck by a vision of three women. Like the cheerleading scene-as-epiphany for Lester Burnham (Kevin Spacey) in *American Beauty* (Alan Ball, 1999), there is a slow track up to the object of lust, and the trio seem impotently hypnotized by a vision of beauty with close-ups on each man, a nonnaturalistic level of perfection and coordination of the women's movement with provocative wringing of clothes in slow motion, all the time their own wet clothes clinging tightly to their bodies. Ignoring McGill's formal set of introductions, the women just keep singing, slowly approach, and offer him alcohol. The lyrical content of their echoing song, including the line "You and me and the devil makes three," underlines their role as temptresses, and certainly the way they squeeze Delmar's face suggests that he has lost control of his own faculties. With the shift into more discordant whistling, the frame fades to black. Rather than Homer's Circe, who turned Ulysses's men into pigs, we have nameless beauties, which also sing spell-binding songs and apparently transform Pete into a toad.

There are also clear parallels with *Sullivan's Travels* (Preston Sturges, 1942) in which a film director called Sullivan (Joel McCrea) sets out to make a gritty documentary about the reality of poverty in the United States during the Great Depression but ultimately rejects the project, learning that escapist fantasies can do more to cheer the spirits of his audience. The title of the original film was to be *O Brother, Where Art Thou?* In a sense, the Coen brothers give us the film Sullivan never made but blended with his later understanding about the value of fantasy. Thus serious elements are juxtaposed with a lighter tone and neither is allowed to dominate completely. It makes for a slightly unsettling mix at times, but compared to other Coen work perhaps accommodates more comfortably their tendency toward the quirky and eccentric alongside dark humor.

The cinematography of Roger Deakins evokes his work on *The Shawshank Redemption* (Frank Darabont, 1994), another tale involving prisoners, escape, and lyrical beauty of the American South. It is the first film to be entirely digitally corrected, so that the film's lush colors (it was shot in a Mississippi summer) are converted to the look of an older sepia tone to deepen a sense of nostalgia and pleasure in countryside that was less forgiving at the time.

What contributed to the development of the film as a sleeper hit is its music, from the opening sound of the chain gang singing, heard before we see it. Despite the presence of armed guards on horseback, the workers almost seem content with the melody and rhythm raising their spirits and sustaining an element of hope. However, although "Po Lazarus" by James Carter, a genuine, original plantation song (the only one in the film) is heard at this point, the notion of a contented group of workers is only a consoling cliché. It soon gives way to "Sweet Rock Candy Mountain," a world dominated by the sweet and artificial. The melody and lyrics seem to ameliorate the lot of the poor and oppressed, but such music is also used manipulatively by disreputable politicians as part of their campaigns. As the escapees listen to music at Walter's house, we hear "You Are My Sunshine," used again at the political rally near the end when McGill

meets his daughters, representing the nostalgic appeal of a more innocent, romantic age. The music is often motivated from within the scene,
not just via the radio. We see several scenes of groups singing, the volume
of which rises and falls as we approach or depart from their presence (like
Mr. Lund groaning badly off-key in his sound booth). This includes
Tommy with his guitar, the congregation by the river, and most obviously
the Soggy Bottom Boys themselves who take an impromptu detour to sing
"into a can" for money.

Generically, the film might even be classified as some kind of musical,
keenly evoking a time when music helped create a sense of a shared culture as well as an increasingly lucrative means to make money. We see
the very primitive mechanics of the recording process and the importance
of the recording contract, even if Delmar can append only a cross to his.
Music has a political purpose too as a way to reach the masses, used by
both ends of the political spectrum as we see the Reform campaign use a
band playing on the back of a truck and later at a rally, and Pappy discovering at the end the way to gain popularity by association, in sharing a
stage with the Soggy Bottom Boys. The Reform campaign especially
seems to focus on upbeat numbers (like "Keep on the Sunny Side") as a
way of associating their brand of politics with optimism and hope. The
music is part of the overt gimmickry of campaigning, like sharing the
stage with a midget and a broom to symbolize standing up for the little
man and sweeping the old politics away. Chris Thomas King as Tommy
is actually a talented musician and played his own numbers, and Tim
Blake Nelson (looking like a slimmed-down Stephen Baldwin) had a
good enough voice to perform his song "In the Jailhouse Now." Clooney
himself, whose actual vocals were performed by Dan Tyminski from
T-Bone Burnett's original song, gives a sufficiently convincing mime to
persuade many viewers that he was actually singing.

The soundtrack stayed stubbornly popular at the top of a number of
different charts and acted as something of a catalyst for a resurgence of
interest in bluegrass, blues, and country. It even went on to win a number of awards at the 2001 Country Music Awards and was voted Album
of the Year at the 2002 Grammies. It also led to the strange situation of
a band calling itself The Soggy Bottom Boys performing and touring
songs from the film with Dan Tyminski on lead vocals, especially the
hit "Man of Constant Sorrow" (which won the Grammy for Best
Single). This was made more complicated by the release of D. A.
Pennebaker's film *Down from the Mountain* (2001), documenting a charity concert, featuring music from the soundtrack of *O Brother* and introduced by Holly Hunter.

There is a strong element of comic absurdity in the narrative, from our first sight of the three escapees, standing upright in a field, and then suddenly diving back down on a shouted warning. Unlike narratives like Erich von Stroheim's *Greed* (1924), where the protagonists are finally shackled together, underlining the negative brutality latent in human nature, here we see a celebration of joy in the ridiculous. Although initially motivated to find some "treasure" as McGill calls it, this is largely forgotten and ultimately revealed as a ruse anyway. The time deadline (that the valley where the money is supposedly hidden will be flooded as part of a hydroelectric scheme) fades in importance, and when the flood does finally happen, what seems like a deus ex machina act in saving the protagonists is predicted right from the outset.

Ultimately, it is not a pursuit of money that motivates McGill but love and comradeship, and there is a sweet earnestness about the hapless escapees. When asked if he knows his "way around a Walther PPK," Delmar replies, "Well, that's where we can't help you. I don't believe it's in Mississippi." The scene of Delmar waking to find Pete's clothes lying on the ground, as if he had been vaporized, is a comic highlight. Delmar concludes "them sirens did this to Pete" and "left his heart" since the shirt appears to be moving. The appearance of a toad does not destroy Delmar's superstitions but only refines them, so that he now believes that Pete has been magically turned into a toad. There is situation comedy in Delmar's subsequent chase after "Pete" and carrying "him" around in a box. McGill remains skeptical that the creature is Pete, to which Delmar calmly replies "Look at him" as if the likeness is obvious.

There is physical comedy, such as the openly false beards that the trio use to get into the rally at the end or the scene where they try and board a train, while still chained together. McGill stands, framed by the open carriage door, and asks his fellow passengers, whose point of view we share, in high-flown language whether any of them are "trained in metalurgical arts." We hear Delmar fall and see Pete being dragged down, but the humor is in the delay before McGill is slammed first to the ground and then dragged out in wide-eyed incomprehension.

Consistent with the era in which the action is set, there is a Marx Brothers feel to some of the three-shots of the escapees and the acting style of Turturro especially who gives several wide-eyed stares to the camera (for example, early on at the sound of pursuing dogs). The fight in which McGill challenges Vernon (Ray McKinnon), his wife's new suitor, subverts expectations. Clooney's character is clearly out of his depth, adopting a very strange fighting style with his hands raised ineffectively against Vernon's more professional stance. Even before any blows are exchanged, McGill moves right up into Vernon's face and sniffs, not as a grand attempt at humiliation but literally because he can smell his favorite pomade, the ultimate indignity. However, swift punches to his nose follow and McGill is literally thrown out of the store. The Coens do not give us the stereotypical western fistfight, cutting away from the action almost as soon as it starts so that we only hear rather than see the blows.

The Ku Klux Klan are portrayed as laughable, and the trio's stealing of uniforms and the ability to infiltrate a rally, despite marching so badly out of step, feels closer to the tone of Abbott and Costello movies. The whole scene seems ridiculous with the Klan members moving in almost Busby Berkeley-style dance moves to uplifting southern music. The reappearance of Big Dan is logical in terms of his character, but the escape of the trio is again nonnaturalistic, first as Dan catches a flagpole, inches from his face, only to then be flattened by a burning cross pushed down on him. The Reform rally acts as a way of drawing narrative threads together as Homer is unmasked as a racist and thrown out, along with his campaign manager, Vernon.

Clooney has a new look here: wild hair (something of a first for him), a defined Clark Gable-like moustache, arched eyebrows, often giving him a wide-eyed, surprised expression, and his mouth often held open (like the close-up of his face as the boy who is rescuing them drives at the wall of the burning barn, or the appearance of Pete, apparently reincarnated as a toad). Eating with an improvised napkin even by a campfire, he is defined by his choice of hair-care product: he is literally a Dapper Dan man, seeking this product out during the course of their journey and asking Walter if he has a hairnet that he can wear as he sleeps. And it even seems to dominate his dreams, waking with the mumbled question, "How's my hair?" He rejects the pomade called Fop, although this describes his character quite well, and he frets that "I don't know how I'm going to keep my coiffeur in order." Clooney is playing with his own image here as a figure known for his hair and signals a willingness to laugh at the excesses associated with grooming a star image. It is important too, though, as it shows that for the first time that he does not necessarily have to be placed in a narrative as an object of female attention.

It is McGill who assumes the role of chief planner and strategist and does seem the most observant of the three (being the first to notice the sound of singing by the campfire). McGill's verbose and formal language marks him as an educated outsider here. Later, he declines Delmar's offer of food, noting "a third of a gopher would only arouse my appetite," and declines to argue with Pete as "the personal rancor in that remark, I don't intend to dignify with comment." The later revelation that he is actually a disbarred lawyer hardly comes as a surprise. In moments of high pressure, however, his fluency deserts him, declaring repeatedly "We're in a tight spot" when they are surrounded in a barn. He can switch linguistic codes as it suits him, lecturing his peers on the "paranormal psychic powers of the blind" only to dismiss the words of "a nigger and an old man" a few moments later with "what the hell does he know."

He is not averse to minor acts of immorality, driving off without paying for gas, stealing a pocket watch from Wash, Pete's distant and untrustworthy relative, and later inventing two more players (unnecessarily adding the detail that they are black) in his band to secure more money from Mr. Lund. There is, however, also a core of decency running through McGill, so that he leads the group to rescue Tommy from the Ku Klux Klan (having chosen earlier to pick him up in the car), and although he lies to the group about the existence of "treasure," he does so in order to win back his wife and enjoy the experience of traveling together en route. Unlike his wife, the suitably named Penny, whom we first see in the five and dime store, he is not driven primarily by money. He has the gift to charm individuals when he needs to but he seems more drawn to values of community and constructs the trio into a surrogate family. He later indignantly declares himself as "the Pater Familia" on discovering the plot to usurp his position.

McGill is the only one of the three who does not race forward to be baptized, marking him as more skeptical. As Delmar subsequently describes him, he is the only one left "unaffiliated." After picking up Tommy, who claims to have sold his soul to the devil, McGill dismisses their conversion ("You two are as dumb as a bag of hammers"). However, although McGill notes that in times of economic hardship "everybody's looking for answers" and religion appears to offer some, the film is not as scathing in its criticism of religion per se as it is of those who pervert it for their own ends (like Bible salesman Big Dan Teague). The offer of forgiveness, redemption, and everlasting life is clearly attractive to Pete and especially Delmar, whose subsequent behavior is marked by a desire to lead a different life now that they are "saved." Although McGill is the natural leader of the three, we do not know exactly how he was caught in the first place, and he is singularly stupid in placing vanity above the risk of leaving clues, his Dapper Dan tins, that are clearly identifiable (and distinctively fragrant). McGill seems to recognize an alter ego in Big Dan, someone else "endowed with the gift of the gab," but his naïve politeness blinds him to the superficial charms of others. He is taken completely unaware during the picnic as Dan breaks off a branch from the tree under which they are sitting and proceeds to bludgeon him before making off with their money.

He is seen as protective toward his children, who are revealed at the Reform rally, as well as naturally affectionate (they instinctively run forward and hug him too). His problem is one of social standing: in the eyes of his wife, he is not "bona fide." For the entirety of the film, he is humbly dressed in the blue cap and overalls of the working man, contrasting with the new love rival who has a more impressive ring to offer. He has been disavowed by his wife, the children now taking their mother's maiden name, and he has been placed in a new narrative that he was "hit by a train." This family element to McGill's character is primarily a plot contrivance to bring the political and romantic subplots together, focused on his former home about to be flooded and where his ring is now housed. The retrieval of this item (the real treasure of the narrative) now becomes the focus of McGill's motivation, determined to show he is more than "some no-account drifter" as she calls him, and allows the dramatic intervention of the biblical-style flood (as predicted by the old man at the beginning).

Although McGill's observation that the store is "a geographical oddity: two weeks from everywhere" is intended more sarcastically at the length of time it will take to order either a car part or his favorite hair product, it also reflects the existential setting of the film as a whole. A little like *Forrest Gump* (Robert Zemeckis, 1994), the plot careers from one iconic image (especially from the American South) to another, including chain gangs, Ku Klux Klan rallies, bank-robbing gangsters, and itinerant workers. However, allusions to a wider social and political world are delivered with a light or comedic touch. The overweight entourage that waddle around Daddy O'Daniel, including his sons, reflect the manipulative nature of local politicians, but the Ku Klux Klan scene and the unmasking of Reform candidate Homer Stokes is mostly played for laughs with the three protagonists rescuing Tommy by means of some slapstick violence. The rows of faces that meet the escapees as they try to board the train are a silent reminder of the millions of itinerant laborers at the time. However, poverty is used more as a comedic backdrop. A friend of the trio, who gives them a meal, apologizes while they eat: "I slaughtered this horse last Tuesday. I'm afraid she's starting to turn."

The pursuit of the trio, which might have ended in lynching, turns more toward cartoonish violence as the barn in which they are sleeping is raked with machine-gun fire, without causing any injuries. The inversion of a barn burning into the hurling back of a torch, and the subsequent explosion of a police van and the rescue by Walter's son driving a getaway vehicle are more like the escapist fantasy of adventure films. The betrayal of friends by Walter to the authorities could seem dark, were it not for Pete's angry insults that he hurls down, standing in plain sight of the police guns; and the pile of books on which Walter's son sits both at the table and in the truck is a visual gag about his diminutive size but also reflects the positive consequences of being educated and being able to think for oneself. The shadowy figure, whom we may subsequently identify as Sheriff Cooley (Daniel von Bargen), pursuing the trio is not given much dramatic life beyond the wearing of dark glasses in which we see the reflection of fire on a couple of occasions and Tommy's description of the devil as "white as you folks, with mirrors for eyes."

Crime is touched on lightly, by implication one optional lifestyle in a time of economic hardship. The presentation of George Nelson (Michael Badalucco) is cartoonish from the outset, driving a car with notes fluttering all around it, politely stopping to ask directions before hurtling off with them on board, commanding McGill to hold the wheel as he hangs out to shoot at pursuing police. Strangely, the potential brutality and danger implicit in the situation are transferred onto animals. George, who has the attention span of a small child, is distracted by some cows, which he irrationally shoots at, hitting some. A few are scared into the road and one is hit by his pursuers. Similarly, later Big Dan's brutality is signaled by his gratuitous crushing of Pete-as-a-toad, which sends Delmar into a rage.

Despite toting a gun and threatening lives, there is little sense that the generic boundaries of the film will be breached by scenes of gore or traumatic violence. Delmar describes George's entrance into the bank with the understatement, "He's a live-wire." George's getaway plan (having explosives tied around his middle), his tendency to shout all his thoughts, including his catchphrase that he was "born to raise hell," and his boast that he wants to break his record of three banks in two hours, all suggest that he is quite a retarded figure. Indeed, when one woman mistakes him for "Babyface" Nelson, he becomes quite upset and broods on this lack of recognition. Not long afterward he gives them each some money and walks off into the dark. Although we later see him at the head of a torch-carrying mob (almost leading it as much as being paraded in shame), he still seems cheerful rather than cowed by the experience (as Delmar says, "Looks like he's right back on top again," unwittingly echoing James Cagney's proud boast as Cody Jarrett at the end of Raoul Walsh's 1949 *White Heat* that he is "top of the world" just before being consumed by a giant explosion). Less a fully rounded character, George is a caricature of the really brutal Capone-style gangsters of the time and Hollywood's representation of them (on whom he models himself). Delmar looks back on some of their bank-robbing adventures with "that was some fun," ruefully remarking that it almost makes him wish that he had not been saved.

The film is also part road movie of an itinerant laborer during the Depression, always on the move with a mythic goal in mind rather than a specific destination with little sense of specific geography, the trio using cars when they can and walking when not. The course of the film seems fairly random but is highly structured. The nonnaturalistic circularity of the narrative, bumping into familiar faces more than once (Dan, George, Pappy, Tommy, and even the whole chain gang on the road and at the cinema), is even commented on by McGill who opines that when George walks off into the night, he is sure they have not seen the last of him. The importance of deadlines is raised only sporadically; the tone in most scenes is relaxed and focusing on small-scale absurdities, so that the narrative becomes a search for Dapper Dan pomade as much as anything else.

Film technology is not intrusive. Coen uses wipes (both oblique and horizontal) to signal a slightly anachronistic film technology, and as Delmar is left mourning the death of the toad (or Pete as he believes it to be) the iris closes on him. The newspaper that McGill tosses into the fire only reveals (to the viewers, not the characters) continuing interest about the identity of the Soggy Bottom Boys and more particularly details of plans to flood the Arkabutla Valley, as it burns and curls open.

The tonal mix is a little jarring at times. The violence meted out to the cows and to McGill and Delmar at their picnic, as well as in the potential lynching of Pete, does not sit easily in the narrative where it takes place. The sadistic brutality of Big Dan squashing the toad in his bare hands, contemptuously throwing it against a tree and then driving off in their car, is just the action of a bully and seems out of sync with the tone of the body of the film. Even though we subsequently see Pete again as part of a chain gang (another miraculous coincidence that McGill and Delmar would pass him), the possibility of suffering has been planted in the mind of the viewer, who has seen Pete whipped if not actually killed. Immediately prior to the flood, the trio were looking at three nooses and three freshly dug graves, irrespective of their pardon from the governor.

However, there is also a strongly lyrical quality to the film, emphasizing the beauty in the everyday. An anonymous figure at his plough is leisurely framed, standing to watch an oncoming truck with a band playing on it; a slow crane shot down past heavily cobwebbed trees focuses on the three protagonists walking toward the camera; a long shot picks out gloriously golden leaves as the trio accept a lift in an old jalopy, and later they pass two boys, carrying blocks of ice. An itinerant life on the road is unashamedly sentimentalized, whereby pies are stolen from window ledges but money left for the impropriety.

By the end of the film, some narrative problems (the men's legal status) are resolved, others (McGill's wife's unreasonable behavior) continue, and all the while the bonds of family and superstition seem to cross one another and occasionally collide. It is a world that does seem to have some order (possibly at the behest of a divine power) but often that order expresses itself in absurdity. Political and religious corruption exists but often this is dramatized by cartoonish (particularly bloatedly overweight) figures, whose pretensions are exposed, ridiculed, and punished in the course of the narrative.

CONFESSIONS OF A DANGEROUS MIND (GEORGE CLOONEY, 2002)

In 1984 TV presenter Chuck Barris claimed that not only was he a household name on such lowbrow game-shows as *The Gong Show* but that he had also been a hit man for the CIA and was responsible for the deaths of 33 people. Clooney was probably attracted by the chance to work with a script by Charlie Kaufman, whose critical stock was high after *Being John Malkovich* (1999) and *Adaptation* (2002), both directed by Spike Jonze. *Confessions* was a smallish film ($30 million) that would not bring down an entire studio if it failed. It allowed him to draw on favors from friends like Julia Roberts, both to keep costs down and work with people he knew. By taking the part of Jim Byrd, he could be on set but avoid the added stress of a leading part. He could draw on his own childhood, growing up on the sets of popular TV shows (reflected in the reference to Rosemary Clooney, his aunt, during the studio tour and her singing over the closing credits); and Steven Soderbergh, his director on the *Ocean's* franchise, was on board as one of the producers.

Jim Byrd sports a moustache somewhere between the Clark Gable style Clooney used in *O Brother* and the fuller Wyatt Earp look in *Men Who Stare at Goats*. With his hair slightly slicked back, Clooney delivers his lines largely in an inexpressive voice with impassive features, becoming less friendly only when Barris talks of backing out. Later, the frostiness of their breath as they talk (in literally freezing temperatures), framed in silhouette, separate from the other trainees, reflects this sudden coldness with Byrd stating that at 32 Barris has achieved nothing with his life. When Barris balks at his first killing, Byrd warns, "You don't play, you don't leave." Like Tyne in *The Perfect Storm*, there is a Jekyll and Hyde quality to his character (he says to Barris that he "could be a great warrior") with not much emotional range in between, also partly because of his minimal on-screen time.

The closest shot on Byrd (still wearing a ubiquitous hat, suit, and prominent moustache) frames him next to British contact, the stiffly stereotypical Simon Oliver (Michael Ensign). When Byrd later warns Barris about the existence of a possible mole, we see Clooney in a less stylish checked suit, but the spy cliché of hearing dialogue despite playing loud music, supposedly to fool listening devices, is deflated with the provision of subtitles. His final shot by the pool has echoes of Rutger Hauer (oddly present in this film as the assassin, Keeler) in *Blade Runner* (Ridley Scott, 1982) in his strange sitting death pose and brother Tony Scott's *The Hunger* (1983) in the scene's use of distorted drums at a moment of death and then a cut to a high-angled long shot without any sound for a second, taking in the bizarre tragedy of the scene.

Sam Rockwell, who worked with Clooney on *Collinwood*, was always Clooney's number one choice as Barris. Rockwell filmed Barris himself over several months, so that the final performance we see in the film is less an imitation or impression but one of embodiment in which gestures and expressions are interwoven with performance. Rockwell still submitted himself to the audition process, including showing some impressive dance moves at his screen test. Clooney preferred casting a lesser-known actor for the role of such a familiar public figure, and Rockwell's performance here and subsequent work such as *Moon* (Duncan Jones, 2009) vindicates this choice.

Rockwell excels at eccentric characters, such as Wild Bill Wharton in *The Green Mile* (Frank Darabont, 1999), and he captures Barris's manic energy as seen in the montage sequence of the pilot for *The Dating Game*, where he acts as floor manager, director, and warm-up man. Rockwell delivers a strong performance of a mind in meltdown, vividly portrayed in jump cuts, with mumbling, hesitant speech, sweating, and panicked shots from his point of view. When Barris is slapped hard in the face by a girlfriend, Rockwell swings around, open-mouthed to face the camera, and is held in an iconic freeze frame, an emotional loser and figure of fun like the final appearance of Ned Ryerson (Stephen Tobolowsky) in *Groundhog Day* (Harold Ramis, 1993). We see Barris's mental deterioration, perhaps deriving from a murderous career, and the appearance of former victims at his own wedding has a slight Banquo-like feel, even though Barris never really has the truly tragic stature of a Shakespearean hero like Macbeth.

The movie opens with, and is sporadically interrupted by, real figures from Barris's TV career, talking in interview mode about him. Such footage—including host of *American Bandstand*, Dick Clark; host of *The Dating Game*, Jim Lange; and *Gong Show* regular, Jaye P. Morgan—using high contrast and infrared film (at the suggestion of cinematographer Newton Thomas Sigel), clearly sets it apart from the body of the narrative and gives the film some semblance of documentary. On the DVD commentary Clooney mentions *End of the Road* (Aram Akavian, 1970), a film also concerned with a mentally unstable protagonist, but the device is also used in more serious films like Steven Spielberg's 1993 *Schindler's List* or comedies like Rob Reiner's 1989 *When Harry Met Sally* or even Clooney's own *Up in the Air*. In a sense, the challenge for the audience is to allocate the narrative to a particular pseudo-director within the film. If the CIA story is true, then Byrd is directing operations; if not, then what we see are expressionist nightmares from Barris's deluded imagination.

The authenticity of Barris's story is left open in the film. There is certainly much about Barris that is childish, from skulking around the set of *American Bandstand*, taking pictures, to nearly messing up the code phrase in meeting Patricia (Julia Roberts) in Helsinki. On the other hand, the reaction of Penny Pacino (Drew Barrymore) in the car at the end, i.e., dismissive laughter, means this is also the perfect cover. The notion of a highly subjective universe is underlined by Barris's opening voice-over, his clearly disturbed mental state, standing unkempt and naked in front of a TV in a hotel room, as well as the narrative construct of his writing down what he has done as a way of giving meaning to his life, what he terms "a cautionary tale." Clooney's visual style complements this sense of a world out of kilter, opting for off-center framing, and extended length of shots, so that along with the dissolves as transition devices, these feel like the stylistic markers of a new scene, although we remain in the old one.

A key part of the authenticity question is whether any other main character interacts with the shadowy figures associated with Barris's double life. Like *The Sixth Sense* (M. Night Shyamalan, 1999), if no one else does, then it could all be a subjective fantasy. Byrd appears suddenly like a ghost on the set of *The Dating Game* in one of the contestant seats, up in the lighting gantry, during which time no one other than Barris interacts with him. This is how matters stand, right up to the scene in which Barris introduces Peter Jenks (an uncredited second role for Robert Burke who also plays a CIA instructor) to bark at the contestants and intimidate them into toning down the innuendo in *The Dating Game*. The appearance of a character across the two plotlines could be seen to validate Barris's CIA story a little further. This is underlined in the later restaurant scene when Penny sees, hears, and almost speaks to Patricia. These two scenes make all the others possible.

However, if Barris's story was true, it might be expected that such a double life would spill over into his everyday life more clearly. Shots like where he greets Penny at the door with a pistol held just out of her sight might seem comic in isolation, but that such an individual could assassinate as many people as he claims seems highly unlikely. On the other hand, it is conceivable that if the CIA pursues the madcap schemes dramatized in *The Men Who Stare at Goats*, it might look at Barris as possessing the kind of profile they could use (an unstable background, an easily suggestible nature, and given to irrational behavior that might act as an effective cover). Clooney does not show us the kills clearly (except the death of Renta on the DVD extras), retaining an element of sympathy for Barris while also adding to the ambiguity of the validity of his story. The victim in the alleyway is shot off-camera, Keeler (Rutger Hauer) is the one who strangles his target in Berlin (manically smiling for Barris's snapshot), and although Barris pulls his gun on the annoying whining contestant in Helsinki, he does not actually fire. As Barris seems to take to the part of spy, he dons the look he associates with such a role (leather jacket, shades, cigars, and permed hair). His concept of Cold War spying is mediated through cinematic representations, so we see a version of *The Spy Who Came in from the Cold* (Martin Ritt, 1965) but with dominant reds as it is shot in color.

Penny (Drew Barrymore) is an effective counterpoint to Barris's amorality. She is portrayed as a force for good, kooky but engaging and clearly deserving of better treatment. Barrymore, a big fan of Barris in *The Gong Show*, plays an empathetic figure, as well as acting as something of a reflection of 1960s counterculture. Their shared playful nature, shown wearing Marx Brothers-style masks in bed, suggests at some fundamental level that they are right for each other. The montage, complete with small jump cuts, as Barris carries her over the threshold of a new house together, upbeat Latin music, and the discreet blurring around their lovemaking, all suggest this is a real opportunity for Barris. However, Penny is a figure of much-maligned virtue, such as the scene in which he talks to the top of her head as she lies on his chest and pulls her up into shot to answer her plaintive question, "Do you even like me?" Penny is crucial to maintaining a redeemable element in his character. Although he reacts angrily to her proposal, he does eventually come back to her (even if it is mostly due to her persistence).

Clooney as Director

As a first-time director, there was obviously a lot of pressure on Clooney to have a credible presence on set, and he prepared carefully with meticulous storyboarding and tried to build confidence with some relatively easy shots to start with. However, there is real ambition to tell his story in an innovative fashion, right from the outset. The scene at the door with Barris and Penny was planned as a split screen but with both speakers facing outward, presumably to emphasize the failure to connect at this point, psychologically rather than emotionally. The use of a range of film stock, cross processing (the use of processing film in chemicals normally used to treat other kinds of film), and shots that are not explained fully at the moment they appear (the prostitute singing happy birthday) all present a challenging viewing experience. Flashbacks in black-and-white infrared film are juxtaposed with more lurid color for shots of the hippy counterculture as we criss-cross about 50 years of time in the narrative, often with sudden leaps back to Barris's childhood, in washed-out sepia tones. Clooney is not afraid to use Kane-like extreme low angles, like when Barris picks up some forms for management training, suggesting the character's grandiose dreams. Clooney uses lightweight, mobile cameras for brief, albeit gimmicky, shots like the one from the point of view of the tray on which Patricia carries the poisoned tea.

Barris's fragmented character is conveyed by several shots in which he looks into reflective surfaces, including TVs in a store, inspiring his move to Manhattan to seek a job in the television industry. Later, he is seen in reflection, staring at the names of the NBC chief executives, displayed behind glass. As Penny lies in the bath, talking to him, he is staring into the bathroom mirror, clearly not listening, even being bluntly rude about "dating bullshit" and caring what other people say. Later, we see Penny's face momentarily reflected over that of Tuvia (or possibly this is Barris, raised-as-a-girl), disturbingly suggesting that he never really gets over his strange obsession with the young girl; and also in the very opening scene, there is the faint, even ghostly reflection of Barris himself in the smooth grain of his own door.

Clooney also uses some ambitious long takes, involving large numbers of extras as Barris arrives at NBC first as a visitor as part of a tour and then disappears out of shot only to appear seconds later, leading his own group out of shot and then reappearing eavesdropping on stagehand Debbie (Maggie Gyllenhaal) describing her ideal man, which he instantly resolves to become. Time is telescoped as well as showing Barris's drive to succeed. Later as Byrd explains his idea of Barris's chaperoning role as cover for European operations, Clooney shoots the scene in long shot, refusing to cut closer so that we hear their conversation but only see Barris speaking to Byrd's back, seen from outside the glass of a control room. This makes Barris seem more isolated and not only forces viewers to pay closer attention to the dialogue but is preceded by continuous dialogue on the floor of *The Dating Game* and then the lighting gantry as if Byrd can flit ghost-like from place to place.

In particular, Clooney tries ambitious theatrical transition shots in which rather than cutting or using some elaborate postproduction process, he opts for flyway scenery and actors moving once they have left the frame. This might reflect nervousness over cost or unfamiliarity with the technical nature of some processes, but it also rings true with the period in which the film is set, when such effects were not yet possible. He zooms into an extreme close-up of Barris's eyes in the bathroom, where he has the idea of *The Dating Game*; there is a turntable effect to an adjacent set and then a zoom out to the presentation of the pitch for the program itself. Later, we pull back from a shot of the pilot that Barris has made to the stony silence of the board of ABC executives, unimpressed by the thinly veiled innuendo on a primetime show. Wes Anderson, with whom Clooney would go on to work with on *Fantastic Mr. Fox* (2009), uses a similar effect for his AT&T series of commercials in 2007.[3] Later, we pan slowly from left to right and then back again across contestants on *The Dating Game*, who change by the time we return to them (we have actors, including Brad Pitt and Matt Damon, rapidly swapping places) almost like the schoolboy gag of appearing in a photo twice by running from one end to the other. The effect of suggesting a repeated process and the passage of time is similar to a jump cut but less intrusive.

A similar effect is used to take us from Barris on the phone to TV executive Larry Goldberg (Jerry Weintraub). Barris steps to the edge of the set and we see Goldberg speaking from an adjacent set, effectively giving us a split-screen effect but in reality rather than by a technical trick. Clooney then pushes this theatrical device a stage further by having Penny dance across both sets, in a literally impossible action, underlining the subjectivity of what we are seeing. Like the ABC tour guide scene, Barrymore then has to run around the set to be in shot again as the camera tracks left back into the domestic scene. There is an effective juxtaposition of the snapshot of Barris's literally colorless parents and his mother's monotone observation to her unresponsive husband that they need a new icebox before the scenery flies away to reveal the color and vibrancy of one of Barris's TV shows in which the star prize is a new freezer.

Fly-away scenery is possibly overused, appearing again in Barris's fantasy while auditioning terrible talent show acts, as the wall behind the contestants slides back to reveal the church square where he killed Renta (both original scene and fantasy, shot on location), and then he fantasizes about blasting the singer in front of him with a shotgun in an act of wish fulfillment. However, we zoom into an extreme close-up at the sound of a gong as he has his eureka moment and dreams up the premise of *The Gong Show*. All the way through the narrative there are some examples of creative shot composition. When Barris is thrown out of the bar onto the street, we see Byrd exit the bar and begin to address an apparently empty space before Barris stands up into the shot. As Barris walks into the extreme foreground, Byrd is framed as a tiny devil-like figure on his shoulder.

In among some visual bravura transitions, there are also scenes like Jenks's barking at the contestants where Clooney just allows his actors to perform without any gimmickry. In this scene, Burke's head bobbing and manic delivery, eyeballing certain individuals while dismissing others, and walking off before his speech really reaches its conclusion as if he could not be bothered to finish it, all work really well.

The scenes that Clooney ultimately chose to delete also tell us something about him as a director. He certainly seems ruthless, willing to cut good performances (the bellboy exchange with Barris), spectacle that must have taken time (and presumably money) like the Mexican procession, or the expressionistic explosion of Mr. Flexnor's head on delivering bad news to Barris who pretends to shoot him with his finger. It is not quite in the league of David Cronenberg's *Scanners* (1980) but it is still an example of a stunt or effect, like the excerpt of a piano falling on a contestant and her dog in "How's Your Mother-in-Law?" which Clooney is prepared to lose if it takes his narrative in a direction he does not want. This suggests a strong sense of personal vision and a necessary willingness to sacrifice material that does not conform to that. The loss of the scene in which we see Renta actually killed might have made us believe Barris's story a little more, but like Penny's suicide attempt, this would have shifted the narrative toward a more clearly dark and tragic tone and made Barris a less empathetic figure. A bigger loss is the sequence leading up to Barris's discovery of Penny's suicide, in which Clooney uses a triple split-screen, so that we see Barris's actions within the house from three different camera positions, running simultaneously, giving us the unusual effect of appearing in two frames at once and possibly reflecting Barris's fragmented psyche and his fractured love life.

In all of the deleted scenes, there is still some visual panache on show. When Barris meets "Old Tuvia," as he calls her, on an ill-advised date with the focus of his childhood obsession, Clooney uses freeze-frames at the moment of their meeting at the door and rather heavy-handed symbolism of the woman willingly eating strawberries in a provocative fashion, which feels too much like obvious wish fulfillment on the part of Barris. An amusing scene of Barris's growing paranoia shows him pulling a gun on a car that appears to be following him, only to reveal two young fans. Barris's offer of an autograph is funny and shows the sudden switches in tone of his character, but perhaps the film would struggle to accommodate this.

Some of Barris's walking around the back of the TV set is included in the finished film, but the additional footage cut from this shows the direction that the original Kaufman script might have taken, complete with a *Malkovich*-style opening of a door onto a bricked-up wall and the sound of audience laughter, as if he is a small Kafkaesque figure trapped in a surreal universe. He undertakes an expressionist journey through key images in his recent past, including the church square where he killed Renta, the Berlin alleyway, and a shot of a sky that is apparently moving but is really a piece of scenery being carried through the shot. By choosing the theatrical option of a physical illusion in front of the camera in real time, Clooney keeps an element of theatricality in the film and also makes Barris's character seem more believable. It is harder to dismiss what he sees and does as subjective illusion when the fabric of the film remains in front of the camera rather than in postproduction trickery.

It was Clooney's securing of Roberts's name that persuaded Miramax to allow the casting of Rockwell. In a virtual parody of a film noir femme fatale, Roberts wears her hair up, heavy red lipstick, big hats, and big boots and sits forward into the light on command to catch her prominent cheekbones (or create her own effect in the scene where she sits in the dark in Barris's apartment until turning on a lamp above her head). The montage of Barris's growing romance with Patricia, intercut with Penny over an Elvis impersonator's version of "Can't Help Falling in Love," does suggest Barris's confusion between the two women; and the plot twist, with Patricia admitting to killing Keeler and thereby exposing herself as the mole, is neatly done as Barris falls to the floor, apparently poisoned, only to reappear healthy in the center of shot as Patricia herself is suddenly struck down.

Clooney's childhood involved time on TV sets of game shows (his father, Nick, was host of *The Money Maze*) and he effectively intercuts audience and contestants with playback cameras and extracts from real shows to break up the conventional lines of continuity, so that in these scenes we occupy several different viewing positions, giving the sense of a vibrant, unpredictable atmosphere. This also required some creations of fake footage, which also then had to match activity in the fictional studio—all for only a few split-second glimpses but it reflects Clooney's attention to detail. This is also expressed in the gag of naming two of the CIA trainees "Ruby" and "Oswald," the latter being unable to fire more than a single shot before his rifle jams out on the range.

It seems Clooney is most influenced by American conspiracy thrillers of the '70s, such as Alan J. Pakula's *The Parallax View* (1974) and *All the President's Men* (1976) or Mike Nichols's *Carnal Knowledge* (1971), like the shot of the whining contestant asking for Barris's help with the girl, paralleling Jonathan (Jack Nicholson) and Sandy (Art Garfunkel) in Nichols's film. Clooney claims that the similarity of the alleyway scene to *The Exorcist* (William Friedkin, 1971) struck him only later but this seems a little odd, especially since the earlier shot of Barris walking away from the contestant as he stands under a prominent single street lamp and the whole notion of Barris selling his soul to a tempting devil-like figure in Byrd evoke the earlier film quite strongly. The prime reference to *All the President's Men* is the use of silhouettes or at least insufficient light to see faces clearly, as when Barris is caught cheating by Penny. Here, it is Penny's dignity that is more important, and also it avoids a literally awkward moment for Rockwell to convey. There is another nod to the same movie in a deleted scene in which we see a more collaborative form of working in the TV studio, like the conference call in Pakula's film.

From *The Parallax View* we have the juxtaposition of Keeler's assurances that everything will be fine to a shot of him on a mortuary slab, like the character of Lee Carter (Paula Prentiss) being assured by Joe Frady (Warren Beatty) that she will be fine and the next we see of her is as a corpse, supposedly the result of an overdose. The influence of Sidney Lumet's *Fail Safe* (1964), discussed in chapter 7, is seen in the tight shot on Flexnor's eye. The small musical cues, particularly via a few somber piano notes, are inspired partly by Pakula's *Klute* (1971) and Bob Fosse's *All That Jazz* (1979). The only slightly more modern film Clooney mentions on the DVD extras is *The Princess Bride* (Rob Reiner, 1987) in reference to the game of bluff in which Barris and Patricia switch the signals, showing which cup is poisoned.

Like Barris's book, the film is an ambitious blend of thriller, comedy, conspiracy thriller, and love story, all in the framework of a delusional fantasy. It is hardly surprising then that it is a little uneven in tone or that it struggled to find an audience, mis-marketed primarily as a thriller. The choice of a script by Kaufman (whose involvement dates from around 1997), who was a known quantity in terms of his experimental and boundary-stretching nature, seems a mixture of courage, hubris, ambition, and naiveté. Perhaps Clooney's decision to moderate some of the more extreme elements of the script was the only way to bring it to a wider public, and at this stage of his career, it may not really have been his deci-sion at all. In Kaufman's original, Barris gets the poisoned cup from Patricia, but this would hardly tally with the continued life of Barris the author and make the events in the film clearly a fiction. Kaufman had planned to use a voice-over by Barris himself, which would have under-lined the unreliability of the narration more strongly and emphasized his sense of regret about his life, but perhaps for his first directing experi-ence, Clooney opted for coherence and may have been wary of extensive voice-over use. For a directing debut, wanting to make the film one's own and being unwilling to cede too much hard-won control is perhaps under-standable. Clooney's next directing project, *Leatherheads* (2008), also included difficulties over the script, but by the time of *The Ides of March* (2011) it looks like Clooney has settled into writing with a partner who he feels most comfortable with and can trust: Grant Heslov.

Kaufman disavowed any linkage with the film, unhappy that Clooney publicly praised his script and then made changes without the writer's involvement. However, this is still an ambitious film, in content, tone, and style. Sigel states his belief that, even acknowledging the film's com-mercial performance (it took only $16 million in the United States), over time the film will be reappraised and find its audience as a cult film: a view with which this writer would agree.

THE GOOD GERMAN (STEVEN SODERBERGH, 2006)

This film remains something of an anomaly in Clooney's work. It is part of his collaboration with Soderbergh, partly funded by their production company Section Eight, and reflects an ongoing seriousness about films that without his interest might not otherwise get made. What makes this example different is its complete immersion in a particular style. Despite the fact that a number of Clooney films are set in the past, this film is the only one to attempt to overtly use the exact film style of that period (something Clooney only touched on with *Leatherheads*).

As we see Churchill, Truman, and Stalin draw up a new map of Europe in postwar Berlin, so the hero Captain Jake Geismar (Clooney, uneasily blending the role of jaded military officer and crusading journalist) is attempting to map out the boundaries of relationships, past and present. He cuts a subdued figure with trousers slightly too short for him, empha-sized in occasional long shots, complete with the ubiquitous cigarette, which he is more often holding or stubbing out than actually inhaling.

Soderbergh goes beyond merely alluding to the style of wartime movies; this is not a pastiche or a parody. For the DVD release, Soderbergh uses the aspect ratio of the time of 1.33:1 and is actively re-creating the look of a 1940s film for a serious rather than ironic purpose. The film appears in black-and-white but was shot in color because this allows a faster film speed and the use of green screen technology. The basic lighting codes evoke the 1940s use of chiaroscuro pools of light and shadow, like the first meeting of Jake and Lena (Cate Blanchett), where she is turned away, her face half in shadow, and he has a bar of light that plays across his eyes (also when he finds her file later).

Wide-angle lenses with deep focus allow for some composition in depth and means there is little sudden movement through the frame as the choice of lens would have a distorting effect on such action, like Clooney emerging from behind a tree at the discovery of the body.

Incandescent lighting throws real shadows, which produce shots that are harder to match that those taken on sets flooded with lighting, but it also means that Soderbergh, who often edits his own movies too (under the name Mary Ann Bernard) and acts as his own cinematographer (in the name of Peter Andrews) had a rough cut ready within a couple of days.

There are other small anachronistic devices like boom mikes, which necessitate a slightly stronger delivery and projection for the sound to carry, self-conscious low angles (like when Jake walks to Lena's flat), blurred vertical wipes to signal transitions device, and an iris narrowing on the name of Schaeffer (Dave Power), who knowingly orders Tully (Toby Maguire) as Jake's driver, hoping that by putting the two together they would lead him to Emil Brandt (Christian Oliver). The early sequence of Tully and Jake in the jeep is initially shot from the backseat with the two placed in the dead space of the T-frame, delivering their dialogue facing away from the camera, like very early sound films. The crude back projection here and later when Lena meets Bernie Teitel (Leland Orser) distracts from the dialogue, which is important in both scenes.

Like the extreme low angle of Lena as she passes a picture of Stalin, there are self-conscious stylish flourishes, like the symbolism of the cracked photo of Emil, a broken individual who has lost his moral compass, as well as suffering an estranged marriage. As Jake is left on the landing looking at the departing figure of Lena, he is framed against a huge hole in the wall behind him, featuring a moonlit sky, which seems the kind of painterly picture composition at odds with the dominant style here. The choice of a cinema as a place for Lena to meet Emil (an addition to Joseph Kanon's 2001 novel of the same name) seems designed for its iconic filmic potential rather than a practical arrangement with shafts of light from the projection room and the cliché of rising smoke and a crushed cigarette as evidence of someone watching them.

The echo in the final scene of Michael Curtiz's *Casablanca* (1942) is overt in the promotional material for the later film. We have a rain-soaked night scene at an airport, featuring the separation of lovers, one of whom is an American, against the background of the Second World War. However, the woman boards the plane alone as she is unworthy of his love, a fact Jake finally realizes as she confesses the full extent of her collaboration, betraying 12 Jews in exchange for her own survival. Despite a kiss on the cheek and a final exchange of looks as she boards the plane, the pair part for good. Her complicity in Nazi crimes is made deeper in the film by conflating her character with that of Renate, a "Greiffer" or "grabber" in the novel, used by the Gestapo to identify Jews trying to evade capture. Like *Casablanca*, the film is shot almost entirely on a studio back lot and soundstages and focuses on the under-belly of wartime corruption and exploitation. However, the discordant, somber theme music, the very slow pace of the credits, and the revelation of Lena's collaboration make the final scene less the beginning of a beautiful friendship than clearly the end of one.

The sequence in the sewer, not in the novel, clearly motivates some mise-en-scène, evocative of Carol Reed's *The Third Man* (1949). However, we see Lena and Emil sitting on upturned boxes enjoying a moment of shared food and comradeship, which seems warmer than any-thing we see in connection with Jake. Unlike Reed's chase of a doomed man through the shadowy tunnels, here there is an unlikely amount of light, especially unmotivated underlighting, throwing up watery shadows across the faces of the estranged couple. Emil complains about the air but it feels more like a romantic hideaway than a sewer.

Any substantial novel converted to a screenplay of 110–20 pages will need to cut some material, but some of the changes that Paul Attanasio's script makes are curious. There are limited exterior shots, with very similar bombed-out buildings being used for both Lena's flat and the area around Jake's billet, so that when Jake spots the boy with a toy boat and realizes that Tully's body could have been dumped elsewhere and floated to Potsdam (a fairly obvious possibility overlooked in both book and film), the precise geography of where this takes place is unclear. In the book, Gunther has a large map of Berlin on his wall, and some sim-ilar visual reference points here might well have been useful and would have made the detective element of the narrative easier to follow.

The adaptation builds the role of Tully as Jake's driver and makes Lena much more culpable, which both erode the centrality of Jake as the hero. The opening of the book as Jake's plane arrives in Berlin, the description of the city, and the conversation with a congressman could have been a

succinct introduction to the political maneuvering that the hero is flying
into and given a much stronger sense that Jake knows the city (a fact we
are later told in the film, rather than feel). In the novel, Lena and Tully
never meet. Lena is nursed back to health by a patient and loving Jake,
motivating scenes of a romantic and sexual nature, and closes with Emil
and a son (Erich), cut from the film, being given safe passage to the
United States. In building Tully's part in the film, it diminishes Jake,
whose expositional dialogue about his experience of politics, the camps,
and Berlin makes his blindness to Tully's duplicity even more ironic.

In the film, it is Tully who is seen first as Lena's former partner (which
we see before we even know of any connection with Jake). Tully's virtual
pimping of Lena to anyone who will pay partly motivates her shooting
him, but the film blackens her character to the extent that she cannot
form a close emotional bond with the hero without compromising him
morally and dramatically in the eyes of the audience. By showing us more
of Tully (a character who is then removed from the narrative), the film
feels more seedy, with Jake only a bit-part player rather than the male
lead. The film, although generally expressed through Jake's point of view,
also includes voice-over comment from Tully (threatening to dominate
the opening section where he boasts that "war was the best thing that
ever happened to me") and even later briefly from Lena.

By making Lena cold and distant (several of her scenes have her
speaking while facing away from Jake) as well as morally reprehensible,
the film prevents the relationship with Jake from developing. In the
novel, the sexual scene between Jake and Lena as she takes a bath
evokes the bathroom scene in *Out of Sight* but there is no similar chemistry here. Likewise, the link with *Solaris*, of a man having a second
chance at love, does not really come alive as their relationship seems
stillborn from the outset. When Jake finally meets Lena in the bar, there
is limited eye contact (she hears his voice before she sees him), and
whereas *Solaris* spends the body of its narrative exploring what a pair
of lovers feel about each other, here the meeting is instantly and
brutally interrupted by Tully's vicious beating of Jake, and the narrative
momentum in the novel provided by the murder is lost by it occurring
25 minutes into the film. The book uses Brandt's father as the repository
of the all-important documents, but in the film Lena has them, making
her level of knowledge clear (and increasing the cruelty too in reducing
the allocation to slave workers from 1,100 calories in the book to 800 in
the film).

Jake, like a typical noir detective, is at the mercy of forces beyond his
control (as Teitel says at the end, "You've been wrong every step of the

way, why stop now?"). However, it is as if Soderbergh cannot allow his hero to be the complete "patsy" as Tully describes him near the beginning; and in the second half of the film, Jake miraculously discovers the ability to pursue a line of investigation with vigor, even though he misses the biggest clue of all in the shape of Lena. Jake is denied another female sidekick (the photographer, Liz, in the novel) to whom he might show his more emotional side, and although Blanchett can exude glacial charm, it is hard to imagine Lena and Jake in love, in the past or now. Thomas Newman's score, which epitomizes the somber and elegiac mood of post-war construction, reflects this sense of being frozen in emotional aspic, ending fairly much where it began. The oft-repeated line of dialogue "there's always something worse" serves to deny characters much empathy as the viewer is just waiting for the next betrayal.

Rather than the book's focus on revealing the atrocities of the Nazi rocket science program, in the film we have a conspiracy narrative based around the figure of Jake. He only gradually realizes how he has been used to lead the Americans to Emil Brandt, who can then be conveniently eliminated, allowing German scientists to be adopted by American military without the taint of Nazism. The film is quite a bleak view of political expediency with Breimer (Jack Thompson) slapping a newspaper into Jake's hands at the end, underlining the link between the spy games in Berlin and the wider point about ending the war more quickly by using atomic weapons. The difficulty of winning the peace is an interesting subject, but Jake's pseudo-film noir dialogue (talking of "the good old days when you could tell who the bad guy was by who was shooting at you") seems strangely naïve from one who has reported on the war for several years.

Expositional dialogue, placed in the novel in exchanges with Breimer, is shifted in the film to bizarre exchanges with a helpful barman (Tony Curran), so that Jake pours his heart out about background information and his thoughts and feelings across a bar (including his theories about a murder and secret files), while other customers mill around, to a minor character who has no bearing on the plot other than finding a place to stay for Lena later. In the book, no one really pays Jake any attention—he really is a lone investigator. The film plays up his importance, so that on leaving a room at the Potsdam press pool, several key players, including Sikorsky (Ravil Isyanov) Breimer, and Teitel, are all shown turning to watch his exit, implicitly hoping that he will lead them to Brandt. Later, Jake and Lena play out a strange prostitute-and-client scenario with Lena prepared to go through with it but Jake pulling back at the last moment, telling her to keep the money. The generic boundaries of a

wartime film cannot accommodate changes in sexual politics in the intervening years to the present day without a sense of awkward compromises.
The film struggles to find a space for a romantic relationship between Jake
and Lena, and clearly once she has pulled a gun on him on the stairwell,
this becomes even less likely. With a surviving husband, who is ennobled
through his repentance and Lena's support of him, to bring Jake and Lena
together becomes impossible.

There is also a sense of style being prioritized over plausibility, such as
when Jake is allowed to wander by the site of where Tully's body was
found. First we have the cliché of miraculously finding a clue at the scene
of a crime, then the introduction of some random violence as a guard hits
him with a rifle butt, only to then have an expositional chat with
Sikorsky while being stitched. The speed with which Jake, having wan-
dered outside the Potsdam conference for a smoke, spots Tully's body, at
around two seconds of screen time, does seem ridiculous. Jake and
Sikorsky exchange an eye-line match over the body and Jake gives a
slight shake of the head, but rather than suggesting an investigator struggling to accept what he is witnessing, this just seems unmotivated and
odd. Clooney's reaction on being told that Lena was raped takes
Soderbergh's direction about muting demonstrative acting to an absurd
extreme, as there is no visible reaction to what must be a major revelation
to him. Emil is caught and stabbed by Gunther, whose role is translated
from a principled policeman who saves Geismar's life in the novel to a
Russian stooge, ridiculously following Bernie and Jake to the records
office, like a Marx Brothers routine, especially with his bald head and apparent lack of speech.

Soderbergh's stylistic experiments throw up several contradictions. The
audience is not from the 1940s and may find it difficult to process genre
signals from an era with which they are unfamiliar. The inclusion of
Tully's profanity, his brief but brutal sex scene with Lena, and the violence of his beating of Jake outside the club or his punch to Lena's
stomach—all this would have been unthinkable in films of this period.
At times, the film feels like a wish fulfillment for Soderbergh, a fantasy
of how his career might have been different if he had been part of the
studio system in its heyday. However, this also includes a level of naiveté
or nostalgia. The level of control that someone like Soderbergh has over
his films (producer, director, editor, cinematographer, sometimes writer)
is light-years away from Curtiz's relatively restricted role at Warners.
Films from the period may have used voice-over but usually with a central
narrator and a motivated reason for any further fragmentation, whereas
here we drift from Tully to Jake to Lena and back to Jake.

The adoption of stylistic limitations has the feel of a Dogme manifesto but for a single film project. The use of fixed 32-millimeter, wide-angle lenses prevents any reliance on zooming to create a sense of drama but allows the kind of composition in depth like when the camera pulls back slowly through the legs of spectators and then cranes up so we see Gunther exit the crowd in the background with Emil's body still lying in the foreground (the clapping of the crowd providing an ironic commentary). Wider-angle lenses increase the scope of the frame so there is not the focus on cutting between close-ups and instead a more leisurely cutting style with actors walking into a space and delivering lines to another character within that shot, i.e., closer to the experience of everyday life rather than the rapid cutting between tight close-ups. However, there is also plenty of shot-reverse shot patterning (like the final exchange between Jake and Lena), stressing reaction shots, and the speed of cutting is still quicker than the average shot length of the 1940s.

Rather than opting for how most films are shot nowadays with multiple cameras, generating plenty of so-called coverage, meaning the film is really created in the editing room, Soderbergh shoots most scenes with a limited number of cameras, selecting shots carefully, in theory making the performances more intense, exact, and purposeful. The fact that there are no extras on the DVD reflects that Soderbergh's method of working produces fewer deleted scenes and a tighter shooting schedule but perhaps also suggests an unwillingness to dwell on the overpowering stylistic elements.

The Good German has the slight feel of reality shows where participants willingly live supposedly realistically in a given historical period. Soderbergh's search for lenses from Panavision without the modern antiglare coating, of the type used by Curtiz, may be interesting but throws up all kinds of contradictions about countless other areas of production, like cameras, makeup, or even the editing tools used, which do not derive from the period. Even if Soderbergh succeeds in making a film so much like an old one, an audience may wonder why not just watch that instead.

CONCLUSION

This book uses direct quotation from Clooney himself relatively sparingly. Perhaps rather cynically, interviews by stars and directors all too often seem little more than extensions of promotional material and a mythologizing of public personas. In relation to From Dusk Till Dawn, Full Tilt Boogie (Sarah Kelly, 1997), purporting to be an objective documentary on the making of the film, is actually filled with uncritical coverage of the cast and crew, who are allowed to present themselves as they wish, Clooney and Tarantino hamming it up as if in an improvised interview, although their responses are clearly rehearsed. It is not polished like a standard DVD "Making of-" featurette, but in a sense that is the point: it is parody of that kind of presentation, trumpeting its low-budget credentials. So we see interviews with a range of crew members, hear about problems with unionization and sand storms, with the overall feel of a video diary, trying to capture the mood on set.

The films in this chapter are all challenging because of their mixed generic natures. *Three Kings* might have been placed here (or indeed in chapter 6 as Clooney's first political film) but it seems more natural to put it in the next chapter as, in premise at least, it is a heist movie. Clooney seems increasingly drawn to films that seem to offer straightforward pleasures of a particular genre, only to offer something more challenging, such as *Solaris* or *The American*, or resist generic categories altogether, like *Michael Clayton*. It is in such films that we find some of his best work as an actor (see chapter 8).

CHAPTER 5

Heist Movies

OUT OF SIGHT (STEVEN SODERBERGH, 1998)

Jack Foley: It's like seeing someone for the first time, and you look at each other for a few seconds, and there's this kind of recognition like you both know something.

This is Clooney's first experience with Soderbergh, with whom he would go on to work with on the *Ocean's* franchise, *Solaris*, and *The Good German*, and also with a nonlinear narrative (a feature of all of these films). Clooney plays Jack Foley, an armed robber prepared to carry a gun, but the tone for his character is established from the outset. Here, it is wit and charm rather than brutality that is his preference, fooling the teller into handing over money with a plausible lie about a fictional accomplice holding a gun on someone. After a botched escape attempt in which Federal Marshal Sisco (Jennifer Lopez) just happens to be parked in front of the spot where an escape tunnel comes up, she and Foley are forced to get in the trunk of a getaway car.

In the trunk, Foley and Sisco experience a scene of physical intimacy. It is strangely romantic, lit with a single-sourced red-orange light, with both characters facing the camera so that they can talk but we see only Sisco's facial reaction or Foley's admiring glance down the length of her body. It is also intensely sexual. Soderbergh's camera adopts a male voyeuristic perspective, looking her body up and down and featuring a close-up of his hand on her hip. Foley, after several years being surrounded only by brutal males, is in forced close proximity to a character played by Jennifer Lopez, famous for her curvaceous body, in a short leather skirt. Having just returned from dinner with her father, she is made up smart in contrast to his grimy disguise. Like the repeated rear-entry sexual positions of *Crash* (David Cronenberg, 1996), such proxemics allow juxtaposed close-ups of faces while at the same time suggesting distance between a couple (she is a federal agent after all). This was the audition piece that Lopez read, acting out the scene with Clooney on a couch, and it is not hard to imagine how good that was. That said, it was difficult to get right, particularly since originally it was a six-minute-long take and there were over 40 attempts before Soderbergh was satisfied. Test audiences did not react well to the single take so the scene was reshot.

The scene establishes a stylistic mode used for exchanges later in the motel bathroom and subsequently in the hotel. Lighting is limited, red-orange in color, and often from below (motivated from the table lamps, for example). The low-angle shot up out of the trunk of Foley looking down approvingly at her lying form is reversed later in the motel as she looks down at his naked form in the bath. Sisco remarks that she never really understood Robert Redford and Faye Dunaway's lead characters in the film *Three Days of the Condor* (Sydney Pollack, 1975): "You know, the way they got together so quick. I mean, romantically." It is a personal thought about the progress of a relationship and obviously a self-aware reference (an actor talking about films), but it works here since their relationship is a slow-burn affair and this is certainly the touch paper.

Like *Jackie Brown* (1997), *Out of Sight* is based on an Elmore Leonard novel from 1998 and adapted by Scott Frank, who had already scripted Elmore's *Get Shorty* (Barry Sonnenfeld, 1995). There is a little bit of Tarantino-style riffing on popular culture and in-jokes like Michael Keaton's uncredited cameo as Sisco's unimaginative boyfriend, Ray Nicolette, directly reprising his role from *Jackie Brown* (Quentin Tarantino, 1997), and a mug shot of Clooney borrowed from his role as Seth Gecko in *From Dusk Till Dawn*. The later bizarre accidental death of White Boy Bob (Keith Loneker), shooting himself as he trips up the stairs, also feels like a nod to the accidental shooting in the car in *Pulp Fiction*. However, in the trunk scene Frank's script puts both characters together in an unusual but dramatically plausible way, and neither character lists cultural references to appear cool or as part of a persona that is trying to be hip or ironic. There is a slight nod to the leatherwear of *Shaft* (Gordon Parks, 1971) or *Jackie Brown* in Sisco's wardrobe and also to the strong female detectives in such narratives. The scenes in which she trusses up Chino (Luis Guzmán) with a high-heeled foot on his back or smashes the arm of an abusive boyfriend of a witness later with a baton or the climax or where she hands over the house with a crop of dead criminals to the arriving backup, all underline her status. The birthday present from her father of a gun defines both her and the nature of their relationship, bound to law enforcement.

The trunk scene is a clear updating of screwball conventions. The hero and heroine from different sides of the law are literally thrown into close proximity and learn some unexpected truths about their common humanity. Opposites attract, certainly, but there is more here. This is really pillow talk with the quick-fire banter suggesting an emotional as well as a linguistic connection. Neither character can talk like this with anyone else: Foley's girlfriend, Adele (Catherine Keener), does not understand his coded language from prison, and Karen's predictable FBI boyfriend, Ray, proudly wears a sweatshirt emblazoned with "FBI." Her father (Dennis Farina, a real former cop) asks him if he wears one with "Undercover" on it to which he humorlessly replies, "No." Foley is able to make her laugh, something no other character achieves.

Often romance in heist movies struggles to be anything more than an unconvincing interlude between action scenes but here it is the whole basis of the plot. In following scenes, Foley and Sisco separately cannot stop talking about each other, and the narrative has the pair tripping over each other (a device going as far back as at least the Victorian novelist Thomas Hardy). As a marshal, whose job involves pursuing fugitives, this is perhaps not surprising for Sisco, but there are domestic scenes—Sisco with her father and Foley with Buddy (Ving Rhames)—where they happen to see separate photos of each other in newspapers. In interviewing Adele, Sisco looks at framed photos of Foley, in a sense checking out a prospective partner. He has her wallet, giving the viewer visual information about her but also allowing him to call her at home. Outside Adele's flat, Foley spots Sisco in his side mirror and cannot tear his eyes away from her rear as she drops her keys. Later in the farcical FBI raid, where the marshals stealthily approach via the stairs, he comes down the elevator. As the doors open to allow an elderly woman out, Foley exchanges a glance with Sisco, sitting in the lobby. It is a moment of recognition, not just of their identity but of their relationship as Sisco raises her radio to her mouth (her sense of duty) but says nothing (what her heart dictates). Foley is left standing there, giving a clumsy wave, cut off by the closing door, an awkwardness accentuated by his hopeless disguise of a red Hawaiian shirt.

In the motel, Foley wipes steam from the bathroom mirror, revealing his torso but also a sense that he is trying to work out his feelings. Meeting Sisco has disorientated him. Like a fantasy, she appears in his bathroom, as if willed by his thought. He appears completely vulnerable (perhaps part of what she finds attractive about him) but his pose is broken as he opens his eyes and hauls her into the tub (shot from directly above) with Sisco clearly not resisting. We then cut to Sisco in hospital, subverting expectations and suggesting that this was actually *her* fantasy. Scott's script clearly describes this as her dream, but Soderbergh denies us conventional fictive markers like a wobbly screen, making his audience work to piece the narrative together.[6]

Later in the hotel, we have a glimpse of the norm that Sisco has to tolerate as a sequence of well-meaning but uninvited men approach her. She looks at her reflection and the snow falling in the darkness outside (a computer-generated effect) as another man appears, his head cropped from view. The underlighting of the table, the fact that Foley is now smooth-shaven, smartly dressed, and not drunk, the close-ups of his eyes, and his romantic gesture of placing his hand over hers—all of these factors work in his favor. The following love scene is conveyed with freeze frames before we fade to black. From trunk to motel room to here, the relationship has progressed to a more complete consummation. There is also a use of flash-forwards to the love scene itself, like Nic Roeg's *Don't Look Now* (1972), intercut with shots of them still in the dining room to convey a disorientating sense of intense sensuality.

Particularly key is the earlier scene in Detroit, of the gang lead by Maurice Miller (Don Cheadle) minus Foley, carrying out a horrific attack on a rival dealer. Soderbergh gives the viewer only a few, brief distorted images of the violence and in a subsequent scene images of the police investigating the crime scene. The full power of the scene is writ large on the shocked and numbed expression of Glenn Michaels (Steve Zahn) on the gang's return, their nonchalance contrasting with his obvious petrification. Clooney's role then is of a criminal but is of a different league to the sadistic gang who brutally murder another prisoner, kill the victims of their housebreaking, and plan to rape Ripley's maid, Midge (Nancy Allen) in the final attack. Foley uses firearms initially only to threaten, and eventually chooses to fight back against the gang rather than take flight with Buddy and removes the bullets before confronting Sisco, provoking her to shoot him, albeit not fatally. The final scene with Sisco, revealed as the driver of Foley's prison van, leaves open whether she only wants to see him, talk to him, make him aware she will wait for him, or help him escape once more.

It is Foley's ability to observe and plan that sets him apart from his other inmates. Like Andy Dufresne (Tim Robbins) in *The Shawshank Redemption* (Frank Darabont, 1994), Foley uses his learning to his own advantage (literally flattening one of Maurice's henchmen in prison with a book). We see him watching the set up boxing matches, noting the potential target of Ripley (Albert Brooks), so that when he is outside prison it is his quick thinking that keeps him at liberty. In the scene in the library, where Miller tries to intimidate Ripley, it is not until Foley speaks, calmly complaining about the noise, that we are even aware he is in the scene at all. In the final raid, he is the one who finds Ripley and the hiding place of the diamonds (the fish tank) rather than being distracted by the appeal of food (Bob) who tries to empty the refrigerator or sex (Kenneth) (Isaiah Washington) attempting to rape the maid.

The film might include some typical features of the crime genre (a robbery, a fixed boxing match in prison, a climactic crime), but in each case Frank's script and Soderbergh's realization of it give us more. Even in prison, Michaels is so feeble that he cannot lift any of the weights in the open-air gym area. The nonlinear narrative effectively blends flashbacks to prison signaled by captions and later drops scenes unannounced into the narrative that can then be placed in order retrospectively—for example, Foley's disastrous interview ends with anger on the streets and then a glance up at the bank, last seen in the opening sequence. Such a structure makes the film harder work but more rewarding for the viewer as well as explaining in this instance why Foley seemed a little underprepared, since his decision to rob the bank was spontaneous, and also reflecting that this is what he really is. Like Butch and Sundance, he tries to go straight but circumstances seem pitted against him. In crime films, even when he plays someone on the wrong side of the law, Clooney's character is contrasted with a greater brutality, like Maurice Miller and his gang here, and performs some final sacrificial action to redeem himself (killing Kenneth and, along with Sisco, shooting the gang, respectively).

THREE KINGS (DAVID O. RUSSELL, 1999)

Barlow: Are we shooting people or what?

David O. Russell's account of the chaos in the wake of the ceasefire at the end of the 1991 Gulf War places Clooney in the role of Major Archie Gates, leading a band of soldiers to appropriate some of Saddam Hussein's gold. Clooney found Russell's methods difficult, like his constant filming, even during rehearsals and meetings, leading to a well-documented confrontation over Russell's treatment of an extra. Russell was under pressure himself from Warner Brothers, who were concerned at how overtly political the film was becoming, and original writer John Ridley, who was contesting Russell's scriptwriting credit, but Clooney has yet to work with him again.

Derek Hill states that "the moral choices . . . are sophisticated, paradoxical and messy in a way that is rare for such a star vehicle,"[1] and certainly the initial presentation of the U.S. military is hardly flattering. Troy Barlow (Mark Wahlberg) approaches a figure standing on the roof of a house, representing the dilemma of any soldier in armed combat. His colleagues barely seem prepared for such decisions: there are two whip pans to other soldiers, standing in open sight, one trying to remove sand from the eye of another. The man is at some distance, he does present a weapon, and without the benefit of combat experience, Barlow's mistake in firing is perhaps understandable. Less sensitive, his fellow soldiers, represented by Conrad Vig (Spike Jonze), take pictures and congratulate him for having shot "a raghead." The men seem ill-prepared and ignorant of the political and military situation.

The scenes of celebration at the end of the war, represented by the pumping iron, lazing on huge air mats, the water fights, the posing with guns and flags for photos, and the presence of Snap's "The Power," all seem like a fraternity house party, disconnected from any notion of suffering. The camera whips past a group of prisoners, representing a reality that these soldiers, and we the viewers, must soon face. At this stage, Barlow is happy to dress up as an Arab: for him, it is just a form of fancy dress. It is a sequence of joyful, albeit insensitive, male bonding and a nod to Wahlberg's dance moves that are shown more fully in *Boogie Nights* (Paul Thomas Anderson, 1997). Reporter Adriana Cruz (Nora Dunn) is trying to put a more articulate spin on what she is witnessing, describing how the war was about "exorcising Vietnam with a clear moral imperative," but an interviewee answers more bluntly, "We liberated Kuwait." Cruz, as an experienced journalist, is looking for a story, searching for meaning in what she sees but there is the suggestion that such meaning is absent here.

The main characters are introduced via freeze frame and a brief piece of on-screen text that appears as if typed. Vig, inexpertly performing karate moves, "wants to be Troy Barlow." His admiration, bordering on hero worship, is his prime characteristic, along with his blind stupidity, both of which contribute to his death later, running to help his friend. Gates is shown in typical action, having sex with a junior reporter. The fact that the woman instantly fires a work-related question at him seconds after they have finished suggests this was just a meaningless diversion for both of them. Like Cruz, she too is looking for a story but will use other means to get it.

We have in the group a cross section of the military. Gates is a high-ranking, experienced officer in an elite section of the army; Barlow is a young officer (Sergeant First Class) with leadership potential, trying to do and say the right thing (his action later in trying to stop Iraqi children running onto mines is typical); Chief Elgin (Ice Cube) is a willing foot soldier, representing an Afro-Caribbean demographic, following orders and the guidance of God, and Vig represents the lowest level of army recruit, without a high school education but also given to moments of literal insight denied the others by their upbringing. The officer class seem barely in control of their men. Captain Van Meter (Holt McCallany) is unaware of the men getting alcohol and later, in conjunction with Colonel Horn (Mykelti Williamson), they seem farcically unaware of the whereabouts of several soldiers and key items of equipment. However, perhaps the true measure of Horn and Van Meter is that at the border confrontation later they support the humanitarian efforts to save the group of Iraqi dissidents; that is, they do what good they can.

There is also a linguistic war in progress. Incomprehensible orders are barked simultaneously through two megaphones at cowering Iraqi prisoners. Vig unthinkingly mentions a "dune-coon," and when reprimanded by Elgin states that the mixture of "pro-Saudi, anti-Iraq type language" is confusing and adds that the captain (Barlow) uses these terms. One way in which Clooney's character seems separate from his men, apart from coming from another division, is his refusal to use such terms. His rank as a senior Special Forces officer allows him a certain freedom: he walks, unchallenged, into the tent and demands the map. Quickly, he recognizes that he cannot cut the men who found it out of the deal and instantly takes them into his confidence. They become the team and he assumes the mantle of pack leader and chief strategist in the planning of a robbery, as he would do later as Danny Ocean.

There seems a fundamental childishness to many of the antics of the soldiers, like Troy and Elgin arguing first about football teams and later about whether a particular brand of car has a convertible. Gates accepts that he must use soldiers of all ranks, and he shows great forbearance in enduring actions and words that test his patience severely, asking Barlow only, in relation to Vig, "Are you able to control him?" He drives out into the desert (as if he is the only one old enough to take control of the vehicle), a tape of Bach on the stereo, with the soldiers like kids on vacation, acting up in the back. Like McGill looking after Delmar in *O Brother*, Clooney plays a character who takes a paternal care over those much further down the educational ladder, again driving a car with child-like adults. Here, he indulges the game with the football as a kind of version of clay pigeon shooting, until one wired with explosives almost blows the truck off the road at which he pulls up and administers a calmly worded telling-off. He responds to their wishes to see some action by calmly leading them a few paces away from the vehicle to show them bodies, half buried in the sand.

The character of Vig is partly present for comic relief, imagining bullion is "them little cubes you put in hot water to make soup." Like a small child, he has a very short concentration span, asking apropos of nothing whether you have to cut off someone's ears to get into Special Forces, which he terms "SF." Unlike Barlow and Elgin, whose mundane civilian existences we see in rapid montage form, cutting between Barlow dealing with an exploding toner cartridge to Elgin loading airport luggage (explaining his later knowledge of how best to carry the gold), Gates has no other life—he is a professional soldier. This also links Gates with Vig, who also has no meaningful existence outside the military (except for a snapshot of Vig, firing a gun at a range of soft toys outside a decrepit trailer).

Gate lectures them about sepsis, miming a gun with his finger, and pretending to let off a round at Barlow. This apparently childish action, however, is accompanied by realistic sound effects of the bullet flying and a reaction shot of Barlow, apparently hit. We fade to a close-up of Barlow's internal organs, quickly filled with bright green bile, before Russell plays the film backward and the damage is miraculously undone. Back at the opening of the film, a title card explains that the makers of the film "used visual distortion and unusual colors in some scenes." This suggests the film's audience might be confused by such expressionistic devices, clumsily underlining "they intentionally used these unconventional techniques to enhance the emotional intensity of the storyline." This scene, demonstrating the damage that a single bullet can do, is one such scene, but it seems so stylistically out of sync with the film around it that it functions less as a powerful moment on its own than as a foreshadowing of what can happen if you are shot (as happens to Vig and Barlow later).

Clooney's character shows quick thinking in rapidly devising an elaborate cover story to throw Cruz off the scent. However, his plan to practice their approach to the bunker using a cow as a prop proves less inspired, frightening the cow onto a cluster bomb. The explosion certainly reflects the horrors of what such weapons can do, how dangerous the Iraqi landscape has been left, and the simple truth that it could have been them; but the ensuing gore, as they are splattered with remains that rain down on them in slow motion with the head crashing on the hood of the truck, appears primarily to provide cinematic spectacle. As Vig states, it is "like a cartoon." With a Bart Simpson toy on the hood, there is a constant presence of cartoonishness (in emotional responses, in action sequences, and in language) to counterpoint Gates's attempt at injecting some realism.

Before the truck reaches the compound where they suspect the gold is hidden, Bach is replaced by the Beach Boys' "I Get Around" and we have clear shots of the U.S. flag on the back of the truck. There is the sense of exhilaration and self-belief that they are coming as liberators (albeit of the gold rather than the oppressed people). Footage of civilians, especially children following the truck, creates the sense of a rapturous welcome; but more rapid cutting, including increasing use of point-of-view shots from the truck, and shaky handheld shots of the process of tying up the guards suggest the speedy unraveling of the situation. Barlow is soon faced with the reality of unexpected reactions from mothers holding babies, begging directly for help, to a man who tries to hug him rather than offering any resistance.

Generic clichés are also questioned. Breaking a door down with one's shoulder is seen as ridiculous as Barlow just bounces off and Gates has to kick it in. A rocket launched at a tanker leads to the three heroes diving to the ground, expecting an explosion (shown in Russell's ubiquitous slow motion), but instead of gas the vehicle contains milk, which floods the square, knocking them over. In such an inverted, chaotic situation, where mothers try to scoop up milk from the sand, access to food is the new weaponry. What starts out as a heist turns into an aid mission and one with mixed results. Gates's group have to throw a man off their jeep and push back begging crowds, as they leave the compound empty-handed on their first raid.

Gates brandishes a copy of the ceasefire agreement in all the following confrontations, appearing to put faith in the rule of law, although this is just a façade. In the second raid, he claims to be taking back what was stolen from Kuwait, but this cloaking in moral authority fulfills only the first part of the Robin Hood equation: he is stealing from the rich but not planning on giving it to the poor (at least, not yet). He lectures Barlow and Elgin when they start to rifle through jewelry, claiming "We're not thieves," but this has only the veneer of respectability and is patently not true. Gates holds a pistol to the head of a guard, demanding that he reveal the whereabouts of the gold. As the all-important door is found, we do not know exactly how brutal or unprincipled Gates actually is.

Gates's acceptance of the Iraqi officer's offer to help carry the gold clearly compromises him morally: the civilians will be butchered once the Americans leave. To make this clear, the wife of the chief dissident, Amir Abdulah (Cliff Curtis), is executed on the orders of the officer. Gates's key reaction is to put his head on the wheel. He knows now that they cannot remain disengaged from the situation. He gets out of the jeep and walks toward his enemy, which could be seen as an act of bravery or that he has been forced into taking a moral lead; either way, he clearly takes command.

Quickly disabling the guard holding the husband of the murdered woman, we have lengthy shots of the grieving family, a little girl in particular in a powerful microcosmic image of the results of U.S. policy. This is certainly stated explicitly by the rebels in the cave, turning on Gates for starting a war and then not supporting the uprising. In miniature, Gates's actions reflect the wider military and political processes: by killing Iraqi soldiers, they have broken the ceasefire (the very agreement that Gates had trumpeted on entry) and now must bear the consequences, which involve a responsibility to those they have liberated (here, taking the rebels to safety at the Iranian border). There is a tense stand-off as we cut between the two groups of men both with guns drawn, almost western style, with the tension focused on the two leaders. The battle of wills between Gates and the Iraqi officer becomes more physical as Gates grabs the other man's gun so that it fires a round into his foot. At this stage, Gates has shown moderation, limited force, and some statesmanship in taking a moral stance.

However, his subsequent shooting of the Iraqi officer is problematic. Undoubtedly, the man is cruel and has ordered the murder of the dissident's wife, but it is debatable whether Gates as a senior officer is right to act in a way that can only be seen as revenge, shooting the man in the head in the same way (and Russell making the parallel clear with slow motion in both events) even though the man was offering no direct threat to the Americans and could have been just tied up. There is even calculation here as Gates holds his gun beneath the man's chin for a second or two; that is, it is a morally compromised act, not performed in the heat of the moment. A low-angle shot of Gates looking down as clouds race nonnaturalistically overhead produces the vision of the dying man and elevates Gates to the God-like status of the giver of life and death. Perhaps there is the implication of divine intervention, of Gates saving innocent lives (and of Barlow miraculously surviving being shot by his Kevlar vest), but if Gates is a savior, he is a very Machiavellian one. Having made this change of role, despite Barlow's repeated call to "stick to the plan," Gates now orders the political prisoners into the truck, which they commandeer. In a moment, the mission has changed from one of acquisition to one of rescue.

Cruz's sudden bursting into tears at the sight of pathetically oiled birds or the shots of Barlow being force-fed oil with his mouth jammed open with a CD case both make a fairly crude political point about the underlying economics of the conflict, but there are also some more effective images: a coffin full of passports, suggesting where they have come from; the glimpse of Rodney King on a TV being beaten in LA (possibly as a time reference for the viewer or as inspiration for the torturers); the sudden stumbling on a family, huddled together underground, waiting to be tortured; and the bizarre reality of global communications by which Barlow is able to get a call through from one of a box of discarded phones direct to his wife back home. Turning a corner in the Citadel, Gates crashes into a man running the other way, who offers no threat but drops his pile of jeans. Western imperialism collides with Eastern consumerism.

Moral absolutes are questioned as the chief torturer, Captain Said (Saïd Taghmaoui), talks of the death of his baby in an air strike (the shot of falling masonry onto a cot repeated in slow motion), but there is also a suffocating literalism here too. As soon as a character talks of something, we see a shot of it. Barlow mentions his wife, so we have a shot of her at home; he thinks of his greatest fear and we see a wall exploding back home. As the motivation and actions of the enemy are humanized, the only clear villain remains the ubiquitous Saddam, much talked about, much feared, and seen in iconic pictures but not represented on-screen. Possibly after *Hot Shots II* (Jim Abrahams, 1993), he would seem a purely comic figure.

A times, there seems a dissonance between nostalgia for a particular generic form and the more gritty content. The soundtrack seems to hanker after a purer heist narrative like the original *The Italian Job* (Peter Collinson, 1969) with freestyle jazz drumming accompanying some of the loading of the gold and Barlow's search for a truck.[2] The ubiquitous Western music reflects a sense of cultural imperialism, and its use in scenes like the entrance to the refugee camp gives the characters the appearance of figures in a pop video or models on a catwalk, walking in time to the beat. Elgin's more openness to Eastern influences, reflected in his willingness to kneel and pray alongside Muslims, is reflected in his taste in music in the car, much to Vig's disgust but to the contentment of his two smiling passengers. Russell uses the Carpenters' easy-listening classic "If You Leave Me Now" from the in-car stereo as the luxury vehicles approach, but it also bleeds over the subsequent exchange of gunfire. Vig manages to lock himself out of one car, which also contains his gun. Luckily, a stray bullet shatters the glass and he can reach in to retrieve it, at which point the volume of the Carpenters' song rises on the soundtrack.

Some effects suggest elements of an action movie, like the scene in which Elgin throws an explosive football at a helicopter, the brief exchange of fire earlier where the path of the American bullets are slowed down so that we hear them thud into their targets, the flight from the compound and the attack from bazookas firing gas, or the truck crashing into a minefield, but such scenes seem contrived for the pleasures of spec-tacle. Clearly, any director would want to get the most from his stunts, but Russell's use of slow motion becomes almost predictable in depicting any act of violence.

Gates eventually locates Troy and shoots two soldiers who raise their weapons and wounds the chief torturer, who is unarmed. The force he uses here is proportionate to the threat. However, the handing of his pistol to Troy means that he is explicitly condoning killing former captors. Barlow's choice to shoot wide saves both men from the moral ambiguity of when revenge tips over into cold-blooded murder. Gates goes back to rescue his fellow soldier at considerable risk to himself with no prospect of material gain. It is unclear if he always intended to search for Troy, feels a sense of residual guilt (in involving soldiers, who have little training and no combat experience), or responds to the pleading of Vig, but Gates performs the role of military hero, even if this is con-trary to his training. There may be an element of some hubris here too. He may be highly trained, but attacking a compound containing an unknown number of soldiers with only a handful of men seems a little foolhardy.

As a microcosm for the war as a whole, the heist conveys a powerful sense of an apparently easy mission with clear aims, which is then rapidly compromised into a dangerous mess by the complexity of local and regional politics. When Gates and Troy emerge into daylight, there is a pan around the scene outside the compound for several seconds without music, as we also survey a scene of destruction, framed with a fluttering Iraqi flag. Unlike the first sight of him with a junior reporter, Gates remains a professional soldier once in the field. The shot rotating around Gates as he looks out into the scrubland underlines that he remains alert and aware there is still danger, and he reacts quickly to Vig being shot, riddling his attacker on the ground with bullets. The speed and effective-ness with which he puts his head to Troy's chest, diagnoses a hole in his lungs, and improvises a device to relieve pressure on internal organs is like a positive version of the sepsis sequence (as well as injecting a new narrative impetus into the narrative with the need to relieve the pressure in the valve every 15 minutes).

The reality of bullet wounds is conveyed by the speed with which Vig loses consciousness and the reduced sound that accompanies shots of Troy looking up at Elgin and Gates as they try and treat them. Alternate point-of-view shots from Vig and Troy's perspective as they are lying on the ground, side by side, effectively conveys their helpless-ness (a device also subsequently used in David Fincher's *Zodiac* [2007], showing the point of view of victims of a serial killer at Berryessa).[3] Gates recognizes death and breaks the news to Troy with a simple "He's gone," and subsequently, as Troy cries over Vig's body, Gates silently crosses himself and the scene ends with a fade to black.

By this stage, the pursuit of the gold has been largely forgotten and eclipsed by the suffering of the Iraqi people, symbolized by a small group of dissidents, Troy's torture, and Vig's senseless death. There are small glimpses of the heist genre but it has been transformed into something more akin to a parable. There is the familiar element of the division of the spoils, but here it is an almost biblical scene of the group of Iraqis lining up to receive a bar of gold each as payment for their help. The manner in which Troy introduces the Iraqi refugees to his fellow officers marks the breakdown of barriers that the main characters feel with those they have saved and who in turn saved them. When the medical assistance arrives, Cruz, who has eventually found her story, asks if he has the gold, to which Gates replies evasively, "We helped a lot of people."

Three Kings is not a film without weaknesses. The resistance shelter (with a tepee-like entrance clearly above ground) suddenly appearing right next to the site of the accident of the three protagonists' vehicles is patently ridiculous and feels more like the revelation of Q's latest laboratory in a Bond film. However, although it certainly simplifies the complex political and religious situation in Iraq, it also creates dramatically engaging situations. At the Iran border, the dilemma of the Iraqi rebels is made concrete: if they are not allowed to cross, Saddam's forces will slaughter them. The discussion between the American senior officers and the Iraqi leaders is shown in only long-shot, without dialogue, almost like a dumb show.

With the consent of his men, Gates offers to reveal the whereabouts of the gold, if the rebels are guaranteed safe passage across the border. When it comes to a confrontation, Gates puts the welfare of people before material gain (although it could be said that even a single bar of gold would be worth a great deal). Like the scene where he gains the luxury cars, Gates uses his charm to persuade Horn to support the rebels in crossing the border, lacing heroism with self-interest: "Save some people, get that star." In standing by his word, in going back for his men, in showing bravery (not all of which with material reward to be gained), Gates comes to represent what he describes to Horn as "Soldiers' honor."

By the close, we see Elgin and Gates working, ironically, in Hollywood as military consultants and demonstrating fighting techniques on set. Barlow is running his own carpet company with his wife, now with two children. With U2's "In God's Country" coming up on the soundtrack, the ending is decidedly upbeat as if the men have been rewarded for their bravery, selflessness, and possibly entrepreneurial appropriation of some of the Kuwaiti gold.

Hill wonders if the subject matter would have also appealed to Tarantino (who indeed went on to make his own war story, *Inglorious Basterds* [2009]), or "it's something that perhaps a director like David Fincher would have darkly fashioned."[4] The crafting of the bullet sequences through Troy's body may have appealed to the latter but perhaps he would not have adopted Russell's apparent chaotic style of improvised direction. Hill terms it "a morally coherent, visually daring and truly subversive anti-war film,"[5] and it certainly stands as a memorable expression of the delicate balance of tragedy and absurdity that characterizes the lived experience of many veterans.

Along with *The Peacemaker*, *The Good German*, and *The Men Who Stare at Goats*, this is one of several appearances by Clooney in uniform—in all three playing a senior intelligence officer, rather than a front-line soldier. As in *Syriana* (also set in the Middle East), his character understands the political complexities of a situation and goes some way to explain them to his fellow characters (and by extension, the viewers). Despite personal and professional differences with Russell, Clooney shares a strong commitment to try and shed light on contemporary conflicts and, by raising awareness, help to end them. His own particular passion is the ongoing fighting and atrocities that have been committed in Darfur, and he continues to lend his voice to those opposing the situation in that troubled region.

OCEAN'S ELEVEN (STEVEN SODERBERGH, 2001)

Beyond the title, Ted Griffin's screenplay includes few links with Lewis Milestone's 1960 film. There is a plan to steal from several casinos on one night (the Bellagio, the Mirage, and the MGM Grand), led by a charismatic leader, Danny Ocean (George Clooney), with an able sidekick, Rusty (Brad Pitt), and a black member of the gang, Basher Tarr (Don Cheadle). But Soderbergh, forced to ditch original plans to shoot in black-and-white, also cut an original first shot of Rusty framed with a large mural of Sinatra, suggesting he was not keen to underline parallels with the earlier film.

A key difference from the original film is the nature of the cast. In 1960, Frank Sinatra, Dean Martin, and Sammy Davis Jr. represented the epitome of uncontrived cool, the center of the so-called Rat Pack. The cast of the films in this chapter operates in a completely different world. Forty years later, in place of excessive smoking, drinking, and partying we have hard bodies and celebrities sworn to fairly strict exercise regimes. Rather than singers who acted for a little distraction, we have film actors who definitely have no pretensions as singers (except Catherine Zeta-Jones for a brief spell in the 1990s). The three films use musical accompaniments to suggest the Sinatra era (the snatch of Elvis's "A Little Less Conversation" was enough to reanimate global interest in the singer's back catalog) but none of it is produced by the cast themselves. For them, Vegas is purely a place of financial opportunity, not a performance venue. Rather than figures, particularly Sinatra, who operated on the fringes of criminality, we have actors who use their profiles for political activism, such as Clooney's work on behalf of Darfur or Pitt's involvement with post-Katrina reconstruction.

All three films work on the basis of presenting a series of difficulties, and then among potential solutions, fresh problems are thrown into the mix. In the first film, it is Danny's attachment to his ex-wife Tess (Julia Roberts), the current girlfriend of Terry Benedict (Andy Garcia), which is revealed as the driving force for the job. In *Ocean's Twelve*, Rusty's relationship to Isabel (Catherine Zeta-Jones), a cop, fulfills a similar function.

In hindsight, the success of the franchise seems a foregone conclusion but the first film had to establish the tone of interrelationships. The first shot of *Ocean's Eleven* shows Danny blaming his criminal behavior on being "upset" at his wife leaving him, setting him on a "self-destructive pattern." On being asked if he could break away from this, he logically points out that his wife cannot leave him twice. The film establishes then that it is his story, the tale of a man with a troubled personal life but who can charm what has to be said seems a fairly pliant parole board.

Repeated shots of Danny show him fiddling with his ring (underlying his motivation to win back his wife), and we have a transformation of his rough-shaven appearance to the rising shot of him as a smooth operator, now clean-shaven, appearing on an escalator at an Atlantic City casino. He seems a compulsive risk taker and charmingly plausible liar, telling his parole officer on the phone that he has not been in trouble or drinking, although we have just seen him doing the latter. He is mostly dressed in dark, sober colors, often black, such as when he explains to Rusty the basic plan, and even when he is in a shop with Saul (Carl Reiner) is dressed in a stylish mustard-colored shirt. Strong underlighting at gambling tables, designed to make clients as attractive as possible, certainly plays up Clooney's facial features (also used later at the restaurant where he reveals himself to Tess).

The *Ocean's* franchise is a narrative featuring, and designed for, those beyond the 16–24 demographic, and we see the frustration of Rusty

(Brad Pitt) having to babysit spoiled pop stars, who cannot even follow the rules of poker. Although Rusty and Danny argue over criminal strategy here, Danny wins the argument, having substance behind his bluff (symbolically winning the hand), and can see how bored Rusty is in his present position. From the outset, there is an easy, relaxed tone to the banter between Pitt and Clooney based on their well-established personal friendship. They can credibly indulge in the kind of comic self-aware, self-canceling dialogue that is a feature of *Friends*, in which they both had cameo roles, and like in the TV series, as soon as the dialogue heads too far toward sentiment or cliché, there is a countermovement into self-deprecating humor. When Danny delivers his pitch for the plan as they wait for an elevator, Rusty reacts with "Been practicing that speech, haven't you?" to which Danny admits "A little bit. Did I rush it?" A similar style appears in *Intolerable Cruelty*, when Miles interrupts his own grandiose practice speech to a jury, implying a relationship between Donaly and the pool boy with "Did I go too far?"

Soderbergh uses a number of self-conscious camera placements or movements that draw attention to themselves, like the high-angle fixed cameras for shots of cars, such as in Rusty's open-top sports car near the beginning, the rotating shot that follows Rusty eating as the others watch a surveillance monitor, or the cropped shot of Clooney's face as he first surprises Tess in the restaurant (like Foley's appearance at Sisco's table in *Out of Sight*). The staccato effect used in the sequence where Danny watches Linus (Matt Damon) steal a wallet on a Chicago train has the effect of marking it as a digression from the main plot as well as allowing a momentary freeze-frame at the point of the crime and as Danny plants the invitation on him. Soderbergh also uses freeze-frames in the sequel such as the key moment when Rusty jumps out of the bathroom window on hearing that Isabel is about to make a breakthrough in the case.

The elaborate plots of the sequels are sometimes criticized, but the unreality of the whole enterprise is established in the first film with the theft of a device (handily mobile on its own trolley) that can emit an electromagnetic pulse similar to a nuclear bomb. The huge mock-up of the vault at the Bellagio seems unlikely, but as a metaphor for venture capitalism, the whole *Ocean's* series pushes notions of planning to an extreme. Here you really do have to spend money to make money. There is a dissolve from the fake to the real thing, but unlike Kubrick's maze in *The Shining* (1980), Soderbergh does not attempt an exact match. There are small attempts to capture the excesses of Vegas. Soderbergh frames Tarr watching TV coverage of the demolition of a hotel (reasonably modern but now seen as passé) as we see through the window behind him the real one fall.

It is perhaps inevitable that in a film, whose very title suggests a large main cast, Clooney should lose some of the main narrative focus at times. His foolish appearance on surveillance video (in meeting Tess) undermines his role as leader, from which he, albeit temporarily, has to step back. However, he remains cool throughout. The geekiness is outsourced to the ensemble characters, so Livingstone (Eddie Jemison) has the nerves, the Malloy brothers (Casey Affleck as Virgil and Scott Caan as Turk) squabble to the point that Linus begs not be left alone in the van with them, Tarr has an avalanche of British slang, and Reuben (Elliott Gould) personifies sartorial bad taste (complaining about Benedict's casino as a "gaudy monstrosity" while sporting paisley shorts, huge gold jewelry, cigars, and glasses). It almost leaves Danny and Rusty with too little to distinguish them (we never really see Rusty's supposed card skills in action).

After pulling off the job the cast stands wordlessly, looking at the Bellagio fountains in a moment of contemplation. Accompanied by Debussy's "Claire de Lune" (also used at the pool party before they listen to Danny's plan), the shot functions as a curtain call as the characters walk away one by one. In *Ocean's Thirteen*, the team watches fireworks, with Sinatra's "This Town" playing on the soundtrack.

OCEAN'S TWELVE (STEVEN SODERBERGH, 2004)

Theoretically, this is a sequel with Benedict tracking down Ocean and his team and forcing them to repay his money in two weeks. However, it feels a little like the original film on steroids. There are more stars, more exotic locations (this time in Europe), and more elaborate heists, such as the notion of lowering the level of an Amsterdam house in order to steal some precious documents. The slight twist here is Rusty's relationship with Isabel (Catherine Zeta-Jones), which seems fairly knowing from the outset rather than a credible cat-and-mouse element with a female investigator like Norman Jewison's 1968 *The Thomas Crown Affair*. Like the introduction of a rival thief, François Toulour (Vincent Cassell), it tends to overcomplicate an already crowded plot.

Quite why Danny's gang does not all go into serious hiding is a little strange. Danny has changed his name and worked out a routine with Tess as what to do if found, but the others seem to be plying their old trades in familiar places (such as the brothers at a family gathering in Utah and Rusty still working in hotels). As Reuben says incredulously to a fortune-teller at the appearance of Benedict and his henchmen, "You couldn't see this?" The film tends to play fast and loose with the role of Benedict. At the beginning, they are not so fearful of him that (except for Danny) they change identities. Then they do fear him enough to undertake any heist available in the body of the film but then at the end they openly defy him and give his money away.

Life after the success of the first film seems an anticlimax. Danny starts telling a bank employee about being in a bank vault while it was being robbed, the implication being (particularly by Soderbergh's use of jagged little jump cuts as Danny speaks) that everyday life seems dull by comparison. Even the montage of Toulour's ultraluxurious lifestyle seems empty, prompting him into the egotistical challenge to Danny to see who is the best thief. It seems as if the plot itself is exhausted, digressing into a narrative of personal rivalry. It does, however, move the film toward the notion of robbing a single entity (a Fabergé egg) as a matter of personal honor and gives the film a lighter tone than genuine fear at being killed by Benedict's men. However, some of the unity of purpose of the first film seems dissipated with bickering about the name of the original heist, which, unlike the naming scene in Quentin Tarantino's *Reservoir Dogs*, just seems more petulant than funny.

Soderbergh's preference for wipes as a transitional device between scenes (seen in the first film with the elevator doors closing on Danny's face) becomes much more pronounced here, including a 1970s-style venetian blind effect, the hand of a clock, and a *Charlie Angels*-style wipe around the edge of the frame like a maze round into the center. In all three films, particularly in confined spaces (or spaces the director wants to suggest feel confined), Soderbergh uses hand-held camerawork, often in forward and reverse tracking shots following the progress of a character through a room (most obviously casinos but also Isabel in the Amsterdam house).

There are relatively few elaborate postproduction effects, apart from the CGI shot to show the safe-cracking device being winched across the canal (a difficult shot to capture at night) and the hologram of the egg. Soderbergh uses sequences drained of color for any flashback sequences (the final explanation of the deal made with LaMarque), and as in the first film, freeze-frames capture key moments, like Isabel pocketing Rusty's phone, and Rusty's twisted expression of pained self-loathing at his elementary error. There are a couple of Kubrickian devices, like Soderbergh's camera ghosting through walls in the opening scene, tracking to the new character, Isabel, in bed; and at a number of points in the film, he uses on-screen captions to underscore how many are left until Benedict's deadline expires, although this seems a slightly desperate way to import a sense of urgency.

As this is a sequel, there is the opportunity for an increasing sense of knowingness in the plot, with Linus (Matt Damon) pleading with Rusty for a "more central role," which feels a little like Chico (Horst Buchholz) in *The Magnificent Seven* (John Sturges, 1960) with Rusty delivering the same judgment that Yul Brenner states to the aspiring member of the group: "You're not ready." It also perversely inverts Damon's actual request to Soderbergh for a smaller role after his exertions on *The Bourne Supremacy* (Paul Greengrass, 2004).

The additional characters in the sequel, Isabel (Zeta-Jones), Matsui (Robbie Coltrane), and Eddie Roman Nagel (Eddie Izzard), reflect the full diversity of British eccentricity (Welsh, Scottish, and English respectively). Although Coltrane plays his part straight, both he and Izzard (comedians as well as actors) bring a tongue-in-cheek element, particularly the latter, complaining about the cliché of Rusty having a sexy female assistant, only to be interrupted by one of his own.

The scene with Matsui in which Rusty and Danny talk nonsense and then expect Linus to take his turn is presented purely for comic effect, and although it is funny, it adds to the sense of the creating an exclusive club, whose purpose is to tease those who are not fully accepted members. Danny's "If all the animals on the equator were capable of flattery, then Thanksgiving and Halloween would fall on the same date" are followed by Linus's effort, taken from the Led Zeppelin song "Kashmir" (1975). Later at the station, Rusty declares "It's not in my nature to be mysterious" but then goes on to contradict this, claiming that he "can't talk about it and I can't talk about why," leaving Linus far from impressed, giving a mock scared "Oooooh" (a shot frequently used in trailers). Linus is the only one who voices qualms about using the word "freak" and stealing from an agoraphobic victim, prompting the sarcastic comment, "Are you hosting a telethon we don't know about?" The humor here has a slightly sharper edge at times, which in the first film was directed only toward those used to taking it. The mistake of Yen being sent in a bag to the wrong European city is superficially funny, and a subsequent shot of Yen bouncing for joy on his bed like a small child suggests that he does not seem to bear a grudge, but Virgil's gag about him being a "bag man" could have had a more tragic outcome.

The films are not afraid of dramatically dead time, which is often filled with substrata of neurotic patter, either between the Malloy brothers or more often surrounding Danny. Waiting for a train, he asks a series of characters how old he looks and more particularly whether he looks 50, making fun of the running joke that people generally take Clooney for older than he is, even though he is actually fairly close in age to Pitt. A similar scene has Rusty and Danny in a two-shot, sitting facing the camera, drinking wine, apparently watching *Happy Days* in Italian. Rusty delivers some soul-searching dialogue involving a girl and removing a tattoo and Danny's only comment is "That guy doing Potsie's unbelievable." In *Ocean's Thirteen*, Rusty surprises Danny in his hotel room watching *Oprah*, drinking wine and appearing to cry, although he claims he just bit into a pepper. For several seconds we just watch them, watching TV as Rusty also starts to become emotional, with a sniff. Partly parodies of men in touch with their feminine sides, it is also a reflection of the star persona of each man that can accommodate such moments.

We have a glimpse of Clooney's flat stomach as he coolly dresses, intercut with Toulour's more energetic stretching routine (including some Capoeira), the full significance only becoming apparent later as we see him dance through the laser beams that guard the egg. By the time of *The American* (2010), it is Clooney who will show us more yoga-based routines, which help to keep both actor and the character he plays in shape.

However, the sequence in which Tess is miraculously turned into Julia Roberts only partly works. In literature, the idea of real people appearing or authors stepping into their own stories is an increasingly noticeable feature of writers from Vladimir Nabokov to Martin Amis to Douglas Coupland, but the medium of film seems more resistant to such boundary breaking. As Tess says, "It's just wrong." However, Linus tries to assure her, "You're like an object. No one actually knows you," which rapidly proves ironic as Bruce Willis (also playing himself) does recognize her. The sense of stars playing versions of themselves does reflect the reality of modern stardom and ironically could be seen to reflect the image of Clooney in particular (see his commercials in chapter 9). Life and art collide as we later see Clooney sipping wine, looking out from Toulour's palatial villa on Lake Como (using his own as a location), and ultimately giving Benedict's money away to charity in the kind of high-profile philanthropy that he and Pitt support. However, if Tess can pass for Julia Roberts just by putting on a hat, why does no one comment on the fact in the first film? Linus has a couple of interrupted questions to Rusty in the second film but it is not like an embarrassing secret; one might expect a visible reaction in other characters much earlier. If reference starts to be made to the real lives of actors, why does this only apply to Tess/Julia Roberts? Why does no one notice that Danny Ocean looks like George Clooney? The fact that only Bruce Willis is playing himself here underlines the inconsistency even more.

More problematically, why bother with the whole Julia Roberts idea at all if the real egg has been switched (which is revealed at the end), arguably undermining the point of much of the body of the film? Toulour may lose the bet in the strictest sense of the word, since Danny's team get the egg, but the question of who is the better thief is hardly settled since the contest is grossly unfair in terms of numbers (although Toulour knew this in proposing the challenge). But more importantly, LeMarque (an uncredited Albert Finney) tips off Danny as to the whereabouts of the real egg; i.e., they cheat. Toulour does break the cardinal rule of loyalty among thieves by betraying them to Benedict, but it feels more like Toulour is positioned as the villain because of his arrogance, the fact that he is French, and, possibly, the most important point: he is not George Clooney.

The involvement of Milena Canonero (with whom Soderbergh and Clooney had worked on *Solaris*) adds to the sense of classic European design (as well as finding some great ill-fitting trousers for Brad Pitt to wear as a room cleaner) but also perhaps that the look of the film is more important than the coherence of its narrative. The final blurred freeze-frame of Isabel falling off her chair laughing reflects a cast at ease with one another but perhaps also the sense that these films are being made more for the pleasure of the participants than the audience.

OCEAN'S THIRTEEN (STEVEN SODERBERGH, 2007)

Rusty: Relationships can be—
Danny: Oh yeah.
Rusty: But they're also—
Danny: That's right.

The fact that the cast (and director) know each other so well and that this is the third film in the series means that dialogue can be even snappier, often incomplete, and employ even more in-jokes and pseudo-criminal terminology (some real, some not). Even the dialogue is explicitly filmic as Roman commands Danny to "Run it for me. Give me the big picture." There are running gags through the franchise, such as the heavily tattooed character (Scott L. Schwartz). He appears as a supposed thug in the first film, only to let Danny escape, and resurfaces in the second as legal counsel to help free Frank (Bernie Mac) from jail. In the third film, he appears (uncredited) taking a large bundle of chips during the mini-earthquake.

The films neatly sidestep the whole notion of whether a casino robbery is a victimless crime by giving us a despicable casino owner to steal from (*Ocean's Eleven*) and then repay (*Ocean's Twelve*) and then an even more unprincipled, egotistical owner, Willy Bank (Al Pacino), for *Ocean's Thirteen* who has cheated Reuben, something of a father figure for

Danny. Thus we have personal motivation added to the unpleasant ego-
ism of Bank wanting a Five Diamond Award for the opening of his new
hotel. Here we have the wish fulfillment of breaking the bank and of turning the tables on those who normally stack the odds in their own favor.
The unfeeling capitalism of the symbolically named Bank is represented
in the way he casts Reuben aside and barks at his employees; and his man-
ageress, Abigail Sponder (Ellen Barkin), echoes his own values: we see
her sacking a waitress for having a body mass index adjudged to be is
too high. Beneath the glamor of the casino world lurks much less refined
motivation, reflected in Frank's instructions to prospective employees for
his new gaming system, who can create the right level of sophistication by
raising their hemlines three inches.

Tendencies in the first two films are greatly exaggerated here with a
hugely overly complicated plot involving multiple cons (tampering with
dice in Mexico, altering gaming machines, even engineering an earthquake) with narrative exposition delivered via an extended conversation
with Roman, intercut with shots of these different problem areas. There is
the familiar introduction of fresh obstacles (Benedict's command to steal
the diamonds as well as break the bank or Weng's refusal to climb into a
shaft) and apparent problems that transpire into solutions (Livingstone's
nervous performance as a croupier emerges as a deliberate ploy, so
Roman can enter and replace the machines with doctored ones).
Commitment to the group overrides everything else as the film opens
with Rusty walking away from the middle of a robbery after getting a call
about Reuben.

There are still some good lines. Linus's bullish performance on the
phone and refusal to hand over to Danny or Rusty is undercut by his final
words, "Bye Dad," or the hotel reviewer (David Paymer) thanking Bank
personally for throwing him out after being hectored out of his room by
the Malloy brothers, including the accusation that he has "nose cancer"
and cannot detect his own bodily smell. There are several effective comic
situations, like Linus as Lenny Pepperidge, "communicator" for Mr. Weng
(Shaobo Qin, who also plays Yen), browbeating Sponder for having kept
them waiting at the airport for seven minutes, an effective portrayal of
the standards of hospitality that accompany excessive wealth. Linus's
prosthetic nose making champagne flutes difficult, Saul's almost-
imperceptible slap on Bank's butt as he passes him in the casino, or the
daredevil costume sported by Cheadle as a fake Fender Roads, which is
loud enough to distract him from the TV monitor, showing the faces of
the gang rapidly being altered by Turk's hacking skills: such moments
are largely enough to distract the viewer from the unwieldy plot.

Part of the pleasure of the third film is the pain inflicted on hotel/restaurant reviewers who may not always seem fair in their columns and a sense of Schadenfreude that the man in question here has to suffer the kind of poor service that less special customers might well experience on a more regular basis. The glimpses of factory conditions in Mexico are brief and the rapidly escalating mini-revolution is played for laughs, but this is the first time in the franchise that we have a sense that the wealth and privilege of the characters, high-rollers and criminal gang alike, are based on other low-wage economies.

There are some neat little creative touches, particularly relating to sound. In *Ocean's Twelve*, when Tarr's fledgling music career is interrupted, Soderbergh bleeps out all of his swearing and then this becomes an act of Benedict in the control room. In *Ocean's Thirteen*, Bank reads a poetic thank-you note that we hear on voice-over from the sender, until the sentiment and the woman's voice is suddenly interrupted by a bored Bank, who rips up the note.

The film is full of visual gags, like on-screen text, showing the extent of individual winnings next to customers, and the size of Bank's losses includes a gag, putting 5150 next to Clooney (shorthand medical code for an individual with mental problems) or the so-called "Gilroy" as a term for the hormone patch (a reference to Tony Gilroy, writer of the *Bourne* franchise and also writer/director of *Michael Clayton*, released the same year as *Ocean's Thirteen*). The running gag that at different points almost the whole cast seems to understand Yen's Chinese without any problems is also extended here as Tarr's techno-babble about problems with the drill that we expect to overwhelm Rusty receives a crisp comprehending answer. The in-jokes that pepper the final exchange between Danny and Rusty, that Clooney should keep his weight down (after *Syriana*) and that Pitt should settle down and have some children (as Pitt has done with Angelina Jolie), perhaps signal that this is a logical place to call time on the franchise. It has become a source of lucrative income that the cast (and Soderbergh) could tap again at some point if funding for less commercial projects were needed.

A deleted scene would have given us more of Clooney's fantastic Village People-style handlebar moustache and some ill-fitting false teeth and also a great line in which Rusty's story about a girl being surprised by him appearing without a towel is interrupted by Danny saying "Those are the waters" to which Rusty gives a knowing "Oh yeah" only to be corrected by Danny, "No, those are the waters," pointing to an ostentatious water feature in the foyer of Bank's casino.

WELCOME TO COLLINWOOD (ANTHONY AND JOE RUSSO, 2002)

Jerzy: As a film, it's a disaster.

Clooney himself, despite posing prominently on the DVD case, appears in only three scenes as Jerzy, the master safecracker: the scene with the projector, the rooftop demonstration, and briefly at the funeral for Cosimo (Luis Guzmán). It is really only a cameo rather than his conventional star vehicle. Indeed, the film is an ensemble piece, in which there is no single main role. Observing the film of the jeweler's (which he describes above), the amateurishness of the team is readily apparent with the final number of the combination repeatedly obscured by someone blocking the view. Jerzy appears in the extreme foreground of the viewing scene, wheeling himself closer to the screen and from darkness into light, revealing a look close to Everett in *O Brother* with his hair tousled and his face often set with a slightly wide-eyed expression.

On the rooftop, the absurdity of the situation becomes even more apparent. Despite cloaking himself in the aura of a teacher ("I have a class to teach"), the only wisdom that he has to impart involves a handheld circular saw, which you have to crank for around three hours to make a small hole (supposedly) in the side of the safe. He will have nothing to do with explosives (possibly the source of his wheelchair-bound existence) and hails his method as the cleanest if not the quickest ("It's the method I was taught. It is what I believe in."). He appears once more at the funeral home in a laughably bad disguise as a Hasidic rabbi, which supposedly prevents him being identified by Detective Babitch (David Warshofsky) who is watching the scene from a car across the street. The irony of Jerzy's own appearance seems lost on him as he calls the others idiots for being so easy to identify.

Instead of his usual role as the leader of a heist, here Clooney is the possessor of supposedly specialist knowledge, but in keeping with the lack of talents in the rest of the group, he is as much a loser as they are. He is a joke to local children who tease him by shouting that the police are coming, sending him into a blind panic, throwing a sheet over the safe. His spluttering at the children ("fucking midgets") is funny but also underlines his impotence to do anything about it. The clap he gives in the projector scene at being offered a part on the team is partly the stupidity of the offer (given his wheelchair-bound situation) but also his frustration at his own situation. Jerzy is an absurd version of Jim Byrd from *Confessions*, also advising the group to "Watch your back," and Seth in

From Dusk Till Dawn whose tattoos, which had been visible on his neck, are subsequently revealed more fully by his wearing just a vest.

Clooney was the last cast member on board, and his scenes act as additional rather than central material to the plot, which could function without them, but nonetheless he adds some comic depth in keeping with the tone of the whole. Clooney seems absent from the DVD extras package, which is perhaps logical given his small on-screen time, and then he appears behind the camera, pulling faces at the Russo brothers during their segment. It seems that both he and particularly Soderbergh, who first saw their film *Pieces* (1997) at the Slamdance Festival, were drawn by a style, sensibility, and method of working (Joe is also an actor but they operate as two heads speaking with one mind) that seems like a younger version of the Coen brothers.

The Russos acknowledge the debt to *Big Deal on Madonna Street/I soliti ignoti* (Mario Monicelli, 1958) at the end of the credits. The Russos maintain small elements in the film that hint at the Italian source material but there is really only a residual element (casting an Italian, Jennifer Esposito as the maid, Camilla), and the terminology, which seems drawn from a blend of gangster movies and adolescent slang, is altered a little (their dream crime, their "Bellini," and the notion of a patsy to take the blame for a crime, a "Mulinski"; Riley, played by William H. Macy, later claims the Bellini is starting to look like a disaster or "Kapuchnik"). The much-used term "Bellini" does not appear in Monicelli's film (he uses "Peccora" or sheep for "Mulinski") and stems from a local Collinwood story about a man, given a job at the Federal Reserve, who mysteriously disappeared (presumably with some of the money he was responsible for incinerating). Some names are changed slightly (Peppe becomes Pero) and some are shifted to make a more subtle allusion (Michael Jeter's character is called Toto, the stage name of the actor playing Clooney's part in the original).

There is a running use of anachronistic jazz/Italian music, but for many audiences this may not place the film in an exact chronological period but signal more an indefinite mythical past.

Stylistically, the Russos allude not so much to the specific era of the original version but further back to the era of silent film. The credits with their use of bordered intertitles, the opening four-shot without dialogue and all the characters facing outward to the camera, and the imposed graininess on credits for the DVD featurette all feels very like the aesthetic of the period 1895–1905. The film is punctuated by fairly simple visual gags, especially in the climactic robbery where they drill through a water pipe, breaking into the wrong room, and then blow themselves up by lighting a faulty gas cooker. However, this latter mistake does not lead to bloody injuries or loss of limbs, just cartoonish blackened faces.

Cosimo is typical of how laughable the group is. He is first seen trying to steal a car while eating a cheeseburger, catching his scarf in the door, setting off the alarm, being unable to start the vehicle, and being too slow to escape arrest. Pero (Sam Rockwell) easily tricks him into revealing the details of his Bellini; Cosimo escapes prison only due to a guard having a heart attack; and he himself dies pathetically, walking in front of a tram. Throughout the film, he calls everyone a "son of a whore" but at his funeral is ironically revealed to literally be one himself. Riley, who is seen carrying his newborn baby around for most scenes, steals a camera (also in Monicelli's film) by using a fake arm but then later has his arm really broken by the man he stole from, appearing on the night of the robbery full of tranquilizers. The practicality of Toto (Jeter) coming on a physically demanding break-in is absurd from the outset, and predictably his frailty and fear of heights lead to him being carried across the rooftops, losing his pants on the way. The absurd appearance of Leon (Isaiah Washington, who had worked with Clooney in *Out of Sight*) with his cravat, pipe, bow tie, and even sporting a dressing gown in his first scene although it takes place outside, apparently on wasteland, underlines his ridiculous pretentions to some kind of Oscar Wilde-style persona. Pero is planning a boxing career, although he is downed with one punch, and his line in seductive power is more persuasive for its energy and irrepressibility than for its coherence (he tells Camilla that he has a "degree in . . . learning" and explains a kid spitting on his shoes that this is just a game they play with each other).

It is an inverted version of *Ocean's Eleven*, where each member of the team has no particular criminal aptitudes at all, and the narrative details their step-by-step progress toward failure (which we see from the very opening shot, to which we return at the end). The supposedly well-planned job is composed of a series of pratfalls, closer to the style of a Laurel and Hardy comedy. The coal chute entrance only leads to a pool of drainage water, Toto falls off the ladder onto Pero's face, Leon's elaborate attempts to cut a circle out of a window make the whole pane shatter, and Riley's plaster arm knocks over a statue that then lands on Toto's foot. There is an anachronistic feel to the crime being proposed, robbing a safe, but there is no brutality or technological know-how on show here as there is in the final house-breaking sequence in *Out of Sight*.

In this, *Collinwood* feels a little like Wes Anderson's *Bottle Rocket* (1996), which also features ordinary characters dreaming of criminal greatness but with no ability to plan or execute even the simplest of crimes, as well as the accompanying musical selections of Mark Mothersbaugh. The pause in the climactic job in *Collinwood*, where the would-be robbers sit down and take turns explaining what they would do with all the money, money we see they are never going to gain, is typical of the dreamers that people Anderson's films. The final shot of the film, the sign welcoming visitors to the town with the sarcastic afterthought scrawled beneath "the Beirut of Cleveland," also feels like a flipside of *Syriana*, which in some senses normalizes that region.

Actors of the caliber of William H. Macy would not waste their time on poor scripts, and although Clooney or Soderbergh are not credited as writers, they both worked with the Russos for several months on its preparation. The jokiness of the DVD extras with Sam Rockwell interviewing cast and crew, the rap "Your mother's a whore" complete with video, and the shots of the cast (including Clooney) playing basketball reflect a film that appears to have been fun to make. The numbers (a budget of around $12 million and a U.S. gross of $340,000) might cast such fun as a little self-indulgent or suggest that a well-made film, based on a strong original, was not marketed strongly enough to reach an audience who would appreciate it.

CONCLUSION

I love it when a plan comes together.

—Hannibal (George Peppard) in *The A Team*

The attraction of the *Ocean's* franchise for the actors concerned is fairly clear. The chance to work with a large number of A-list actors, a director known for his unconventional indie work, and a remake of a famous title (if not a great film) all give this, like Danny says to Rusty near the beginning of the first film, the appeal of something that has "never been done." After the audience reaction to the first film, they become part of a commercially successful franchise, playing characters that are mostly likeable as well as able to enjoy the kind of lifestyle they are portraying with actors who are also their friends. The characters of Tess and Isabel, dropped without much ceremony in the third film, and the starchy but fairly easily distracted Sponder (Ellen Barkin), seem additions rather than central to the franchise. The group, like the original Rat Pack, is predominantly male. Basically, women are present only as a one-trick scam (Tess as Julia Roberts), for slapstick (Sponder, amorously befuddled by drugged by Linus's hormone patch), or as a force of law and order, which can be charmed or corrupted (Isabel, who joins the gang at the end of the second film).

There is no real attempt at character development. As Rusty says to Saul in the first film, "Guys like us don't change. We stay sharp or we get sloppy. We don't change." This means there is a slight feeling of diminishing returns across the three films. There are only so many times an apparent threat can morph into a fellow conspirator before viewers suspend their disbelief that the planned heist will fail. Using Linus's mother (as the fake U.S. Marshal, Molly Star) in the second film and his father in the third (as an FBI officer) stretches things a little. Across the three films, the whole dream of Vegas seems to shrink. Waxing nostalgic about Reuben and how the town has changed, Danny states, "They built them a lot smaller back then," to which Rusty ruefully observes, "They seemed pretty big."

However, much of the appeal of all three films is not in the actual gaining of money. None of the films go as far as criticizing Vegas as a symbol of excessive luxury, but the second film does underline that once obtained, unlimited wealth does not guarantee happiness. Like a murder mystery, the prime pleasure (for both characters and audiences) is in considering a series of apparently impossible problems and producing a sense of catharsis in the audience that arises when those obstacles are overcome.

There is something purposely anachronistic in the style, the music, the language, even the portrayal of violence in the films. Unusually for this genre, there is absolutely no sight of blood, and the worst that is likely to happen if a plan fails at any point is arrest and detention (as seen in the second film). As Roman says, Rusty and Danny are "analog players in a digital world." When Toulour pulls a pistol on the rooftop at the end of *Ocean's Thirteen*, Linus says with incredulity "a gun?" and it is revealed to contain no bullets. Despite the money at stake and despite talking about the levels of protection, the SWAT team of the first film never fires a real shot, Reuben's flashback about the most recent failed attempt to rob a Vegas casino freezes as the police presumably shoot the man down, the man who is bundled out in *Ocean's Thirteen* is rammed into a machine out of sight of camera, and although featuring Al Pacino in the third film, there is no sense (unlike his gangster characters in *The Godfather* or *Scarface*) that he will order a hit in revenge. Although the plot opens with his reneging on a promise to Reuben, it closes with him apparently (and rather unbelievably) willing to accept his loss, simply because any potential killers "like me more than you" and Bank "shook Sinatra's hand." The whole *Ocean's* series operates under quite different generic imperatives than Martin Scorsese's *Casino* (1995) with its underbelly of extortion and murder. The notion of a bloodless, stylish crime caper (especially the second film with its European settings) evokes a bygone era of films like *The Italian Job* (Peter Collinson, 1969), where planning and cool is privileged over technology and brute force.

CHAPTER 6

State of the Nation

Governor Mike Morris: Integrity matters.

—*The Ides of March*

FAIL SAFE (STEPHEN FREARS, 2000)

This live Cold War TV drama dramatizes the consequences when, due to a technical fault, one group of planes cannot be recalled and go on to deliver their payload to their given target: Moscow. Although there is no longer a technological need for a live performance, clearly, from an actor's point of view, the sense of danger and the ability to play a character in linear fashion without the retakes of film are worth considering, and certainly the cast that director Stephen Frears attracted all seem enthusiastic about the idea. The performance happens in real time, and in rehearsal Frears gave notes akin to working in the theater. However, in several other ways, it is different. The whole cast is not on a single stage or within direct eye contact with one another, and a key dramatic element, the presence of an audience, is also missing.

The production was split between two huge sound stages at Warner Brothers, and we cut between the four main settings (the presidential bunker, the Omaha War Room, a New York think tank, and the fatal cockpit of the Group 6 bomber, piloted by Grady) and a brief introductory scene in the bedroom of Lieutenant Blackie (Harvey Keitel), which establishes where his wife and child will be later on that day. Thus, with at least three different sound stages being used, it becomes less of a linear performance for the actors and more of a linear accomplishment for the producers; that is, it is arguably more of a technical accomplishment than an artistic one. Much is made in interviews about the edginess of performing live, and certainly the possibility of making a career-defining mistake in front of millions of viewers could be said to add this. However, if watched on DVD, the viewer already knows that the performance worked, so much of the edginess has gone.

The historic nature of the enterprise is hailed by Walter Cronkite as "a giant step" in the introduction, and certainly it is true that CBS had not entertained such an idea for nearly 40 years. However, as with Soderbergh and *The Good German*, it is debatable whether the adoption of anachronistic technology in itself delivers art that is any more profound than using state-of-the-art means. In retrospect, it feels more like the attempt by television to market a gimmick, one that marks it as distinct from movies certainly, but still, in 2000, a gimmick. It becomes a technical achievement and a must-see TV event of that particular season.

The second question here perhaps is why remake this particular film in a similar form to the original with the same title, scriptwriter (Walter Bernstein), and fundamentally the same narrative and audience: Lumet's 1964 version with Henry Fonda and Walter Matthau was clearly made for American viewers (rather than primarily European or other territories). Therefore Clooney is not updating a classic in technological or scripting terms. It seems more of an homage to one's own cinematic heroes for a new generation, unfamiliar with the original film or with the nuclear issues that may have receded a little from public consciousness since the flashpoint in the early 1960s but that still remain relevant (underlined by the intertitle at the end). Rather than the robots and spectacular fight sequences of the *Terminator* series, this film, which explores the same basic thematic territory (men create machines that they cannot recall, leading to nuclear strikes), the emphasis here is on tense dialogue exchanges and looking up at screens depicting the inexorable route to catastrophe.

On the DVD extras, Richard Dreyfuss (playing the president) talks up the educational value of the film in dramatizing the absurdity of the Cold War for current and future generations, who find it hard to understand. Certainly there is a dated feel to the president's offer to bomb New York as a sign to the Russians that the Moscow bomb is a mistake. Above the absurdity of the ideology of mutually assured destruction, it also taps into notions of post–Second World War moral strength. It is hard to imagine any president of the modern era having the courage to make such a decision. There is a nostalgic element here too for a pre-Nixon era, when the president seems honorable and will trust certain key individuals, often those he has known for a long time, like Blackie, who serve their president without question, even to the point of dropping an atom bomb on New York (where his wife and daughter happen to be visiting a theater). The presidency is let down by hawkish advice and a flawed system, rather than being corrupt in itself.

Clooney's role, Colonel Jack Grady, seems one that dovetails with his *ER* persona, engaging in banter with his son (also looking forward to *Michael Clayton* in this respect) and apparently sensitive to the obsessions of youngsters (here talking about a chameleon). However, once in the air it is the intransigence of Clooney's character (or the mindlessness of his training perhaps and the ideology that it represents) that leads to the bomb being dropped on Moscow, despite a personal plea both from the president and from his own son (a scene using Grady's wife is cut from Lumet's original), including the private joke with the ironic punch line "Only fools are positive." The cutting in the cockpit is progressively closer with early dialogue obscured by oxygen masks. The masks are then removed and we have close-ups of the three pilots (one played by Clooney's longtime collaborator, Grant Heslov), shifting to extreme close-ups of three pairs of eyes during the appeal by Grady's son.

The production still represents a strong viewing experience. The usual, and often lazily employed, means to inject suspense into TV drama (rapid cutting between close shots, underscored by upbeat music) are dispensed with here. A relatively small number of cameras focus on wider shots, often two-shots, for longer periods of time than average shot lengths to-day with very little movement, and there is no music (even at the end). The production picks up little points of style from the past, such as the old-style Warner Brothers logo at the beginning or the reading of actors' names over footage of them at the close. The fade to black between acts every 20 minutes may feel odd but the original transmission would have had commercial breaks too.

The choice to film in black-and-white references Lumet's version and also alludes to the early days of television drama, underlined in Walter Cronkite's address to camera, a figure associated with truth and the documenting of modern political history. Lumet used negative footage for some of brief cutaways of military action, primarily because he could not find the stock footage he wanted. In the remake, Frears cuts to stock 16 mm footage to show the jets falling into the sea or the launch of the Russian missiles, which seems particularly odd in juxtaposition with the black-and-white body of the film, and he also imports letter-boxing from cinema (not in TV from the '60s). At the same time as talking up the edginess of performing live, there is also a countermovement, minimizing risk by using double-mikes to make sure no sound is missed, and the film was pulled out of the sweeps period, ostensibly to give time to make the production as good as possible but also to reduce pressure on whether it was perceived as a success or failure.

It is noteworthy that apart from guest appearances in *ER*, *Fail Safe* is the only example of TV that Clooney has agreed to star in post-*ER*. It reflects his attachment to the original film as well as interest in helping to deliver a live TV project in the role of producer. It is also the first of a series of films featuring content that is explicitly political, leading on to *Confessions, Good Night, and Good Luck, Syriana*, and *Michael Clayton*. After having some experience with live TV on *ER* and having grown up in the world of live TV, Clooney is able to blend an attachment and possibly nostalgia for one particular film with the medium of his childhood viewing of TV. The attraction of Frears as director also reflects Clooney's glowing clout as a producer and his ability to draw a big-name cast, both factors that would allow him to persuade studios to finance projects over the coming decade.

GOOD NIGHT, AND GOOD LUCK (GEORGE CLOONEY, 2005)

This is a story about five episodes of TV.

—George Clooney[1]

Clooney's second experience of directing was always going to be slightly controversial, focusing on the specific battle between broadcaster Edward R. Murrow and the junior senator from Wisconsin, Joseph McCarthy, who created an atmosphere of panic and fear in America in the early 1950s by his increasingly strident crusade against those he deemed to be subversive elements in American society, particularly those seen as Communist sympathizers. For Clooney, the film is a chance to pay tribute to one of his own personal heroes, as well as a tribute to his own father who impressed on him the value of Murrow and of individuals like him, prepared to make a stand over key principles. It also allows him to contribute something to the ongoing debate about personal freedom, particularly in the wake of 9/11, and leave behind a statement of belief in liberal ideas. The frame story underlines this idea of a tribute, which is literally a dinner in Murrow's honor. However, a lighthearted evening turns more somber as Murrow characterizes the television of that era as designed to "distract, delude, amuse and insulate," which he partly blames on the producers, i.e., his own industry, but also audiences with their "built-in allergy to unpleasant or disturbing information."

The opening sequence shows the ongoing tension between what is real and what is fictional. Cowriter Heslov (present on set as studio director Don Hewitt, who would go on to create the iconic 60 Minutes) and Clooney filmed the main cast and extras while in costume for about an hour without their being aware of it, catching some natural exchanges over dinner table chatter, which are then edited together to convey a sense of spontaneity. As in *The Deer Hunter* (Michael Cimino, 1978), the effect is to introduce the characters en masse before we get to know them better, and the sequence also emphasizes the collegial nature of the workplace, with willing teamwork valued over egos. It is the views of such chattering classes that are at stake in the battle between Murrow and McCarthy. Stylistically, it sets the tone with Dianne Reeves singing "When I Fall in Love," long lenses picking out some details in sharp focus and others left blurred, a key way in which our attention is directed through the course of the film, and the ensemble nature of the piece with Clooney only gradually emerging as one face among several in the pose for a group photo.

Clooney's first choice for cinematographer, Newton Thomas Sigel, with whom he worked on *Three Kings* and *Confessions*, had a clash of schedules, so he opted for Robert Elswit, with whom he had worked on *Syriana*. Like Soderbergh would later do in *The Good German*, Clooney tried to acquire old equipment used on films that had the look he was aiming for (here Jean-Luc Godard's 1960 *À bout de souffle*), but after testing a number of different combinations of cameras, lenses, and film stocks, he opted to shoot with color film (black-and-white would need many more lights, which would not work with the amount of reflective surfaces in the main set) in 35 mm with long lenses to try and re-create the documentary feel of Robert Drew's *Primary* (1960) and *Crisis* (1963). This mostly works, but it is hard to make the office sets for Paley (Frank Langella) seem imposing in black-and-white without recourse to the kind of expressionist devices (wide-angle lenses, distorted sets, and specific lighting devices as in Orson Welles's 1939 *Citizen Kane*) that the naturalistic set and the limitations on lighting created by using so much glass all effectively rule out.

Music producer Allen Sviridoff helped Clooney select Dianne Reeves as the singer, whose voice sporadically punctuates the narrative, establishing the mood of the time and lyrically commenting on the main action. Via a long take, we follow a couple of minor characters walking around and through the CBS studios, introducing us to the fictional world of the narrative, as we hear and then finally see Reeves singing "TV Is the Thing This Year," motivating the sound when we reach her performing live. Later she sings "I've Got My Eyes on You" after Murrow's open attack on McCarthy, not just reflecting the course of the plot but allowing time for the audience to dwell on it and to provide respite between the dense speeches of Murrow as well as giving a useful sense of the space within the studio (since she is singing live in the scenes where she appears).

As a modernized version of Arthur Miller's *The Crucible* (1953), the film acts as a useful introduction to the perils of McCarthyism, particularly to younger generations unaware of the ease with which civil liberties can be eroded. Both Murrow and Clooney show the power of using the personal to exemplify the general, focusing on Milo Radulovich, a lieutenant in the air force, who was deemed guilty by association with his father, who himself was labeled a Communist by McCarthy for subscribing to a Communist-sympathizing Serbian newspaper.

The performance of David Strathairn (whose participation was not actually confirmed until only a few days before shooting) is also attributable in part to Clooney's direction, a role paralleled in his position behind the scenes as Fred Friendly. Originally written with Clooney himself in mind, it was surely the correct decision to stand aside as Clooney has found in all four of his directing roles so far; directing oneself as the star of a picture threatens to destabilize the overview that a director needs as well as compromising the quality of performance he or she can give. The weariness that he exuded for *Solaris* might have worked in that instance, where the circumstances were personal and emotional, but part of Strathairn's power is to suggest a careworn demeanor at the erosion of ideas and principles that he holds dear. Despite being a nonsmoker himself, he is seen (like much of the cast) smoking throughout and does so believably. In part to assuage feelings of guilt about making smoking look attractive, Clooney included the Kent commercial, which seems incredibly dated in its exhortation to buy a product, increasingly deemed antisocial.

Clooney's belief that actors should not play famous people leads to the use of real film of McCarthy. This belief seems to suggest that an actor might make him too engaging and thereby risk shifting the emotional identification away from where a director wishes it to be focused or that it represents a manufacturing of reality to suit a given political agenda. The film uses McCarthy's own words (even if judicious editing greatly affects their meaning) and reflects Murrow's own technique of focusing precisely on this in order to undermine the senator's approach. Clooney's argument might also dictate that Murrow should not be played by an actor, but at the time perhaps Murrow was known as much as a voice on radio as a face on television. Furthermore, for the film to work we have to identify strongly with Murrow's character, which Strathairn achieves by small gestures to show the strain he is under. Clooney's character Friendly is made more pleasant in his playing of it. The real Friendly, physically much more imposing than Clooney, and generally remembered as more aggressive and bombastic, is the kind of director figure that Clooney has striven to avoid (both becoming himself or working with), particularly after his experience with Russell on *Three Kings*.

Murrow used the case of Radulovich in a broadcast of his flagship current affairs program *See It Now* on October 20, 1953, to focus the minds of viewers on wider issues of the suppression of civil liberties. In the relatively new medium of television, using a focus on individual stories and edited compilations of actual testimony, punctuated by commentary from Murrow, created a potent mix. Clooney follows a similar strategy. The decision to focus on a specific moment in Murrow's life allowed the flashpoint with McCarthy to act as a microcosm for the country as a whole and also made the narrative more dramatically focused.

Like the good journalist that his father was and that he trained to be for a brief period, Clooney did attempt to double-source everything. Even light banter is based on accounts from those present.[2] As Strathairn notes about Clooney, "He's really the Edward R. Murrow of this production and Grant is the Fred Friendly," and the pair did follow in the footsteps of their fictional characters by pursuing painstaking research.[3] However, once little tweaks appear (such as adding a comment about Murrow's work on migrant workers, despite the fact that his key work on the topic, "Harvests of Shame," did not appear until two years after the night of the speech), perhaps assertions about complete historical objectivity are harder to maintain.

The script was originally written as a TV movie, possibly even to be performed live, like *Fail Safe*, and was closer to a more conventional bio-pic format. At the time (around 1998–99, according to Heslov), Clooney did not really have the industry clout to get such a heavyweight project made but his interest continued, and by the time he came back to the project, having converted Heslov as well by this point, the two of them knew more about the subject and had worked on more projects together, including *Unscripted* and *K Street* (both 2003). *K Street*, although it ran for only one season of 10 episodes, is an interesting experiment, including up-to-the-minute script changes to reflect the political mood of a given week and a consequently more flexible improvised way of working. Clooney, also credited as cameraman, could indulge his interest in the workings of Washington, with live TV and comedy. Since both

Heslov and Clooney are also actors as well as producers and directors, they can bring an extra dimension to how they talk to actors and explain what they want from them.

The issue of balance arises directly in the film when Sig Mickelson (Jeff Daniels) accuses Murrow of "editorializing," in that he is departing from standard CBS practice and not showing two sides to an issue. Murrow's defense, that in this example there is no credible opposing case, raises the question of whether striving after constant balance only legitimizes the indefensible and produces bland programs in the name of objectivity. There is a constant game being played over cooperation, with Friendly claiming that footage the two military officers want to see is not yet available and they trying to intimidate him, casting Radulovich as a security risk. Friendly's direct challenge to them to name who knows the exact charges against Radulovich, and whether they were elected or accountable, is precisely the kind of scene that Clooney-the-leading-man might be expected to have, but with this isolated example, Friendly's political credentials are underlined without stealing the limelight from Murrow.

The drama of live television creates a great sense of theater. There may be a script, written by Murrow himself, but no autocue as yet, just a piece delivered straight to camera, directly into people's homes. We see Murrow, sitting, foot tapping, suggesting a rare bout of nerves, steeling himself for his follow-up attack on McCarthy. Friendly's position below the desk motivates the low-angle shots of Murrow, whom we see partly through Friendly's perspective here. Political and personal moments coalesce and it feels a little like the child at the feet of a parent, possibly Clooney himself playing in studios as his father, the local anchorman, got ready to deliver the news. Like the musicians who accompany Reeves, including Matt Catingub who produced Rosemary Clooney's last album, there are a number of small but significant personal touches to the production, climaxing in Clooney's choice to premiere the film in his hometown of Maysville, Kentucky.

The film is a rare example of a narrative where ideas and words predominate. The film takes place almost exclusively in the CBS studios. There is no action in the sense of chase sequences, only a suppressed romance between a married couple, and the resolution, though complete in terms of starting to bring McCarthy to account, is still relatively downbeat in Murrow's bleak warning about the future of television. The narrative dramatizes a standing up for principle, knowing the potential risk but not the audience reaction, until the phones start ringing, showing the support of the public. As Murrow says, "It occurs to me that we might not get away with this one." The close of Murrow's program on

McCarthy ends with rapturous applause from the control room, reflecting a sense of euphoria, relief, and also the sense that this is very much a theatrical performance on the part of Murrow.

The film celebrates a different kind of heroism: a quiet, articulate kind rather than the usual variety we are offered. The idea, as expressed by Murrow that he and Friendly would be prepared to split the cost of a commercial between them in order for a controversial broadcast to go ahead, would be hard to imagine today. It is also a film that keeps things back: obvious outpourings of emotion, unnecessary exchanges of dialogue, even whole scenes. We never learn exactly what Paley says to Friendly when he asks him to stay behind (it is reported a few seconds later as a desire to lay some people off) or exactly what the lawyers say to Palmer Williams (Tom McCarthy) except that he is subdued after meeting with them.

William Paley represents the commercial and political pressures on a TV station, stressing (through Mickelson) that they are reliant on sponsors, who may have military contracts. He does, however, warn Murrow about the tactics McCarthy will use (personal attacks on individuals rather than what they are saying) and promises that the corporate interests of the company will not interfere with editorial ones. He also warns Murrow that "we don't make the news, we report the news," suggesting he is uncomfortable with CBS's reporting becoming the story itself. The film touches not just on the moral responsibility of the media but also on its power to influence viewers and listeners. Even the Kent cigarette commercial is prefaced by some flattery of the average viewer of *Person to Person* as not easily persuaded by advertisers, before the program proceeds to try and do so. An idea of Langella's, we see Paley walk into a darkened and empty studio, shortly after McCarthy's rebuttal, possibly suggesting that he may have to say goodbye to his empire shortly. Structurally, the fates of Murrow and McCarthy run parallel. McCarthy stays in the Senate but like Murrow is somewhat put out to pasture, moved away from the center to the periphery of things. Paley's final exchange with Murrow and Friendly underlines how their professional relationship has shifted, so that Murrow is offered only a five-episode series on Sunday afternoons.

The slide into celebrity culture is already signposted in Murrow's own banal interviews on *Person to Person* with figures like Liberace. Clooney has some fun (as with the clip from *The Newlywed Game* in *Confessions*) using some material, which now seems absurd, as Liberace talks about settling down and showing some romantic interest in Princess Margaret. The compliment from a member of the studio crew "Good show" is met by a withering look from Murrow and silence as he remains sitting as the studio lights gradually go out—he knows exactly the kind of program he is being forced to make. Later, he is seen sneaking glances at 45 degrees to his interviewee (Gina Lollobrigida) of McCarthy being subjected to the same kind of questioning that he forced on others. At the same time, the film accepts the commercial reality of television, not just for the channel but for the individuals concerned. Murrow has to admit to Paley that the patronage of CBS helped him put his children through school and on balance has allowed him to do many things that rival channels might well have refused. For his part, despite being old friends through the war, Paley seems unhappy that his star has been eclipsed by Murrow's notoriety.

We also see in Don Hollenbeck (Ray Wise) a parallel for Murrow, someone who might share and support the same principles but does not have the personal strength, or perhaps luck (his wife has just left him), to stick to them without paying a price. The fixed grin that Hollenbeck sports through most of his scenes, twitching slightly in the bar later as Shirley reads the critical reviews, only serves to underline its opposite: that here is a man near breaking point. The pressure from critical journalists like the unseen Jack O'Brian had been present for several years on the real character, who found it increasingly hard to bear. Words can be used to speak the truth as in Murrow's campaign but they can also injure and at extremes even kill.

Using two long lenses (as he also does in *Confessions*), Clooney often racks focus, so that our attention is very much directed by what is sharp on screen, no matter where it is in the frame. Hence, in Murrow's own counterrebuttal we shift attention from a side-on shot of him in the studio to his image behind on the monitor, looking head-on at the camera. In the newsroom meeting, the slow zoom into Murrow sitting in shadow, thinking, as others argue around him about the legality of McCarthy's tactics, underlines his greater vision of the situation. He cuts through their focus on small details with the wider picture (that McCarthy will come after him personally). Correspondingly, in the following scene there is a slow zoom-out from Murrow, a lone figure at a typewriter, working at his all-important closing argument, like a lawyer in a high-profile court case.

The flip side, which is not completely ignored here, is whether Murrow's campaign (and therefore Clooney's film in dramatizing this) becomes something of a personal crusade, losing sight of wider pressures. The scene between Joe and Shirley in bed together, with Joe wondering "What if we're wrong?," does show the presence of doubt, even among those who suffered the most detrimental consequences for themselves personally. The fact that Murrow shows some surprise at the revelation of the secret marriage suggests that he is perhaps too focused on his battle of principle to notice more personal things around him. In the bar, he is framed in sharp focus, biting his nails in apparent worry, looking up at Hollenbeck, blurred in the foreground, but if he senses the strain the other man is under, he does not say or do anything to try and prevent the other man's suicide. The film does not duck opposing views, such as the military's faith in the judgement of superior officers, the presence of Bobby Kennedy on the McCarthy panel questioning Moss, and Paley challenging Murrow about whether people really want a "civics lesson" rather than entertainment.

Clooney's own performance (hampered by a back injury sustained during *Syriana*) is relatively low-key, with relatively few close-ups, so that he is a backroom presence, guiding proceedings in the newsroom but doing so in a way that leaves the story as the central character rather than his orchestration of its telling. The iconic exchange with Murrow, when he crouches down at his feet and taps his leg with a pencil just before they go on air, reflects not a subservient relationship, despite the low angles used, but the camera tends to stay on Murrow: it is his show and it is his words that are spoken, supported technically and morally by Friendly. Mickelson derides the cliché of being "all in a big boat together," undermining Friendly's position at this point (a brave line for a writer/director to include about his own character). The real Joe Wershba describes the actual relationship being closer to "hero worship" on Friendly's part and Murrow's sometimes patronizing disdain.[4] Clooney shifts this more into the buddy territory of wise-cracking equals (akin to his own relationship with Heslov). The film would perhaps struggle to hold audience attention if the plot deviated too far from the razor-sharp precision of Murrow's words on camera. Generally, the scripts were actually coproduced more heavily by Friendly but the film emphasizes the shift in the attacks on McCarthy toward Murrow working alone.

At the news by phone of Hollenbeck's suicide, Clooney's head drops. However, both what he hears and then what he says to Murrow is not audible, so that we focus on the actor's reactions. We cut to Reeves singing "How High the Moon" (a song present in the film's conception from the very outset) to establish an elegiac mood, and this bleeds over the following scenes, describing Hollenbeck's actions and the words of a reporter, the unseen O'Brian, who is hostile even in recording Hollenbeck's death. Murrow is framed looking at Reeves through glass (specially placed for just this shot), so that her reflection is partly seen superimposed over his face. It is a rare example of quite an artful shot, but here the emotion of the moment justifies it rather than seeming self-indulgent. Murrow's succinct on-air obituary is contrasted with O'Brian's tasteless hostility.

To secure financial backing, Clooney had to add 5 pages to the original script of 85 pages, but probably most of this length is pared back again in production, with a focus on the silences, like the slight awkwardness of Friendly and Paley in the elevator. Cut out or down are Wershba interviewing Radulovich, Murrow talking to Gina Lollobrigida, the second scene between Murrow and Hollenbeck, lengthier questioning of Annie Lee Moss, and some of the banter between Friendly and Murrow before McCarthy's rebuttal is shown. In all these cases, the substantive details are present elsewhere and anxiety is better conveyed by silence than nervous chatter. Some reaction from Murrow and Friendly during McCarthy's rebuttal is also cut, which would have had Friendly deliver the line "We've got him, Ed," which might have seemed too premature and triumphalist. Without it, there is more tension as we are unsure exactly how the public reaction will play out. Clooney cuts some of Murrow's speech where he mentions his coverage of Soviet atrocities during the war, which perhaps would have confused audiences and drawn them away from the focus on an American story in the present.

The subplot of Joe and Shirley Wershba (Robert Downey Jr. and Patricia Clarkson, respectively) and their secret marriage (which Heslov suggests he and Clooney did not know about until they actually met them), symbolized by their daily removal of rings, does have the effect of creating a parallel in a personal sphere at a time of growing cultural paranoia, particularly Shirley's line about looking over her shoulder at work before answering what seems like a perfectly innocent question.[5] However, just because something really happened does not make it dramatically compelling in fiction, and such etiquette existed long before McCarthy. There is a repressive element in wider society at work here. Later, Murrow concedes that McCarthy "didn't create this situation of fear, he merely exploited it." Perhaps it could be said that the throwing off of McCarthy's influence allows people to question other subjective codes of behavior, but these scenes act as a hiatus in the main plot, rather than adding a great deal to it. The film does not really explain how their secret is exposed at this precise moment. The suggestion is that everyone knew and it reflects a bowing to extended pressure. The script talks of a "melancholy" at the moment when they are presented with their ultimatum, but the film as shot plays up a quiet relief that they do not need to hide anymore.[6] Although in real life, the pair went on to be successful producers, in the world of the film, without this information their future remains uncertain.

The newsroom scenes are certainly informed by Clooney's own upbringing, and his love of films from the 1970s like *All the President's Men* (Alan J. Pakula, 1976) is reflected here in overlapping dialogue (even scripted in parallel columns), panning around a group of passionately committed young men, with only the speaker in clear focus. As part of the preparation process, Clooney had the props department give out stacks of actual newspapers from the period, from which the cast had to pitch stories as in a real newsroom.

Murrow is initially framed slightly side-on, with the camera he is addressing in the left side of the frame so we have a sense of a program being made, but as the narrative gathers dramatic momentum, Clooney uses more shots straight down the lens of the camera, giving us the experience closer to a TV viewer of the time. There are a large number of shots of Murrow framed against monitors, some showing himself at that moment speaking but also of his supposed guest. For this, Clooney and Heslov need to carefully select and coordinate quite a large amount of real footage that needs to be timed so that it creates the sense of a genuine conversation taking place. At times, this meant using footage of the real Murrow, as in the Liberace interview, but the image is too small (and the match with Straitharn too good) to see any difference. In Murrow's longer speeches, there is very little camera movement beyond a slow zoom for a closer, more dramatic climax.

The postshow scene in the Pentagon bar, one of the few location shots in the film, as the group waits for the early editions of the papers, originally carried more dialogue but Clooney cuts nearly two pages of anxious small-talk, opting for a longer silence, underlining how the initial euphoria (more effusive in the film than the script suggests) and laughter fall away and for several moments they consider more soberly but silently what might be the reaction to what they have done.

Rather than a montage of moments from television history, which was shot, Clooney and Heslov opt to end the film within the context of the film and return to the frame story. Giving the last words to Murrow himself means the film ends on quite a bleak note with a warning and a simple fade-to-black. In his closing remarks, Murrow encourages his peers and by extension the wider viewing public to "exalt the importance of ideas and information," arguing for a mix of programming, with some educational content mixed in among the entertainment.

Part of the difficulty in criticizing *Good Night, and Good Luck* is similar to a potential response to a film like *Schindler's List* (Steven Spielberg,

1993), whose moral authority is such that criticizing its form seems petty. Like *Fail Safe*, it deals with real events, in portentous black-and-white, and both clearly have a strong remit to educate a younger generation, possibly ignorant of a series of cataclysmic events in mid-twentieth-century history. The film is a nostalgic look back at a time when American culture had figures in the media whose faces and voices represented a sense of informed trust—someone, like Walter Cronkite (actually recruited by Murrow at CBS), who would tell the viewers the truth. There is a sense in which the Academy not only appreciates a film about a closely related industry but that in acknowledging it in award terms, it accepts the truth of Murrow's words, that is, that it can accept a chastening word from one of its own about the educational function of visual mass media.

Rather than trying to produce a bio-pic, Clooney and Heslov focus on a specific, career-defining moment in Murrow's life. The film, like Murrow's own shows, manages to condemn McCarthy by extended use of footage of the man himself, browbeating witnesses and then later in the Moss case high-handedly excusing himself after only seven minutes, assuming his job is done. Annie Lee Moss may or may not have been a spy, but in a sense this is not the point. Like John McClellan, the Democratic senator from Arkansas who stood up for the principle of not trying individuals "by hearsay evidence," Clooney suggests that it is the denial of her constitutional right to face her accusers that is at stake. Branding Clooney as unpatriotic is as unconvincing as those accusations leveled at anyone who questioned McCarthy and his methods. Any film adaptation involves editing and selecting material, so the notion that there is a single truth in a situation is specious. However, Clooney does admit that the script radically compresses the time between Murrow's programs and the Senate investigating McCarthy from a few months to the very next day, thereby exaggerating the immediate power of the protagonist's broadcast. Similarly, the Murrow/Paley exchange really took place several months later.

It is also true that McCarthy contributed to his own downfall with his browbeating arrogance, descending into incoherence while ranting at witnesses and particularly in his rebuttal, calling Murrow "the cleverest of the jackal pack" at the point when Murrow's stock with the American viewer had never been higher, after his war reporting from London during the Blitz (the source of the film's title and his closing farewell phrase) and his growing audiences for the more mainstream populist content on *Person to Person*.

It is ironic that the film should win an Oscar for best original screenplay, when arguably the biggest achievement in *Good Night, and Good*

Luck is its adherence to sources, including extensive film footage of McCarthy hearings. During their research, Clooney and Heslov realized that documentaries such as *Point of Order* actually edited together testimony from different days, so in a sense they had to act as documentary makers themselves and go back to primary material, often in quite a poor state. Rigid Oscar categories can often seem problematic, and perhaps Best Adapted Screenplay would be a better description, albeit from multiple sources. Murrow's comments about "If none of us ever read a book that was dangerous . . . ," ending with "the terror is right here in this room," and Wershba's tongue-in-cheek response all derive directly from Wershba's own recollection of the exchange. On the other hand, the film should not be criticized for a lack of creativity when it takes great pains to be accurate to a series of specific events in an extremely limited setting, meaning it is really closer to docudrama than an overtly fictional narrative (with male actors instructed not to wear makeup). A film about journalistic integrity needs to be similarly principled in its script and production. Clooney had key personnel available, like Milo Radulovich himself, Friendly's sons and wife, and members of Murrow's family, Ruth and Casey, at the initial read-through and even at times on set to advise about accuracy; he also enjoyed the company of individuals who, for him, are unsung personal heroes. Material has been assembled that produces a compelling narrative, despite the script including some fairly meaty content, linguistically, culturally, and politically. It is essentially a film of ideas and juxtaposed speeches to give a sense of the importance of the drama being played out for the hearts and minds of the American people but also perhaps to show the potential power of the emerging medium of television and the tragedy that it is so rarely used to its fullest potential.

CONCLUSION

The success of this film looks forward to other explorations of journalistic integrity, like *Frost/Nixon* (Ron Howard, 2008), which also starred Frank Langella playing a lugubrious figure of authority and likewise featured a climactic TV interview, which reflected the political life of the nation as well as the power and importance of investigative journalism and asking sufficiently probing questions at the right time.

For Clooney the prime responsibility of a director is to get the casting right (as much a job of a producer) after which actors should be allowed to get on with their jobs as professionally as possible with minimum disruption from the ego of the director. Clarkson describes Clooney's comments to actors as "incredibly eloquent and succinct."[7] The notion of a bond between the supporting cast, most of whose parts were not offered up for audition, was also helped by the fact that Reed Diamond (John Aaron), Tate Donovan (Jesse Zousmer), and David Strathairn had already worked together on *Memphis Belle* (Michael Caton-Jones, 1990). In terms of the dialogue, Clooney tries to give it a sense of a period feel by avoiding unnecessary exposition, effusive outpourings of emotion, and a certain understatement (possibly reflective of the wartime culture). At the same time, Clooney can get away with clichéd description in the shooting script, like "you could cut the tension with a knife," since he knows he is working among friends and he himself is directing.[8]

In terms of Clooney's career, as an actor it marks a further step in his maturity as an ensemble player, but more significantly, as a cowriter and director it showed that he could embrace an important, complex issue and produce a well-made piece of cinematic art. At the same time, the DVD audio commentary, where he jokes several times about his 1997 award as "The Sexiest Man Alive," shows that he still finds it hard to watch himself on film or take himself too seriously. As in *Confessions*, special effects are mostly achieved by theatrical, mechanical means in front of the camera, but planning had to be even tighter as the shooting schedule was only a third as long. The effect of the elevator opening onto different floors is created by production designer Jim Bissell using a relatively simple rotating effect, so that the doors open onto a different environment.

It is true that Murrow was not the only critic of McCarthy and that the film does focus on his battle alone, ignoring attacks on McCarthy by print journalists (such as Joseph and Stewart Alsop) or the delay that Murrow took in deciding to take on McCarthy (the real Fred Friendly was less patient), and it certainly compresses the effects on McCarthy's downfall. It makes Murrow's stand seem slightly more heroic perhaps than it was; but that apart, as a defining moment of what broadcast journalism is capable, it is still a brave film to make. For a budget of only $7 million, an extremely limited setting, in black-and-white, and with language that is dense and unforgiving in its lack of exposition (explanatory, colloquial intertitles, such as "That's the Evil of it," were cut from the shooting script), it is an ambitious film, determined to be faithful to its sources. Whereas what was at stake in *Fail Safe* was literally the survival of the world, here it is ideas about moral truth and integrity, calling people to account, and the potential of the medium of television, which hang in the balance, arguably more difficult issues to make the viewer care about. Like Murrow's success with *See It Now*, Clooney's film effectively uses the personal to bring out wider political concerns without falling headlong into a didactic history lesson. Television, and by extension its big-screen relative, can definitely still be more than "wires and lights in a box." Clooney's early work might well fall into the type of programming that is being criticized by Murrow, but post-1997 he has moved toward a more high-minded view of what films to make and most have an aesthetic or political core that mark them as more than just mere entertainment.

On the audio commentary, Clooney terms Langella's scenes as "Shakespearean" in their weighty tone and Murrow uses a key quote from *Julius Caesar* in expressing his view that all of society bears some responsibility for allowing McCarthyism to spread ("the fault, dear Brutus, is not in our stars, but in ourselves"). The text, and the notion of betrayal, anticipates Clooney's forthcoming political film, *The Ides of March* (2012), based on Beau Willimon's 2008 play *Farragut North* in which Clooney plays presidential hopeful, Governor Mike Morris. Production was delayed after the cultural euphoria surrounding Obama's election, making a downbeat tale of political infighting and cynical manipulation around a Democratic primary in Ohio seem out of kilter with the public mood. Luckily, for Clooney, if not for Obama, such sentiments quickly evaporated so that the global release of the film in an election year is a timely comment on an unseemly battle for power. The use of a poster glimpsed behind Morris, clearly similar in style to that used in the Obama campaign, links the fictional politician with contemporary Democratic campaigning strategies, and although the implication is that political expediency cuts across all parties, it is the scheming within Democratic ranks that is the film's subject.

Like in *Confessions* and *Good Night, and Good Luck,* Clooney takes a peripheral role, partly to ease the pressure on his own direction. The prime focus is on press secretary Stephen Meyers (Ryan Gosling) and his moral trajectory from young idealist ("nothing bad happens when you're doing the right thing") to ruthless blackmailer. In the process, it emerges that Morris has had a brief affair with an intern, Molly (Evan Rachel Wood), clearly paralleling events in the Clinton administration. As journalist Ida Horowicz tries to warn Meyers that as a politician, Morris "will let you down, sooner or later." It is perhaps the depth of Meyers's naiveté, verging on hero worship, that makes the tarnishing of Morris's image much harder for him to accept. Grubby behavior in one arena is reflected in another: campaign manager Tom Duffy (Paul Giamatti) rejects Meyers as a potential defector once his cover is blown, Horowicz threatens to reveal a meeting Meyers had with Duffy unless she is told some insider gossip, and Meyers loses interest in Molly, failing to meet her after dropping her off at an abortion clinic. Finding Molly's dead body in a hotel after her despairing suicide, his first reaction is to steal her phone to cover his tracks.

This is the first time Clooney has played a public figure and perhaps echoes why he routinely refuses any suggestion that he himself could pursue a political career. A little like Archie Gates clutching a ceasefire agreement in *Three Kings*, Morris claims in a TV debate that "my religion is a piece of paper: the Constitution." Morris's moral platitudes delivered to a crowd at the end are seen as hollow, but so too is Meyers's position. Molly is sacrificed by his character but also perhaps by the narrative as a whole. Her pursuit of Meyers (though pregnant), her need for money despite coming from a rich background, whether her death was deliberate or accidental—all need a little more detail to be wholly convincing. The object of his admiration (Morris) is diminished but so is his own integrity, something trumpeted in Morris's campaign rhetoric. Meyers's blank stare into the camera at the end of the film reflects not only the opening scene where he is testing a microphone with phrases about religion that he appears (at that point) to believe in but that by the end he has literally become the thing he despised only a few short weeks before.

Clooney's interest in politics extends beyond the screen. In September 2006 he addressed the UN Security Council to urge greater action over the disputed Darfur region of southern Sudan. He traveled to China and Egypt in December that same year (and again with friend Don Cheadle in 2008) to press leaders there to exert any political influence they may have over the same issue. Clearly, any celebrity making political statements is open to criticism of being ill-informed and just following the latest trend in supporting a given cause. To his credit, Clooney has stuck with this single cause for a long time, informing himself better so that he can answer detailed questioning and agreeing to interviews even when he does not always have a new film to promote. It is also an expression of his dissatisfaction with entertainment-based news (although ironically he is part of that) and an attempt to focus on a story with some hard visual information to back it up. This was taken a stage further in 2010 when he agreed to be involved with the Sentinel Satellite Project, which used high-quality satellite photography to record any potential war crimes that might be taking place in southern Sudan.

CHAPTER 7

Spies Like Us

It was as if the CIA lived in a parallel universe.

—Bob Baer[1]

Clooney certainly seems interested in the intelligence work of shadowy government departments from the more realistic *Syriana* to the openly absurd *Men Who Stared at Goats*. In *Confessions*, as Jim Byrd he plays a role that politically he may reject but is dramatically interesting. Byrd claims that killing enemies of the state for the CIA represents "honest work for good pay" but we do not really see this. The precise reasons for the assassinations are never explained to Barris or the viewer, we do not see much evidence of the gratitude of the nation, which Byrd promises, and the training the wannabe killers receive seems amateurish and played for laughs. Instructor Jenks (Robert John Burke), as a tyrannical drill sergeant, accidentally injures a volunteer in demonstrating combat skills. Barris himself draws cartoons, while supposedly taking notes on torture techniques, and then is seen later boarding buses with all the other trainees, dressed as stereotypical spies in identical long coats and hats.

In *Three Kings*, Archie Gates, a senior intelligence officer, recognizes the attraction of weapons-based technology, the frustration at missing the experience of combat, and the immaturity of many of the men he is surrounded by, reflected in comments such as, while looking at the map, "That's what makes Special Forces so bad-ass: we got the best flashlights."

Clooney's tiny cameo in *Spy Kids* (Robert Rodriguez, 2001) as chief of OSS (Organization of Super Spies), Devlin, indulges in tongue-in-cheek playing with conventions of the genre, a tiny strip covering his eyes, supposedly to disguise his appearance. The strip moves as Devlin speaks, but in a neat visual gag he picks it off his face. Several features of other Clooney roles coalesce here. He is dressed in a dark, sober suit and holding a position of authority but deflates that with some wit.

SYRIANA (STEPHEN GAGHAN, 2005)

Danny Dalton: Corruption is our protection. Corruption keeps us safe and warm . . . Corruption is why we win.

"Syriana" is a genuine term used by think tanks in Washington to envisage a possible reshaping of the Middle East, but the film is at pains to point out the flaws in attempting to fashion countries in one's own image.

Syriana has a complex structure with at least five different interwoven narratives. Clooney plays Bob Barnes, an experienced CIA operative, who has followed orders over many years without question but now finds that despite (or indeed perhaps because of) his loyalty and his knowledge of the complexities of the politics of the region, he is a dispensable liability. He is told to "go easy on the memos" by his political masters, who do not want to have to deal with genuine complexity or nuanced intelligence. They would prefer a top-down imposition of a reality they would like. As seen at his interview for a safe desk job, he is unwilling to avoid uncomfortable truths about Iran not moving in the direction of democracy, which is what powerful lobby groups want to hear. His experience in Beirut (the subject of dismissive laughter within his earshot even before he is called into the room) is seen as a clichéd way to boost a résumé rather than taking it at face value.

Bob is nearly always framed in isolation, walking with a cup of coffee or his battered case as his sole company, sitting alone waiting for Prince Nasir (Alexander Siddig) to be abducted, or, after realizing his misplaced loyalties, driving to meet his death out in the desert. He seems to have no friends among his coworkers, and his son clearly resents being moved around when all he craves is some normality. Bob's wife is mentioned in passing by security consultant Stan (William Hurt), noting that any relationship with two individuals who have such a level of security clearance is doomed to failure, suggesting that a career in intelligence is largely incompatible with family life. Bob suffers for his loyalty, serving his political masters, believing in the greater good they represent. Gaghan denies us the easy pleasures associated with spy thrillers. There are no chases or clear-cut boundaries between good and evil with a climactic conclusion in which the hero defeats his adversaries. There are multiple story lines, which remain unexplained by a voice-over, shadowy characters who may be seen only once, and plenty of dialogue to which audiences need to pay attention.

Clooney, his face obscured with a full beard, shaved his hairline a little and put on 35 pounds for the part. We see him twice in long shot walking toward the camera, shoulders slightly hunched, his free hand by his side and jacket done up tightly to emphasize his portliness.

He often appears distracted, not looking directly at whoever is addressing him, like at the party and later when talking to his son, looking at a blurred figure partly off-camera, which suggests an air of habitual distraction, with the scene ending with Clooney looking mournfully down and off left at nothing specific. He is a product of his job, unable to look straight at people or give straight answers. He claims his wife is only a secretary but that would be no reason why the family has to live in Islamabad. His son storms out, muttering, "Both my parents are professional liars." When asked why they cannot live a normal life, Bob replies, "It's complicated," which might also be the tagline for the film. In both political and personal spheres, we are denied easy answers or indeed any answers at all. Threads of the narrative are often juxtaposed rather than literally interwoven. Bob sees Nasir only indirectly in the mirrored surfaces of the elevator in the hotel and face-to-face just before they are both killed by the missile at the end.

As a hero, Bob is problematic. His first sequence in the film closes with an explosion that he has engineered, killing some arms dealers in Tehran. Effectively, he is a hired killer. Later we see him in the grisly planning of the assassination of Nasir, coldly instructing Massawi (Mark Strong) to drug him and have him run over by a truck at 50 miles an hour. The business of carrying out state-sponsored murder should make him deeply unsympathetic but we also see more engaging traits. He is technically competent, e.g., testing the missile, appears morally concerned at the destination of the second missile (although seconds later we see that he had hoped to kill the recipient of both), and his action in peeking behind the curtain at what lies in the back storeroom could be seen as curiosity, bravery, or foolhardiness since he instantly has a gun placed at his temple. He is prepared to go back into Hezbollah-controlled territory at some risk to himself, withstand torture without giving up names, and most dramatically, at the close tries to warn Nasir of the impending threat to his life, although the drive out to the desert and the attempt to flag down a motorcade are somewhat at odds with his calm and considered demeanor up to this point. Like the act of leaving himself open to being snatched and tortured, he seems somewhat naïve. Whiting (Christopher Plummer) later states that "your entire career, you've been used" but Bob must know this. We might expect someone with Bob's extensive intelligence experience, who had taken part in assassinations himself, to know about satellite surveillance and anticipate the final attack.

Rather than being treated as a hero who would not betray his political masters (close-ups of his fingers are the only sign of his torture), Bob is put under investigation and excluded from the intelligence community, electronically and then directly and personally as he is forced to visit Fred (Tom McCarthy), his boss, at his home. The cold calculation of Fred is clear in the climax where he oversees the missile strike. Killing Nasir and anyone else around him, including Bob, is just collateral damage. The speed and ease with which the CIA distance themselves from Bob and discredit him, blaming him for the opening attack (in which he was only following orders), and translate his independence of opinion into the notion of a loose cannon, reflect a deeply amoral organization, which appears to operate according to no higher moral standard (and possibly less) than those it is supposedly fighting (reflected in Dalton's speech about the benefits of corruption). The final shot of Bob is in the photos that are carefully packed away as his desk is cleared. He is framed next to colleagues, who have now betrayed him. The voice-over from the video of the suicide bomber is heard as we zoom in to Bob's face, suggesting that it is really he who "died of pure heart."

The amoral machinations of oil executives, lawyers, and intelligence officers closely parallel one another, and the system of supposed regulation is hardly objective. At the beginning, Bennett Holiday (Jeffrey Wright) seems to be a man of principle and determined to expose corruption, but by the close he has revealed only sufficient levels of corruption to "give the appearance of due diligence" and takes his seat at the Oilman of the Year dinner, applauding alongside those who have exploited the situation dramatized in the film. The name of the winner, Connex Oil CEO Leland Janus (Peter Gerety), might well suggest the two-faced nature of the business. Corruption goes as far up the scale of command as anyone has the determination to look. Exploitation of the poorest in society seems like an acceptable price to pay for increased profit and influence. As a direct result of a corporate deal in America, thousands of miles away in the Gulf of Persia Wasim (Mazhar Munir) and his father are casually sacked by megaphone from a refinery and simultaneously threatened with deportation if they do not leave. Economic hopelessness contributes to radicalization of the young (Wasim and his friend are initially drawn to a madrassa by talk of food and the possibility of a respect and direction in their lives). Ironically, continuing instability in the region ultimately benefits the large oil companies by increasing the demand for their sought-after commodity.

The fact that Clooney's role was first offered to Harrison Ford, who turned it down, might suggest that *Syriana*'s original conception was closer to Tom Clancy adaptations like *Clear and Present Danger* (Phillip Noyce, 1994), which features a CIA operative (like Clooney's character here) fighting corruption and backstabbing within his own organization, including state-sponsored assassinations. There is a similar sequence involving a car containing the hero being driven into a terrorist-controlled area, with narrow streets and armed men looking down from rooftops, and which also turns out to be a trap, albeit not in an overt rocket attack. In the earlier film, we also have an explosion as the male hero Jack Ryan (Harrison Ford) walks away from it, a virtual cliché of the action genre (present in *From Dusk Till Dawn* too). However, in Gaghan's film the explosion is initiated by the hero, and he is not blown to the ground but walks calmly away, his job done. It is the callous nature of international assassination that his film explores, not the need for sporadic explosions for little narrative purpose other than to increase the level of spectacle (we are also denied a climactic explosion as the screen just fades to white when Wasim's boat strikes the Connex oil tanker). Action is unpredictable (the final missile attack) or directed in an unexpected direction (Bob rather than Nasir is snatched).

Like Noyce's *Patriot Games* (1992), Gaghan includes a sequence of high-tech satellite tracking to dramatize an American covert strike (in the earlier film via an SAS attack on a Libyan terrorist training camp). There is something of a blend of the two scenes from Noyce's two films with satellite footage (here even with a shot of a joystick, underlining the computer game comparison) intercut with multiple camera positions in and around the cars, including a sepia-tinted flashback of Nasir as he remembers seeing Bob in the elevator (almost like the cliché of life flashing before one's eyes the moment before death). However, whereas *Patriot Games* includes jingoistic whooping, Gaghan's film focuses on the human figures on the ground, before, at the moment of impact, and importantly afterward as Bryan (Matt Damon) staggers from his car to see the burning crater, which is all that remains of Nasir's car. Gaghan shows us the personal consequences of a remote-control kill as Bryan stumbles off toward the city on a journey that will take him all the way back home to his wife and child.

Ridley Scott's *Body of Lies* (2008) feels like a version of *Syriana*-lite. Set in the same part of the world, it also features a CIA character who put on weight for the role (Russell Crowe), a hero (Leonardo DiCaprio) tortured and about to be killed but miraculously saved, the use of surveillance footage portrayed from the American point of view like a video game, and a charismatic supporting role from Mark Strong as head of Jordanian intelligence. However, Scott's film features a tedious number of scenes with characters talking into cell phones, a narrative that is fairly linear, albeit complicated, and a greater focus on intelligence gathering rather than wider concerns with oil and radicalization.

Although Gaghan, who had also written *Traffic* (2000) for Soderbergh to direct, received an Oscar nomination for Best Original Screenplay, the script is informed by Robert Baer's nonfiction account of the U.S. intelligence services, *See No Evil* (2002). The character of Bob Barnes is a surrogate for Baer who also has a cameo in the film as CIA Security Officer #2. However, Baer describes himself as not "in the least the sort of type-A personality who wanted to go out and charm the world," which is usually seen as a key component of Clooney's acting style.[2] Clooney met Baer, but like Rockwell in *Confessions*, his performance here is less of an imitation than trying to capture something of his essence (easier perhaps since Baer is not a known personality like Chuck Barris). The book might almost be Clooney's character's backstory, explaining his discontent with the American intelligence services to the extent that Baer suggests that he could do his work best the further away he was from Washington politics. Like Clooney's character, Baer is also an experienced agent and is the subject of a criminal investigation, instigated largely for political motives rather than any proven wrongdoing. He too is questioned by anonymous men in suits (Secret Service men rather than CIA staffers) who "could have passed for twins."[3]

There are small references to events in the book. Baer's use of a Mercedes taxi as cover in Beirut becomes the transport used by guerrilla groups in the film to carry Clooney's character through the back streets of that same town when he foolishly returns, thinking he is safe. There is a single mention of a member of a Gulf royal family (without specifying which one) who tries to overthrow his cousin, who is the emir, but the detail of the rivalry between the brothers in *Syriana* comes from Gaghan's script.[4] Baer's book describes the shady deals by businessman and lobbyist Roger Tamraz, whose amoral activities are reflected by any of the figures working for Connex. The CIA, in Baer's book and in *Syriana*, is portrayed as a tool furthering the careers and private fortunes of the political elite, rather than protecting the American people. Baer's book does not describe in detail the grassroots recruiting of specific terrorists but rather the dangers that such movements like this could pose to a toothless and unprepared CIA, which seems focused (in his view) on politically influenced big-name targets and reliant on electronic surveillance rather than the work of experienced case officers. *Syriana* plots potential consequences of these failings.

Deleted scenes would have shown us Bob's wife (Greta Scacchi) at an airport, a Tehran café, and the hospital, but their removal does keep the focus on him and the political situation with the cost to his family carried more effectively in the single scene with his son. In the airport scene, shown in passing on the featurette but not as part of the deleted scenes, we see Bob asking his wife what she would do if she knew something bad was going to happen and could stop it. Bearing in mind Bob was in charge of the assassination of Nasir until the operation went wrong, his sudden conversion does seem strange, and a little more of this kind of material might have made this about-face seem more plausible, albeit shifting the ensemble global narrative closer to a personal wrestling with conscience. The deleted café scene, which does appear on the DVD extras, provides some resonance between the couple and underlines the sacrifice that Bob is making at a personal as well as professional level, but it also could be seen as an unnecessary distraction in an already complex narrative. The Asteroids video game, which their son is playing in the background, is more of a loss, as the increasing volume of objects hemming in the spacecraft is a neat image of growing pressure on Bob and his eventual demise by the missile attack.

The script juxtaposes different family groups (Bob, Bryan, Wasim, Holiday, and the rival Arabic brothers) to stress how similar they are all are, making the film akin to a family drama at times. Bryan's family is the most rounded group, especially with small touches like the tactile relationship with his children, holding hands and picking them up at every opportunity, and his slightly overprotective attitude to one of the boys, Max, adding power to the sequence of the swimming pool accident. The actual moment of death or violence is avoided: we focus instead on a long shot of Bryan walking back toward the pool, before we hear panicked screams and his gradual realization of what has happened before he jumps into the pool. Later, Bryan prattles on about superficial differences between Western and Eastern culture, prompting his wife to note that he "sounds strange." The unspoken element here is grief, which neither can articulate, Bryan even echoing the boy's last movements, frowning down into a pool before diving in.

The film in particular juxtaposes different strained father-son relationships. Bob's son has to endure a father who habitually evades the truth and drags the family to strange places around the world without a clear and honest explanation. Wasim indulges a father constantly prattling about the snow-covered mountains of Pakistan, a different form of the American Dream, and a squalid working environment, living in a cramped compound with only rudimentary washing facilities, separated from the rest of his family. However, the network of family and friends is humanized, as we see Wasim playing soccer and arguing about the powers of Spiderman. The scene of Wasim walking through a game of cricket, apparently asking for a bus fare from his father but really hugging him goodbye, has a powerful poignancy. There is also clear family strife among the emirs in terms of a power struggle between the brothers over succession from their ailing father and about the future political direction of the region, literalized in the battle for oil contracts between the United States and China. The least detailed, Holiday's father, who appears repeatedly sitting on the steps of his house, has a drinking problem and is a thorn in Holiday's side, but we see little more than this, even though a wordless reconciliation between them is the final image of the film.

Clooney won a deserved Oscar and Golden Globe for Best Supporting Actor for a performance where he is not afraid to look physically vulnerable. The torture scenes do not shy away from the direct visceral action. Massawi describes what he is going to do and we see him pull fingernails with pincers. There are shots of Bob's feet flinching, his labored breathing, his cries of pain, but these are in addition to direct shots of the act of disfigurement, not replacing them. Punches are repeated, direct, and accompanied by a visceral Foley crunch rather than any spectacular smacking sound. Bob is knocked off his chair and we cut to Bob's oblique point of view from the ground as he sees Massawi walking toward him, brandishing a knife. Throughout the scene he has been stripped half naked, revealing his overweight and untoned torso, and lying on the floor, his trousers with a tight waistband emphasize his paunch.

Alexandre Desplat's score was nominated for a Golden Globe. His main theme, plaintive but haunting, returns at moments of particular drama or wider shots that suggest something of the sheer scale and beauty of the region of the landscape, such as the opening shots of men waiting for buses in the early morning mist or later footage of the huge refinery with workers signaling to each other like Native Americans in westerns.

Clooney seems interested in the human aspect of the intelligence services, in terms of both their motivation as well as the more bizarre practices in training and in the field (as Baer states, "In the end, intelligence boils down to people.").[5] This might involve lengthy and unspectacular legwork. Unfortunately, this does not make for exciting film narratives, and trailers sometimes misrepresent these films as action-driven (such as

The American), leading to some disappointment among viewers when their expectations are not met.

BURN AFTER READING (THE COEN BROTHERS, 2008)

"It's a Tony Scott/Bourne Identity kind of a movie . . . without the explosions."

—Ethan Coen[6]

The film blends farce and family drama with a focus on the private lives of those who work for the intelligence services. There is an A-list cast, several of whom have worked repeatedly with the Coen brothers so presumably they are happy to do so, in a relaxed working environment on material that is different from the vast majority of scripts that come their way.

From the outset, we see Harry Pfarrer (George Clooney) as something of a loser, getting into a needless argument with Osborne Cox (John Malkovich), mostly referred to as Ozzie, spilling food down his tie and talking with his mouth full. Harry belittles his wife's work in front of others and is bluntly taken off to the kitchen by Katie (Tilda Swinton) to allow his wife, Sandy (Elizabeth Marvel), to speak for herself. His tetchy reaction at the party to Ozzie's slightly risqué joke about "discharging his weapon" suggests a literal humorlessness and a general antipathy toward the other man or, as it turns out, a bit of both. He uses the same form of words in small talk, irrespective of who he is talking to (he admires both Katie's and Linda's flooring) and seems bound by habits like his instinctive postcoital urge for a run. Sex seems to be just another form of exercise to which he seems mildly addicted, and stressed about when he is prevented from performing. Costume designer, Mary Zophres, puts Clooney in a plaid shirt with a fairly cheap cut of trousers, and along with his own addition of a gold chain, he has the look of someone lacking wit and sartorial style, almost an anti-Danny Ocean.

The scene in which Harry waves his wife off on her trip to Seattle, only to turn and his smile to drop as he spots a car down the street, effectively shifts the tone from relaxed domesticity to unsettled bemusement and he is framed in silhouetted long shot, alone and vulnerable. The first time he is aware of a car, while out running, small jump cuts and a zoom that is then interrupted neatly suggest his unease. However, unlike films like David Fincher's *The Game* (1997) in which the life of the main character is gradually upside down into a world that might be genuine threat or paranoia, this is not really pursued. Near the end, Linda (Frances McDormand) looks up at a helicopter overhead and feels as if she is being watched by the drivers of cars that pull up alongside or appear to be following her, but this is not the final section of Martin Scorsese's *Good Fellas* (1990) and neither a genuine closing in of security personnel or a descent into overwhelming paranoia is convincing here.

Harry is seen coming out of a Home Depot, framed as if from the point of view of a car, and yet at this stage there is no surveillance on him as the disc has not been discovered in the gym. For an experienced intelligence officer, Harry might well surmise that he is being watched in connection with Ozzie's sacking or at least make some tentative inquiries through contacts at work as to what is going on. Like Katie, we get little real clear view of his competence. He downplays the drama of being a bodyguard, trotting out the fact that he has never drawn his weapon in 20 years, but this feels more like dinner party chatter than meaningful. It does prepare us for the speed and act of shooting Chad (Brad Pitt) perhaps but does not help us in reading this as accidental, an overreaction, or justifiable given the circumstances.

Harry is a moral coward. Talking in bed with Katie, she interrupts his platitudes about mortality, and when faced with the proposal of specific action, separation, and probable divorce, he shies away claiming that it is too hard "to inflict that kind of pain" (sensitivity to the feelings of others, which does not stop him from sleeping around). Similarly, later he tries to portray his sexual opportunism as selflessness in questioning the timing of Katie's proposed divorce of Ozzie. She is not blind to this. When he says that he will be easier to deal with "if he doesn't feel cornered," she asks whether he is talking about Ozzie or himself. In agreeing to eat the food offered him by Linda, he resolves to "live dangerously," but apart from a slight choke, he does not. He appears to be opening up to Linda in admitting he is married but then goes on to claim they are separated, just to get enough moral distance to persuade Linda to sleep with him. The period of time in which he moves in with Katie is slightly surreal, as unbeknown to her, Sandy is only away on a business trip and after a row, Harry goes out to the car to phone his wife begging her to come home; i.e., he is playing at being separated, neatly compartmentalizing the worlds of his wife and various lovers. He may compare favorably to Linda's previous lover, explicitly laughing at part of the same film that left the other man unmoved, but it also suggests a rather cold process of vetting on the part of Linda, going to exactly the same film just to compare reactions.

His wife does call him a "mystery man," but the building of the sex device is fairly bizarre. He might describe himself as a "hobbyist" and someone with an eye for a bargain but that does not explain why he makes this particular item. It is the only thing he takes out of the family home, in an oddly shaped bag, and it is the object he vents his anger on when he finds he has been betrayed, which would suggest he is making it for his wife. We can only imagine, however, what her reaction might have been. Linda seems genuinely impressed ("It's wonderful") and the camera lingers on her reaction, apparently mesmerized.

The character of Harry has elements of previous Clooney roles. As in *Solaris*, we see him cutting vegetables in an echoing home environment, his lover at some distance from him. However, despite the somber strings we hear on the soundtrack, it is relatively late to introduce such a mood shift. Here, Clooney's expression has to encompass guilt and bemusement (he still has no idea who Chad is), and he has no one he can confide in. However, the film struggles to accommodate such an elegiac tone, and his "You know, you really are a negative person" and Sandy's response, telling him "to behave," seem stuck in a PC land of comfortable middle-class squabbling, rather than anything more existential. Clooney and the rest of the cast get the most from the material (which was largely written for them, with the exception of Tilda Swinton), producing some great individual scenes, such as the first mention of the disc. Its exact location shifts in the course of Chad's explanation from the floor to a locker to a locker in the ladies' changing room, stressing that it was hardly a random find, but overall, these often feel more like material for a trailer.

Seen first of all cracking a gym customer's joint in a way that does not sound good, Chad seems almost more a collection of visual and verbal tics than a complete character (bad dyed hair, frequently giving a melodramatic "Oh my God," and trying to sound enigmatic as a blackmailer by referring to Cox's "sensitive shit"). He accepts Linda's insistence that he has to wear a suit to make his blackmail threat in person but still appears on his bike. His dance moves while listening to music, in Linda's flat, on a treadmill, and even in a car while supposedly watching Ozzie's house are all funny but reflect the law of diminishing returns. Beyond physical comedy (like the rabbit punch, which reduces him to silence holding a tissue to his nose in the following embassy scenes), there is little his character can offer as he is not intelligent enough to initiate action. Trying to sound different, not just on the phone but in person by repeatedly using Cox's full name and giving himself the name Mr. Black (a Coen allusion to Pitt's role in Martin Brest's 1998 *Meet Joe Black*), makes Chad absurd, especially the pride that he takes in taking Ozzie literally, when he jokes about them both knowing each other's name.

It is hard not to feel that Ozzie's term for the blackmailers, "a league of morons," might well apply to most of the main characters. The CIA is presented not as seeking to solve problems but simply to make them go away. The description of the disposal of the bodies of Chad and Ted (Richard Jenkins) via dialogue rather than visualizing the act keeps such elements at the level of farce rather than gangster movie, but if life is so cheap in the narrative (the boss is visibly disappointed on being told that Ozzie is not dead), it is hard to care about any of the characters.

There are a number of satirical targets on offer, like soulless Internet dating (after disappointing sex, Linda checks a man's wallet to find a domestic note from his betrayed wife) and call center machines that cannot recognize clearly enunciated English, and the whole notion of exercise culture is seen either as an unhealthy compulsion (in Harry) or an unprincipled business (when Chad and Linda try to extort money from property, which is not so much found as overtly stolen). The script is full of small peripheral details, which seem extraneous but add a quirky depth to characterization, like Katie asserting that "I don't hammer" while beating her fist on the table, or Ted's former life as a Greek Orthodox priest, whose congregation boasted Chevy Chase among its number, or the package addressed to "Oliver the cat who lives in the rotunda." Sandy's book that she is promoting in Seattle is a ridiculous children's version of political processes, entitled *Point of Order, Oliver*, as the main character attempts to interrupt a filibuster.

Characters are surrounded by ambiguities. For example, we do not know if Ozzie is actually good at his job. From his confidence, slight high-handedness to others, and constant swearing, we might assume this to be so. He acts in an extremely eccentric way, from his drinking and falling asleep facedown on a chair to finally storming back to his house, still in dressing gown, wielding an ax. We never really know if he has a drinking problem or just takes to drink after being unfairly shunted out of his job. We do not know if he really was thinking about writing before or just says this to calm his wife down. He acts in a rather grandiose manner, dictating his memoirs on a Dictaphone, but all we hear is halting clichés and his correcting Harry about the terms "lactose intolerant" and "acid reflux" (or later correcting Chad's misreading of "report" for "rapport"), which could be annoying but arguably he is just trying to be precise. Chad and Linda assume they have captured some great secrets but as the CIA boss (J. K. Simmons) points out, closing the file, Ozzie is "not a biggie." He may seem confident in facing down the blackmailers but this is only in comparison to their clueless bungling, especially by Chad.

Ozzie seems a little cut adrift from the narrative, once he has set it in motion. His wheelchair-bound father appears in only a single scene, on the yacht, wordlessly acting as a sounding board for his son to pour his feelings out about the CIA, which "seems like it's all bureaucracy and no mission." It is ironic that Ozzie, the most active in the intelligence serv-ices, is one of the most open characters, whereas his wife is advised by her lawyer that "she can be a spy too." His resolution to write something that he describes to his father as "pretty explosive" only leads to drinking and watching daytime TV in his dressing gown. It is perhaps intended that his character undergoes a gradual mental descent through the course of the film, reflected in his clothing, so that by the end he marches from the yacht to his house still in his dressing gown and clutching the ax. However, he disappears for the central part of the film, appearing only briefly for the ransom meeting or seen performing aerobics while on the yacht. Although it is an ensemble piece, many of the scenes involve only one or two characters, often couples who are not really communicating effectively, so it can take quite a while to come back to Ozzie; but his loss from the screen robs the narrative of a more mature, grown-up voice, even if it is a scary voice, as when he yells down the phone at a bank employee about the apparent loss of his money.

As a spy caper, it has little of substance other than the initial setup and bungled attempt at demanding a ransom. The film opens and closes at Langley, but the CIA scenes seem little more than bookends, opening the file on Ozzie so to speak by sacking him and literally closing it at the end with his body lying in a hospital somewhere, comatose and unable to explain the narrative we have witnessed. Generically, it is re-ally a family drama and perhaps closer to a film like *The Squid and the Whale* (Noah Baumbach, 2005); and as in Baumbach's film, it is not easy to find likeable characters. Katie, Sandy, and especially Harry are all exposed as adulterous. Harry seems able to compartmentalize his life so that random sexual encounters with unnamed women seem to happen at almost any point in the narrative. His promises of fidelity and emo-tional attachment are much the same to Katie (his mistress) as to Sandy (his wife). The scene where he rams a car and wrestles his observer to the ground questions the nature of the narrative we have been watching. He, and possibly we, had thought he was at the center of a spy conspiracy (he demands both of the man and later of Linda, "Who do you work for?"), but the real network of relationships we have here is familial and emotionally bleak (his watcher is a private detective, gathering evidence for a divorce). The man who Harry grabs tells him bluntly, "Grow up man, it happens to everybody."

The figure of Chad is believable in the ease with which he gets himself trapped in Ozzie's house, but the act of hiding in a closet and the Coens' use of his point of view from the partially open door underlines the generic problem here. In the film up to this point, if he is discovered, the worst that is likely is some social embarrassment. This is not *Halloween* (John Carpenter, 1980) and Chad is not in the position of Laurie (Jamie Lee Curtis), frantic with fear at the likelihood of a bloody death from an unkillable monster. Although he has spoken of his job and his gun, there is nothing about Harry that would lead us to expect the reaction of shooting Chad point blank in the face. Harry's reaction, stumbling backward down the stairs, fumbling for a knife, and returning to check the body, underlines what a shock this is for the character himself. This one act puts the narrative beyond the realm of comedy, in which generally there is disruption of equilibrium but in which all disorder can be, more or less, righted by the close. Here, this single act renders such a structural path impossible. *Pulp Fiction* and *Out of Sight* both feature accidental deaths of minor characters by pistol shots to the head, which provoke a moment of absurd laughter. Tarantino uses a bump in the road; Soderbergh, a trip on a stair; but here, not only is the act deliberate but the character removed is engaging in his incompetence. As played by Pitt, Chad is a ridiculous character, hardly deserving of such a brutal death.

There can be few other examples in film history where the camera cuts away from a climactic action (Ozzie cutting down Terry with an ax), the final plot strands summarized rather than shown, and the film just ends, with the camera pulling up and away as at the beginning. It means the last we see of Ozzie is in a burst of anger that must have consequences for him, and Harry running off in a park (supposedly then picked up on a flight due for Venezuela but allowed to leave). As the narrative strands are cut unexpectedly, we have to think back to the last time we saw characters who disappear from the narrative, like Katie examining a boy in her surgery and Sandy apparently indulging in an affair in Seattle. More damaging, the final shot of Linda, arguably the film's most empathetic character, is being thrown out of the Russian embassy, again with no consequence shown or hinted at other than the complete failure of her plan. The agreement by the CIA to fund her operations seems peremptory. The plot also relies on the statistically unlikely chance that in the whole of Washington, Harry and Linda form a relationship over the Internet, thus bringing the two main plot strands together at Ozzie's house. The irony of Linda seeking comfort for the disappearance of her fiend Chad from the very man who shot him, thinking he was some kind of burglar (while both men were in the house of a shared acquaintance, Ozzie), is comic but hard to accept as believable.

The film portrays human nature as strange and ultimately inexplicable, reflected in the irony that both Katie and Sandy describe each other to a third party on separate occasions as "a stuck-up bitch." The framing device of dropping in and pulling out of human affairs like a satellite eavesdropping on human affairs, apparently at random, might fit with the surveillance culture of the CIA but makes the Coens seem a little cold and distant in their view of humankind, almost as an alien species. Humans seem bound up in various levels of absurdity, some comic, some tragic. Ultimately, Linda and Chad pin their hopes and Chad loses his life horrifically for something, which the Russians describe as "drivel" (misheard and repeated by Linda as "dribble").

The narrative by this stage, like Linda, needs "a can-do person"; but it seems that momentum, like Harry, is just defeated. Attempts by Harry to infuse a sense of nostalgia into his relationship with Linda, noting that they are sitting on the bench "where we first met," are at odds with his serial infidelity and the basic problem that their relationship has not existed nor developed enough for such a comment to hold weight. His glimpsing of figures apparently watching him is consistent with his earlier paranoia (with the nice gag of placing her earlier disastrous date on another bench so at least one person really is looking at them), but his haring off away from her and out of the narrative undermines any attempts to take his character seriously. *Burn after Reading* certainly made its budget back ($37 million) many times over (in terms of global revenue), but perhaps in large part this may be due to the strong trailer-like element in the film, allowing promotional material to focus on its quirky strengths as well as name checking the A-list cast.

Clooney termed his roles for the Coen Brothers, from *O Brother* to *Intolerable Cruelty* to here, as "my trilogy of idiots."[7] Miles and Harry have the benefit of relative wealth and status; Everett has neither, having lost what status he had, and is first seen escaping from a penal system, whose agents are allowed to shoot him on sight. The idiocy in *O Brother* is partly explained by educational opportunity, in *Intolerable Cruelty* by the corrupting power of money and the operation of matrimonial law, but in *Burn after Reading*, there seems no real reason for supposedly intelligent individuals (with the exception of Chad) to act so stupidly.

In a sense, all three of Clooney's Coen-directed characters are undergoing some form of midlife crisis, but whereas Miles and Harry take this as the green light for promiscuity, Everett has already made the decision about what is important in life (his wife and family) and the course of *O Brother* follows his pursuit of that goal. For Harry, marriage is a convention he is free to ignore, for Miles its ridiculous nature is the basis of his whole profession, but for Everett it is the one thing to which he holds true. As Miles notes (perhaps with a rueful element of Clooney's own views on the subject), "that's the problem with the institution of mar-riage: it's based on compromise." Everett is willing to compromise; Miles and Harry cannot. Even though annoyed at being declared dead in an accident, Everett still has a respectful view of his wife (trying to win her back by picking a fight he knows he cannot win). Miles's view of marriage is the epitome of cynicism, replying to Rex that Marilyn has him "between a rock and a hard place" with "That's her job." Harry's cynicism is in action, and the vows of marriage are meaningless to him, even though he professes affection to both Sandy and Katie in much the same overblown romantic terms ("I'm crazy about you" and "I adore you") and calls them both "baby."

All three are flawed, and vain certainly. Like Massey, Everett is a law-yer, albeit an unsuccessful one, but apart from the opening ruse of the search for some treasure, Everett does act for the good of his fellow man. By contrast, Miles and Harry are completely selfish, with few, if any, redeeming qualities, perhaps reflecting a shift in indie filmmaking through the mid-1990s onward toward a more dysfunctional view of fam-ily and human relationships generally.

In *O Brother*, although played against the background of real social ten-sions, no one is genuinely hurt (Tommy's and Pete's lynchings are both interrupted). In *Intolerable Cruelty* and *Burn after Reading* however, Wheezy Jo and Chad respectively really do get shot in the head. There is a sliding scale in the graphic nature of the violence too from Joe's ridiculous confusion of an asthma inhaler for a pistol to the point-blank shooting of Chad directly in the face. This latter example is particularly shocking as it is prefaced by the smiling face of Brad Pitt. It seems almost sacrilegious in cinematic terms to reduce in a split second a face associ-ated with male beauty to a motionless corpse.

Comparing the three Coen films, there is an increase in moral vague-ness, random violence, sexual deviance (from Rex's train games, reminis-cent of Nic Roeg's *Track 29* [1980], to Gus Pitch's voyeuristic camera shows for his friends to Harry's bizarre chair contraption), increasingly sexualized language (from *Intolerable Cruelty*'s unsubtle use of "ass" to Ozzie's ubiquitous "What the fuck" in *Burn after Reading*), and an increas-ingly diffuse narrative structure, which struggles to reconcile disparate elements to the point where *Burn after Reading* just gives up at the end. Harry and Ozzie might be disillusioned with their work but they also indulge in womanizing and self-important gestures respectively, which undermines the dramatic impact of their suffering. Linda is an empathetic representation of the dwindling options facing older women (perhaps par-ticularly in the film industry) but there is a built-in limit as to how far her narrative can go: she is not an experienced spy and what she is peddling has no value. Once Chad is brutally removed from the narrative, the film cannot reclaim its comic territory. When the Coens threaded bluegrass through the entire plot of O Brother, they wrote about something they knew and loved. We do not really get the same sense of emotional attachment to practitioners of matrimonial law or the peculiarities of what might happen when the CIA collides with Internet dating and gym workers.

THE MEN WHO STARE AT GOATS (GRANT HESLOV, 2009)

> Neither then nor now, nor ever in the future, can photos tell you what is happening inside buildings or in the heads of the men who occupy them.
>
> —Bob Baer in See No Evil[8]

Like Confessions, this film reflects Clooney's interest in the more unlikely projects of the U.S. intelligence services (here, the notion of psychic spying) and uses a similar subjective, and possibly unreliable, narrative viewpoint. An intertitle proclaims, "More of this is true than you would believe," leaving the question open as to exactly how much that might be. A psychic, Gus Lacey (Stephen Root), who claims to have been trained in remote viewing, shows journalist Bob Wilton (Ewan McGregor) a video in which he apparently kills his hamster by thought alone.

Clooney's performance as Sergeant Lyn Cassady is sound enough, giving him some opportunity to indulge in some physical comedy and deliver some good one-liners, but his part as written does not really allow us to engage in and therefore care about him. Lyn first appears as a shadowy presence, in the dead space of the shot, apparently reading a newspaper but listening to Bob spin delusional lies to his ex-wife from a Kuwait hotel of what dangers he is in covering the war. As in Confessions, a delusional male, given to making up stories of exciting adventures, is drawn to a shadowy figure in U.S. intelligence, who may be a product of a fevered male imagination.

Heslov does a competent but unspectacular job of directing his first film. A bigger weakness is Peter Straughan's script. The narrative structure is basically that of a road movie, punctuated by flashbacks to provide Lyn's backstory. However, the surface narrative in the desert lacks both a goal and a motive, making it hard to care about what happens to Lyn and Bob. They experience a series of events, but arguably these might happen in any order and we are left to wait for the next flashback with its succession of examples of the craziness of the notion of psychic spies. The plot includes a couple of very unlikely consequences: not just Bob sitting right next to the very man that Lacey spoke about, but at the end Bob and Lyn stumble upon a secret base, housing former New Earth Army personnel and a warehouse of goats used for aggressive applications of psychic forces.

A number of features, which in isolation might make an effective comedy or satire, in combination seem to fight against one another: the absurd situations (from Hopwood's opening running into a wall), the juxtaposition of lighthearted music with serious visuals ("Alright" by Supergrass accompanies the title sequence as Bob prepares to go to war, or Boston's "More Than a Feeling" to help Lyn's remote viewing), but most damaging of all is the language. The steady stream of quips and one-liners makes deep emotional engagement difficult. As Lyn becomes more serious and appears broken in the final phase of the film, he retells the experience of killing a goat by staring, for which he feels cursed, but Bob's only reaction is to describe it as "the silence of the goats."

From the outset, the New Earth Army and their capabilities are described using the specific language of *Star Wars* (George Lucas, 1977). Those with psychic powers are "Jedi Warriors" battling the powers of evil. As Bob says of Lyn's extraordinary abilities, "The Force truly was strong with this one." A further layer of self-awareness is added by the casting of Ewan McGregor, the face of a young Obi-Wan Kenobi in the first three films of the trilogy. Thus when Bob is watching TV and we hear a presenter talk of a farm boy who would grow up to be involved in the battle of good and evil, the subsequent cut to a shot of George Bush, rather than Luke Skywalker, is an effective visual gag. When Lyn and Bob struggle across the desert, it is hard not to be reminded of similar treks with the Droids; and Lyn tries the technique used by Obi-Wan Kenobi to evade stormtrooper patrols by making them repeat his suggestions, but his attempt at repeating "You don't want us" to his captors has no effect at all.

Lyn is a laughable figure. His ridiculous martial arts stance when he first challenges Bob, his "sparkly eyes technique," which appears to involve little more than staring, and the so-called "Echmeyer Technique," a diving attack using flailing knives, rendered absurd by him being unarmed when he dives on an Iraqi captor, all undermine his status. He talks of abilities like invisibility but does not demonstrate that, and claims a high level of intuition before driving the wrong way at a crossroads and hitting a roadside bomb. Lyn casts himself as a cursed figure, having received the "Dim Mak" or mark of death from Larry (Kevin Spacey), but a shift into a more morose and inward-looking phase of his character is undercut by the language used to describe it ("like the poem where the guy kills a sea-gull"). Supposedly, he has cancer (motivating the shot of him injecting an unexplained drug) but he attributes this disease to Larry's malign influence.

One of the few clear demonstrations of Lyn's ability is "cloudbursting," causing clouds to disperse, which appears to work, but when he takes his eyes off the road, he and Bob crash into a boulder. He claims to be on a mission but Bob just declares, "You're an idiot." Lyn is able to predict coin tosses but his combat skills, supposedly based on psychic powers, involve throwing Bob to the ground and then claiming "I barely moved." He lec-tures Bob on not giving into fear with gnomic utterances that are revealed to derive from Oprah. It is the death of a goat, apparently caused by Bob's stare, that is the clearest suggestion of substantial psychic powers. He is asked to help locate a kidnapped NATO general, and his subsequent hon-oring by the group, being awarded a symbolic feather, suggests his help is useful. However, later Lyn feels unworthy and returns the feather, and Bill (Jeff Bridges) admits to Bob "None of it was real" and that the feather came from a turkey. Beyond Lyn, it is also unclear what abilities the group has. We see a blindfolded driver in a jeep plowing through cones, forcing soldiers to dive out of the way, and later, asked where General Noriega is, another member of the group replies, "Ask Angela Lansbury."

Bridges does what he can with his character of Bill Janko but he is little more than a hippy cliché given some good one-liners, allowing him to rerun elements of the Dude from *The Big Lebowski* (Coen brothers, 1998). He is court-martialed and stands to object "That's a lie" about mis-using funds but has to qualify his second objection when accused of using money for drugs and a prostitute ("Well, the hooker thing is definitely a lie"). Kevin Spacey as Larry Hooper also has little to do here. He appears, overtly described by Bob's voice-over as "a serpent" entering the Eden-like existence of Bill's New Earth Army. Larry is closer to a playground bully, predicting disaster at a colleague's wedding and faking possession by a spirit. He is more interested in aggressive applications of the pro-gram. We never learn why, making his character closer to Spacey's incarnation as cartoonish Lex Luthor in *Superman Returns* (Bryan Singer, 2006).

There are also overtones of *Forrest Gump* (Robert Zemeckis, 1994) here. Personal developments (Bob's wife leaving him) and events in American history, like Vietnam and especially the 1960s/1970s drug counterculture (hot-tub sex, drug use, and even colonic irrigation), seem to whip past with little sense of their significance. Like Gump's mother, Bob tells Lyn to "find out what your destiny is," and the course of both narratives follows a central character on a personal quest. Bob admits later that he joins Lyn on his mission in Iraq because he was really looking for "something to believe in." Earlier Bob states, "Sometimes there's a need . . . Sometimes people are calling out for something" even if "they don't know it themselves," reminiscent of the runners who follow Gump, jogging across America, thinking they have found a messiah. Whereas Gump is freed from his braces by dancing like Elvis, Lyn as a boy is told not to dance to the Swinging Blue Jeans' "Hippy Hippy Shake" by his father who does not want him to "look queer." Lyn is liberated under the encouragement of Bill, some hallucinogenic drugs, and Billy Idol's "Dancing with Myself" to engage in more uninhibited dancing.

There are glimpses of a darker vision with the kidnapping of Bob and Lyn, in the insensitive, aggressive capitalism of Blackwater-style contractor Todd Nixon (Robert Patrick), and most clearly in the abusive techniques being pursued by Larry, experimenting on a raw recruit, to the point where the man runs onto a parade ground, naked with a gun, and shoots himself. However, even a detainee undergoing sleep-depriving light patterns, reminiscent of abuses, either alleged or proven, at Abu Ghraib or Guantanamo, it is still described by Lyn in the same *Star Wars* phraseology, saying he has seen "the Dark Side." The film tells us nothing about the conflict itself. The sole Iraqi given a name, Mahmud (Waleed Zuaiter), is nearly run over by Lyn, has his house robbed, his wife vanishes, and is prepared to give Bob and Lyn his car, even though he is still repeatedly called Mohammed by everyone.

It is usually assumed that the film takes little except its title from the book but that is not true. Jon Ronson's book is comprised of a series of interviews with soldiers of varying rank who claim to have been involved in some measure with the development of psychic spying for U.S. intelligence. We find in both the quirkier experiments in psychic spying conducted at Fort Bragg, like the existence of a goat lab and the development of a death touch, the "sparkly eyes" technique, and the use of the recruiting slogan "to be all you can be," and both begin with a general trying to run through an office wall, albeit Straughan changes the name from Stubblebine to Hopwood.[9] Name changes include the book's Jim Cannon who becomes Bill Django, complete with revelatory experience in Vietnam and author of the First Earth Battalion Operations Manual. Other names are changed only slightly, so that a psychic who develops a knife-wielding technique is changed from Echanis to Eckmeyer. Elsewhere, Straughan appropriates exchanges almost wholesale, like the "Jedi Warrior" scene, originally spoken by an interviewee, former psychic spy Glenn Wheaton, but transposed into Lyn's dialogue. Indeed,

Clooney's character is a composite of a number of interviewees in Ronson's book: Guy Savelli (who runs a dance studio), martial arts instructor Pete Brusso (who demonstrates choke holds and how to interrupt thought patterns), Sergeant Lyn Buchanan, and Stubblebine, who describes being able to cloudburst while driving.[10] There are differences too. The book makes specific mention of Uri Geller who claims that he was recruited to help U.S. intelligence, the Waco siege, and the training of the 9/11 terrorists. However, the substance of Straughan's script is much closer to the book than has been noted, including all the Star Wars vocabulary and the talk of "Jedi warriors."[11]

By the close, it is debatable whether we have learned any more about the characters than we knew at the beginning. Bob especially is a very flat narrative device, asking questions on behalf of the viewer so that another example of psychic spying can be explained. Bob asks Bill, "Do you believe in redemption?" but the narrative closes not on a rendition of the Earth Army's hippy prayer but a frat house prank of putting LSD in the powdered eggs of the base. Out of context, shots of stoned soldiers giving each other flowers and driving tanks around are funny and it is tempting to think that a more liberal attitude to drugs and releasing some prisoners, heavily symbolized by the liberated goats, will somehow make everything all right, but the notion that this provides any kind of solution to the issues that the film only barely touches on is unconvincing. It is a film with effective moments, but *Confessions* was held together by a powerful schizoid performance by Sam Rockwell. Clooney's part is not substantial enough to know how much sympathy he deserves. Perhaps it ultimately comes down to a more simple issue: we might believe that it is possible but unlikely that Barris killed 33 people but we lack empirical proof that Lyn could achieve something impossible according to the laws of physics as we know them.

The book ends on a downbeat note in which interviewees fail to return Ronson's calls, but the film's final scene seems out of synch with the ironic tone of the rest of the film. Bob is annoyed that his report has been airbrushed into a comedic piece on Barney's theme tune. However, this is effectively what the whole film does with its potentially serious subject matter. What is presumably intended as a rallying call for more crusading journalism at the close actually has the opposite effect. McGregor's self-aware declaration, "Now more than ever we need the Jedi," would be more powerful if similar references had not been used throughout, implying the only hope is the intervention of a fictitious species. Bob ends the film as he began it, indulging in delusional wish fulfillment.

CONCLUSION

Bob Baer talks of the danger that the necessary identification with one's enemy develops to such an extreme that "I was starting to think like the people I was after."[12] Lyn Cassady, Bob Barnes, and Harry Pfarrer all share an intense, emotional identification with a problem, at the expense of the bigger picture (in Baer's case of the 1983 U.S. embassy bombing in Beirut), allowing viewers to identify with a fallible character but also feel possibly slightly superior to them, imagining perhaps that we might have remained more objective.

In Clooney's movies of the last decade, antagonists are often part of a more complex worldview, which might involve shady business in the Middle East (*Syriana*) or legal bodies suppressing information about environmental issues (*Michael Clayton*), or remain largely undefined and possibly only in the imagination of the protagonist (*Confessions*). As in *Burn after Reading*, there is less focus on the job itself and more on individuals, particularly those frustrated with superiors who act from financial and political motives (an element traceable back to his character in *ER*). Even *The Man from Uncle* from which Clooney ultimately dropped out is an entirely logical project for his star persona, offering as it does a blend of the suave and stylish with more surreal cloak-and-dagger elements of espionage.

CHAPTER 8

Existential George

SOLARIS (STEVEN SODERBERGH, 2002)

Snow: I could tell you what's happening but I don't know if I'd really tell you what's happening.

Solaris gave Clooney the chance to work again with Soderbergh in a genre that neither had yet tried, as well as representing the challenge of a remake of a classic text twice over (from Andrei Tarkovsky's landmark science fiction film from 1972, itself an adaptation of Stanislaw Lem's influential short novel from 1961).

The film opens with a close-up of rain running down a window, viewed from the inside. There is no music, no voice-over—few clues that this is indeed a science fiction narrative at all. Our first view of psychologist Chris Kelvin (George Clooney) is sitting on a bed, hunched forward, dressed in a gray undershirt and boxer shorts. His expression is blank, and along with the pathetic fallacy of the rain, the mood is somber. A ghostly female voice-over asks him directly what is wrong and whether he loves her anymore. The scene establishes the tone of the rest of the film: sedate pacing, a hero who appears thoughtful, and a refusal to offer audiences easily won spectacle. Equally importantly, it establishes the notion of a presence that is not physically possible, i.e., that life is an existential experience. Milena Canonero's costume adds unobtrusive touches of futuristic style to his dress, so that he wears only different shades of black (on earth, a long Matrix-style leather coat; on Solaris, a slightly lighter shade of astronaut-like uniform), underlining his status as a figure in mourning.

A loud cacophony of undetermined sound, including a plane landing, takes us to the next scene, Kelvin striding through a crowd in a rain-soaked street. The extreme low angle allows Soderbergh to avoid providing too much detail of a futuristic society (like the later tight shots in the shopping scene) as well as evokes that seminal view of a bleak future urban society, where it seems to rain all the time and where nonliving creatures start to become aware of their own status, as in Ridley Scott's 1982 *Blade Runner*. Rheya (Natascha McElhone) also mentions later that in Kelvin's apartment, there are absolutely no pictures (a key part of the means of implanting memories in Scott's film). There are echoes too of another Scott film, *Alien* (1979), in references to a faceless "company" and more so perhaps *Aliens* (1986), directed by James Cameron (one of the producers of *Solaris*), in the disappearance of a military unit sent to investigate a mysterious signal from a spacecraft and a single individual who is asked for help partly because they have unique skills for this situation but also partly as therapy for themselves.

The strongest link with either of Scott's films is in the visual stylization, which reflects the emotional stasis of Kelvin at this point. It is a future that is cold and hard. The sound of Kelvin preparing his food echoes harshly around his flat, and the *Alien*-style tracking shots through the corridors of the Prometheus (the ship orbiting Solaris) are accompanied by an almost constant low hum of machinery. There are also evocations of *2001* (Stanley Kubrick, 1968) in the slow pacing, the elaborate docking sequence, lengthy shots of the Prometheus turning through space, and the philosophical consequences of interacting with nonhuman species. The colorful control panel lights reflected on Kelvin's visor as he looks out at Prometheus for the first time clearly evoke the "Stargate" sequence.

It is not until some way into the film that we actually see Kelvin address another character face-to-face. We see him on the phone leaving a message, then another phone conversation, but he is facing away from us and we hear only his minimal phrasing (nothing from his addressee). He speaks via an entry-phone screen to security personnel bringing the tape from Gibarian (Ulrich Tukur) asking for help, and pilots the ship alone, not even speaking to an on-board computer. Kelvin's first close-up, looking up at the video screen, shows his face drawn and eyes welling up slightly, as if on the verge of tears. On earth, he seems to lead a half-life, floating among ghosts, possibly driven by his grief or perhaps this is the default setting of human existence. At a bereavement self-help group, he might equally be the therapist or one of the clients. The status of his later flashbacks is suspect as they are subjective, appear in dreams, and apparently under the catalytic influence of Solaris. Cold blue-gray hues dominate the scenes on the Prometheus, contrasting with a warmer brown-orange color palette for the past back on earth, but such a rigid juxtaposition is blurred by sound bleeding across cuts, like Rheya's dialogue on voice-over and the steady hum of the spacecraft. Cliff Martinez's score uses an oriental instrumentation to suggest a sense of wonder, such as when we see Prometheus for the first time, and subsequently to signal a haunting sense of unease, heard at moments where Solaris seems to be exerting its greatest influence.

Once on Prometheus, the narrative appears to shift toward murder mystery, with Kelvin following unexplained trails of blood, and Soderbergh uses slightly shaky camera movement from Kelvin's point of view to emphasize the notion of a personalized subjective narrative. However, such movement, except for the brief chase of an unknown boy, soon gives way to characters sitting and talking. The swift shot of an unexplained blood print on the ceiling or the appearance of the boy do not motivate extended deductive reasoning because there is no explanation. The boy is supposedly Gibarian's child but might equally reflect Kelvin's own desire for a child, which was a key fault line in his relationship with Rheya.

Tzvetan Todorov's concept of the Fantastic, originally conceived in relation to Russian folktales, is sometimes applied to film studies, and is useful here as we are faced with something we cannot explain.[1] However, what Todorov terms a moment of "hesitation" cannot be extended indefinitely and gradually loses its ability to unsettle an audience as it seems that we will be denied a definitive category into which we might place our experience: it is neither scientifically explicable nor a religious vision. As Gibarian says, "There are no answers, only choices," which makes the vast body of the film into an extended moment of Todorovian hesitation and dramatically weakens its ability to hold the attention of viewers over time. A mystery will hold our attention only if we think it can be solved. Talking about it does not help as language seems redundant. The only solution seems to be submission. On questioning the senior physicist, Gordon (Viola Davis) curtails extended debate on events "until it happens to you," echoing the notion behind murder mysteries like George Sluizer's The Vanishing (1988) that you can understand an unknown phenomenon fully only by submitting yourself to it (also part of the Alien franchise).

Sleep seems to be the portal to perceiving creatures, or so-called visitors, that are human in appearance but come from a world beyond our experience, a more philosophical version of the lethal threat posed by Wes Craven's Freddy Krueger. However, at no point does any character articulate what this might mean about humanity, since the visitors are clearly reflections of the desires of the individuals they visit. In Kelvin's first dream, Soderbergh makes the transition from objective reality to a dreamscape by progressively cutting closer on Kelvin's sleeping head, intercut with shots of Solaris with electrical flashes like the synapses of a giant brain and subjective point-of-view shots from Kelvin. This happens without fictional markers indicating that we are entering a dream, like a wobbly screen, but the subsequent scenes with Rheya on a train make sense only as flashbacks to Kelvin's first glimpse of her. This attempt to show on-screen the thoughts of a character is reminiscent of Laurence Olivier's slow zoom into his own head, while delivering the "To be or not to be monologue" in *Hamlet* (1948). In the flashback, we tilt up from the subjective shot of Rheya holding what looks like a doorknob to a clear shot of her face. Such direct looks down the camera lens are used in several of the exchanges between Rheya and Kelvin, which intensifies the sense of a connection between them, excluding the world around them, although at the same time it complicates the consistency of viewpoint, since we also see through Rheya's eyes here.

The romance of Kelvin and Rheya, conveyed via flashback, is conveyed primarily by extended shots of her at a party from his point of view, including a shot of her walking away, juxtaposed with Gibarian's description of Solaris on the voice-over ("It's almost as if it knows we're observing it"), suggesting Rheya's coquettish nature. The snatches of dialogue we hear via voice-over might come from his flashback, from Rheya present in the room with him now, or the sense of an almost telepathic relationship, from either past or present. Soderbergh appears to enjoy playing with the viewer's sense of temporal disorientation. A conversation between Kelvin and Rheya in a later scene fades to black, a conventional marker for the end of a scene, but then fades into the same scene just a few seconds later like a very slow blink.

Rheya becoming increasingly paranoid that she cannot remember being present at her own memories is strongly reminiscent of Rachael (Sean Young) in *Blade Runner* as she gradually realizes that memory is key to what makes us fully human and that lacking this, she is a humanoid robot, a replicant in the language of the film, and Deckard's cajoling that he is only joking feels very like Kelvin's story here to Rheya that her increasing mental unease is just caused by fatigue. Rheya suggests that their continued existence is possible only if they both engage in a form of shared denial, "an unspoken understanding that I'm not really a human being." At the end, Kelvin (now apparently a visitor too) does have a picture of Rheya on his fridge, by implication to help his memory as he is "haunted by the idea that I remembered her wrong." Rheya suffers the existential nightmare of appearing to be immortal (her body restores itself after her suicide attempt) but knowing that she is not fully human either.

Solaris is more convincing as a philosophical provocation than a romantic narrative. The exploration of the concept of a second chance at love is compromised by Rheya's ambiguous status. Viewers cannot invest much emotional weight in the potentially engaging notion of living one's life over again and avoiding previous mistakes if the mechanism of this repetition is only delusional. Kelvin belittles Rheya's belief in "a higher form of consciousness" and lectures her that "we're a mathematical problem and that's that." Kelvin's memory of finding Rheya's body the first time, the crumpled poem held in her fist in in sharp focus, is intercut with his search for her on Prometheus. He finds her ready to submit herself to Gordon's destructive beam, and as Kelvin looks at her face on a monitor, we hear her voice before her lips start to move in synch, suggesting a blend of a fantasy in his head with what appears before his eyes. However, when she looks at Solaris, we cut to a memory of her buying a pregnancy kit, and later during a dinner table discussion, we see Kelvin from her point of view with the sound cut, representing her wish fulfillment. That is, we are witnessing a supposed projection having flashbacks of her own.

A rare moment of tension in the film appears when we cut back to a close shot of Kelvin asleep, in the same position as before but now touched by a female hand to which he does not instantly respond, but upon waking, he leaps from the bed in fear. He cannot bring himself to look at her, keeping his eyes downcast, fearful that she is a ghost or perhaps more fearful that she is real. He slaps himself hard and grabs a nearby piece of furniture before summoning the courage to look up, at which point the tears in his eyes convey a mixture of loss and fear in equal measure.

The visitors are reflections of how the characters remember them. Rheya had seemed suicidal to Kelvin, so that is how she reappears to him. However, in the intervening years since Tarkovsky's film, the notion that our memories can be manipulated and we are living inside some form of construct has been given cinematic expression in a number of ways, from the Philip K. Dick-inspired *Total Recall* (Paul Verhoeven, 1990) to the computer game reality of *eXistenZ* (David Cronenberg, 1999) to Peter Weir's media-controlled world in *The Truman Show* (1998) to the virtual world of *The Matrix* (the Wachowski brothers, 1999). Furthermore, the more precise concept of an alien entity reflecting back the desires of the humans with which it comes into contact has been expressed before in *Sphere* (Barry Levinson, 1998). The element of spectacle that some viewers might expect from a science fiction film is present only in shots of the ship orbiting around the planet and lengthy shots of Solaris itself. There are no action sequences, no explosions, no fights, and only a very small cast. Individual shot lengths are extended and often involve a character sitting or looking, i.e., not moving.

The ending, not in Lem's story, of Kelvin somehow living on with Rheya, both translated into visitors (signaled by his finger now miraculously healing from a cut, in contrast to the opening), might have some logic from within the film as we do not know how such visitors exist or whether they can die. However, it feels like a consoling coda, a romantic cliché, contrived to reflect the Dylan Thomas poem that Kelvin quotes on their first meeting ("Death Shall Have No Dominion") and added to palliate the bleak suggestion that all of our lives are only existential dreams. Perhaps too, this represents a limitation in Clooney's on-screen persona: the idea that a character he plays can crash and die at the close of a narrative is too bleak for most audiences to accept. We have a scene with Kelvin lying on the floor of Prometheus as it falls into the surface of Solaris, and from his point of view, he sees a blurred object approaching, which comes into focus as the small boy from earlier, supposedly Gibarian's son, and who, ET-like, puts out his hand. In close-up, the two hands meet, like a crude version of Michelangelo's fresco "The Creation of Adam," an image of the child that Kelvin was denied with Rheya.

Back in the kitchen on earth, Kelvin asks if he is alive or dead to which Rheya replies, "We don't have to think like that anymore" and "Everything we've done is forgiven," introducing an explicitly moral dimension, which has been largely absent up to this point, in a thinly veiled attempt at some Christian consolation in the narrative. Kelvin's sin (driving Rheya away) is followed by repentance, guilt and purgatory (his experiences on the ship), and redemption (his supposed existence on/in response to Solaris). The narrative explores different levels of grief, via all the characters, not only Kelvin. As Kelvin confronts Snow (Jeremy Davis) with the mystery of two dead crewmen and a further one having disappeared, Clooney's expression becomes slightly more wide-eyed and even slightly crazed as he visibly struggles to comprehend what he is experiencing.

Any potential coherence of cause and effect is broken by problematizing the distinction of reality and dream worlds. Films like *Inception* (Christopher Nolan, 2010), with similar narratives that question their own limits, have compensatory pleasures of special effects and spectacle, neither of which we have here. Stripped of Lem's passages of philosophy, our attention is focused instead on character and especially on Kelvin, who appears in almost every scene. Soderbergh makes this very much into a George Clooney vehicle, but unlike *Confessions* the idea that what we see could all be a subjective dream of the main character is never really picked up. Furthermore, without the sense of cause and effect, there is also little emotional development across the film, which has very few dramatic peaks (apart from Rheya's first appearance and her suicide, although the latter is fairly predictable). The climactic discovery of Rheya's departure from Prometheus or Kelvin's realization that he does not want to enter the escape capsule are accompanied by only some beads of sweat running down his face. This level of anguish is unlikely to be felt by the viewer who may resist the notion of an alien intelligence that acts in a way in which we cannot understand, for purposes we are not told.

Questions of narrative plausibility are not necessarily of paramount importance in a work of fiction. However, where the pacing is very slow, we may find it difficult to avoid considering that if Rheya is a projection of Kelvin's memory, it does not really explain why she is so needy, which she does not seem on their first meeting; why Snow advises Kelvin to lock his door when the visitors can apparently appear at will; why none of the crew, all scientists, suggest or even mention testing these visitors, especially Rheya, except for the convoluted machine that supposedly sends her back where she came from.

The strength (or brutality, depending on your point of view) with which he leads her to the airlock and flushes her into outer space, like human waste, makes his later inability to deal logically with her return seem unconvincing. He does turn away, crying, and we fade to black but he still does this. At this point, he knows and accepts that she is not real. However, later he behaves as if she is and wants to take her back to earth, although little explains this change. The revelation of the death of the real Snow at the hands of his visitor (the unexplained bloodstain from the beginning) would suggest these projections have desires and self-preservation instincts, which the film does not really explain or explore.

Soderbergh cuts down Tarkovsky's running time by a third. He increases the romantic interplay between his hero and projected wife, Rheya (an anagram of Lem's character, Harey), by showing us the key points in their courtship on earth via flashback. These are experienced once on the spaceship, which the hero reaches within the first 10 minutes rather than the 45+ that Tarkovsky takes to build mood and convey the dullness of space travel, of which viewers in 2002 are much more aware. The film, like Tarkovky's version, dramatizes the human dilemma that our knowledge of other people is really only a collection of our own impressions and memories, which we then project onto others.

According to Soderbergh, "*Solaris* required a complete dispersal of all the charm and good spirits that we normally associate with George," and that "it's really a nonverbal part. It's a completely interior performance."[2] However, the lukewarm critical reaction and even less enthusiastic commercial performance reflect, like the planet Solaris itself, what viewers desire and expect from science fiction. The two sightings of Clooney's naked butt originally gave the film an R rating, a commercial kiss of death, but this was reduced to PG-13 on appeal. Marketing played up the romantic and sexual element, but despite a budget of $47 million, *Solaris* drew only $16 million at the U.S. box office. Clooney is due to return to space in *Gravity* (Alfonso Cuarón, 2012) opposite Sandra Bullock, who narrowly missed being cast as Sisco in *Out of Sight*.

MICHAEL CLAYTON (TONY GILROY, 2007)

Henry Clayton: So no one's sure exactly where they are because there're no borders or landmarks or anything.

Clooney plays the title role, Michael Clayton, a troubleshooter at a New York law firm, called in to deal with problems great and small, a keeper of secrets but one who has no clearly defined role in the hierarchy of the company and is under extreme pressure when a top litigator, Arthur Edens (Tom Wilkinson), apparently goes crazy in a meeting, jeopardizing the huge class action case regarding U-North, a producer of agrochemicals.

The film opens with Arthur's call to Michael about his moment of sudden realization that he is "covered in filth" from his years of working for the odious law firm Kenner, Bach and Ledeen, symptomatic of corporate corruption and greed. As an opening monologue, before we have any real plot exposition, Arthur's speech (present from Gilroy's first draft) crackles with metaphoric energy, energized by Wilkinson's powerful delivery, building up to the climactic term "now." Like the later scene with the horses, it is a rare example of a stylistic choice that makes the audience work hard to consider the meaning of what they are experiencing and, in terms of the opening, underlines the script as more literary than we might expect.

The montage of the huge empty office counterpoints the speech well, visualizing the moral vacuum in which legal exploitation seems to operate with impunity. Like the opening of the main plot of David Fincher's *Zodiac*, released the same year, we enter an office space via a point of view from a mail cart. In Fincher's film, a letter from the killer energizes the plot; here it is the pursuit of a document (the incriminating Memo 229) and its ruthless suppression that slowly emerges as the element that holds various narrative threads together. The speech is replayed later in abbre-viated form, bleeding over footage of Michael flying to Milwaukee to meet Arthur and Karen Crowder (Tilda Swinton), their adversary, also arriving and organizing her strategy.

Crowder is first shown trying to subdue a panic attack, sweating and breathing heavily, slumped in a toilet cubicle, and reacting suddenly to the sound of footsteps. Gilroy is not asking the viewer to sympathize with her, but he does show the individual price that is being paid to sustain the monsters of corporate greed. All three of the main roles, Arthur, Crowder, and Michael, are on the verge of a nervous breakdown; the dif-ference is that only Arthur is clever enough to recognize this. When Crowder watches the tape of Arthur cracking up in a meeting and starting to rant and strip off his clothing, she stares wide-eyed with her hand to her mouth in genuine shock as this is exactly how she feels inside too. It is only the ritualistic practice of exact words before speaking in front of others, edging into obsessive-compulsive disorder symptoms, that allows her to function at all and keeps her from similar outbursts. Gilroy shows her stage-managed spontaneity by cross-cutting her practice with the actual delivery of the lines. The suggestion is that her whole life is a per-formance, and although we do not see her practice the lines she uses to Michael in the diner, the implication is that these are rehearsed as well. Gilroy bleeds words from Crowder's final speech across shots of her dress-ing, as if she is mentally practicing this performance too. At the end, when her edifice of lies crumbles, although left in the background and not the focus of our attention as Michael walks away from her, she physi-cally collapses forward, clutching her chest. Ironically, as she herself declares, if you are not ready for the huge amount of responsibility, "then you're in the wrong place," and ultimately Michael can prove that she is. We see little of her boss, but since his signature is on the document that Crowder is desperate to suppress and since she was his protégée for 12 years, we might assume he knows what she is like.

The first sight we have of Michael is a rotating shot around an impro-vised gambling table, part of an underground world, presumably for those leading unfulfilling lives elsewhere needing the adrenaline rush of risk or simply in financial difficulty. As the narrative progresses, we learn Michael has elements of both of these, swearing to his family that he has not gambled in months (clearly untrue). He has led a professional life clearing up other people's messes at a moment's notice, underlined by the hit-and-run episode, and receiving only a modest reward for that. He drives a Mercedes but it is leased; he owes a large sum of money from a failed business venture and has no easy way to pay. Through Crowder's associate we learn that Michael has voluntarily moved from criminal prosecution to wills and trusts and, despite having been with the firm for 13 years, is not a partner. According to Crowder's careerist logic, this does not make sense.

Their one and only meeting before the climax occurs at a restaurant, where Gilroy shows us an exchange of legal sparring, with Crowder lit from beneath, Michael from above, making her seem a little artificial and him calm and businesslike. His position is compassionate and understanding, focusing on the fact that Arthur's wife died recently, his daughter does not talk to him, and all he has worked on for the last six years is the U-North case. When Arthur last suffered a relapse, eight years ago, Michael claims he helped him and watched him get better, the kind of nurturing relationship of which Crowder seems incapable. By contrast, she steals Arthur's briefcase and rifles through its contents. As architect of the case defending the company, Crowder focuses purely on the damning evidence of Arthur's erratic behavior, and when she has made her points, she abruptly walks off, suggesting this was a rehearsed performance and that nothing Michael could have said would have made any difference.

Mr. Greer (Denis O'Hare), the unpleasant driver of the car, who is seeking every way to avoid responsibility for his culpability, is the first of several characters who directly ask Michael, "So what are you?" Crowder ("Who is this guy?"), Arthur (replying to Clayton's assertion that he is not the enemy, "then who are you?"), even his brother, all ask fundamentally the same question, which Michael himself has begun to wonder. To Greer he denies he is "a miracle worker," describing himself instead as "a janitor." There is a hint here of the Clooney from *One Fine Day*, allowing himself to show a slightly smug smile, although generally he does act in a measured, courteous tone with informed comment under provocation. We have a shot of several seconds with Michael just standing and looking at Greer, waiting for his bluster to blow itself out. When the phone rings, Greer jumps; Michael does not. He is calm under pressure and simply points out when his client asks if it is the police, "No, they don't call."

His car accelerates away from the house as if he is keen to place maximum distance between himself and the system of which he is a part. Approaching a junction, Michael signals left and then suddenly pulls right. At this stage there is no explanation given; we can only assume that what he should go back to (office or home life) has little attraction for him.

The episode with the horses is a direct challenge to the viewer. Michael pulls to a stop before he sees the horses, so he is not drawn by a sight of natural beauty. He does not know why he stops, why he approaches the horses on the hillside, and why they do not run away. It is only in retrospect, after the scene with the book, that we might feel that Michael has in some measure apprehended something of Arthur's feelings about the world, and in following his lead (Arthur is very interested in the book), it saves his life. The single horse of the book is replaced by the three on the hill (possibly linked to Michael as one of three brothers), shown lined up, sideways on, and he approaches the animals apparently in a state of driven curiosity. The episode is clearly important (we are shown it twice after all), and each time we see shots of Michael looking down the road behind him on getting out of the car as if he is afraid of being followed. There is no music, dialogue, or voice-over in the scene, no cues for viewers, just the sound of his breath in the air and a close-up on Clooney's mournful face, prefiguring what Arthur says later about the carrying of "a burden." The second time the horse scene is replayed, shots of Michael are accompanied by choral music and he momentarily glances up, suggesting a man who is looking for spiritual redemption.

Clooney himself was not well at the time, and although not contrived deliberately, the weight loss adds to his sense of being haunted. Handheld camera movement follows Michael up the hill, at times from slightly behind him, so we have the horses in shot. At the top of the hill, twice we have an angle down the hill with horses on the right foreground, Michael in the midground and car far away in the background, all in shot simultaneously. There is a moment of silent communication in which Gilroy does not cut suddenly but rotates around his subject slowly, first almost from the horse's point of view looking at Michael and then the reverse angle, up the hill. There is at least one full minute of screen time from starting up the hill to the car exploding, provoking Michael's look of bemused concern before running down the hillside. He is drawn by a force he does not recognize or understand and this specifically saves his life, as if he has a destiny to fulfill in bringing down Crowder and her boss and the explosion gives him the means to do this, creating a false death. Gilroy also scripted the *Bourne* movies, and here we have a car chase of sorts, although Michael seems unaware that he is being pursued, and an explosion, shown twice, but that is motivated by character rather than the pleasures of spectacle.

Gilroy wrote several pages of the fictional novel *Realm and Conquest* (which also appears as a screensaver near the opening of the film), and in collaboration with the production designer, Kevin Thompson, the prop was given the look of verisimilitude with Expressionist-style illustrations. We never see explicit sections of text, and the connection with the scene with the horses is implied rather than crudely spelled out, but

Gilroy's own son apparently likes such books and games and is a means by which the two communicate. It may also allude to debates around the status of Deckard (Harrison Ford) as a replicant in *Blade Runner*, in part informed by a dream sequence, originally deleted but reappearing in the director's cut, where we see a section of another Scott film, *Legend* (1985), and the appearance of a mythical unicorn (linked with the foil creatures that Gaff [Edward James Olmos] makes, suggesting he controls Deckard's thoughts).

There is an explicit link between Clayton's son, Henry, and Arthur as we overhear a strange, illicit nighttime phone call, where the two seem to connect at a philosophical level. Arthur is a pseudo-father figure here, listening in a way that Michael was not earlier in the car when the boy tried to tell him about the book. Arthur is an avid listener. The key point here is the aspect of the game in which a group of characters are drawn to a place "as if they've been summoned" because they have experienced a shared dream (of which they are unaware). This is the force drawing Michael to the field, that he shares the dream of Arthur, of a fairer, more just society, and thereby rejects the life and the lifestyle he has led up to this point. Arthur later uses the term "summoned" to Michael in the hotel room, attempting to explain what he has learned from the boy's book. Whether left deliberately for Michael to find in Arthur's flat or not, the book contains the receipt for the copies of the incriminating memo and the picture of the horses.

Like the lingering shots of Clooney as Bob walking toward the camera in *Syriana*, we have a lengthy shot of Michael walking through his empty work environment, carrying his own bags to a plane with apparently no other passengers. He is a principled individual, framed alone, battling institutional forces of corruption, but is also part of that system. In terms of dress, he seems to be dominated by dark, sober colors that give him almost a funereal air. Crowder is also framed alone (at the gym, in an elevator, and entering a building) but she cannot connect with people like Michael does. He can also be a very charming people person, as when on the phone instructing his young legal team in Milwaukee succinctly but sensitively. He passes an envelope to the man who has been looking after Arthur, offering him tickets to a game if he is ever in New York. He knows how to make low-level corruption and diplomacy work in a spontaneous and interactive way, which we never see Crowder manage.

Gilroy's script links a number of elements. Some are obvious, like the boy's description of a game in which you can be talking to someone who turns out to be your "mortal enemy," which Michael notes "sounds familiar" but is exemplified in the apparently friendly knock at Arthur's door later. Other links are a little more subtle. Clayton's son sarcastically informs his mother that he has had breakfast even though there are no waffles with "It's a miracle" (like his father, he is something of a charming "miracle worker"). In the game, "all the people are hiding in the woods to try and stay alive," which will be Michael's fate shortly after his car explodes. Michael sees the boy off to school with the order to "teach these people something," but the boy does actually have knowledge, which first Arthur values and implicitly Michael comes to understand, if not at the level of conscious comprehension. The man to whom Michael owes money refers to an alcoholic wife as being "like strapped to a bomb" (reminding us of Michael's car). Clayton describes Arthur as "a killer" in the sense of possessing a brilliant legal mind but he will fall victim to unscrupulous men for whom this term is literally true.

Given Michael's clear expertise (demonstrated in the hit-and-run sequence) and the fact that he is in such demand (on call at any time of night), it seems strange that he is in such a financial position. His strained personal and family life and his disastrous restaurant investment all build pressure on him, but the main problem is the lack of precise professional identity, coupled to his effectiveness for an abusive system. When Marty (Sydney Pollack) explains later that he has created a niche, it should be one, given the logic of the system he is in, that pays well. The idea that someone who solves problems for others so well should be fallible in their personal life is a cliché of the detective genre, but that they should be so financially exposed seems unlikely. Gambling is a symptom of his unease with his life rather than the explicit cause of it. The roles that he plays in his job, charming health workers around Arthur, frightening Mr. Greer with facts about police procedure, or holding the phone away from his head for a second while he says he will fetch a pen (although he is already holding one)—all these are just part of his everyday life. Like Miles Massey he is dealing with super-rich clients, but unlike Massey here, as he says to Mr. Greer, there is "no play here, no angle, no champagne room." The stakes are real.

Michael's brother, Timmy (David Lansbury), is an alcoholic who has wrecked the early life of his son but who Michael eventually comes back to as a source of help after he has been supposedly killed by the bomb. His older brother, Gene (Sean Cullen), helps with the final sting operation on Crowder and his final words to Michael, "stay close," underline that family ultimately comes through. Gene underscores Michael's confused identity, in which "all these cops think you're a lawyer" while "all these lawyers thinking you're some kind of cop." He concludes with "You know exactly what you are" but that may not be entirely true.

The security of Michael's whole position relies on superior knowledge. This also means people keep their distance and also underlines his weakness when a lack of knowledge arises (over the impending merger for example). He is not losing his touch but he was never part of an inner circle to be kept abreast of changes. A deleted scene would have shown us a postcoital chat with Brini Glass (Jennifer Ehle), which shows how important he is to the company but would also underline weakness in Michael, in a relationship that is not really more than a stopgap and in which he parades his knowledge about a client (something he never does in the finished film).

The film is full of lengthy two-shots, mostly involving Michael, where actors deliver meaty dialogue in powerful exchanges, interspersed with wider shots or slower panning or rotating movements, such as Arthur and Michael in the cell or later in the alley. In the cell, Gilroy holds the shot on Michael as Arthur rambles on, the anger building as Michael is repeatedly interrupted. His anxious glances outside might convey fear that they are overheard or that their time together will be used up before he has had a chance to speak. When he does get a chance, we realize the frustration is due to Arthur coming off medication, something he had promised not to do. In the alleyway, we have a clear demonstration that "it's not just madness" as Arthur had scrawled on the wall before leaping out of his hotel window. Arthur says he has needed time "to gather my thoughts," to which Michael asks, "How's that going?" We may have a man acting irrationally, carrying a bag with far too many baguettes for one person to eat, but at a moment's notice he demonstrates precise knowledge of the law relating to mental health in the state of New York. It is a good example of an exchange with the minimum of intrusive camerawork, just two great actors delivering powerful lines.

Arthur's speech about the culpability of U-North bleeds across shots of the killers listening in after tapping his phone, and his comment "the last place you want to see me is in court" ironically seals his fate, so that this speech constitutes his summary to a jury we never get to hear. The brutal murder of Arthur, from the knock on the door to his final heartbeat, is all one take, with just a slow zoom in to his foot to show the lethal injection in more detail and only a couple of whispered instructions between the men. With a single hand-held camera we follow the administering of an electric shock at the door, to something being put in Arthur's mouth, to his being carried into the bathroom, to the injection and his pulse taken twice: all within 90 seconds. The killers, Verne and Iker, are described in the script as "flooding in ... like machines" in a bizarre mix of the solicitous (catching Arthur as he falls, carrying him quickly and efficiently, wearing gloves, surgical boots, and even hairnets) and the murderous, with a final irony in the comment, "We're good."[3]

After Michael's brief sight of Timmy, Gilroy initially uses a backseat camera position (a little like that used by Soderbergh for the jeep ride in *The Good German*) with the two passengers, Michael and Henry, in the dead space of the frame. Gilroy shows Michael in close-up, chewing, giving a slight shake of the head as if anger is building up, which eventually bursts out and he pulls over to talk. For all the rhetoric and all the bluster, however, there is an underlying desperation to his assertion that Henry is tougher than Timmy, and the statement "that's not how it's gonna be for you" seems more his worry than the boy's, who just looks back at him bemused. Michael's marriage may have failed, he may not listen closely to the boy's prattle in the car or look at the book he had been given, but he is passionate that his son should have a better life. Michael is only just holding on here. His hug of Marty at the unofficial wake in the bar that follows is held slightly longer than Marty expects, and his repetition "I know it" underlines that he does not know anything anymore and the death of Arthur is a real shock.

The narrative structure, rerunning the section from the gambling den onward, suggests that we, like Clayton, do not know as much about the world around us as we think. Now, we glimpse the man just getting away from the car in time to plant the bomb, we realize why the SAT-NAV does not function properly, and we understand that the stress of Crowder at this point is less connected with speech than with her second assassination, this one very overt. Michael's subsequent appearance to Crowder, a dead man inexplicably resurfacing, has elements of a ghostly visitation and of Tom Sawyer attending his own funeral.

However, he does not walk into the arms of his brother but past him, away from the life he knows but toward what, we can only guess. If his knowledge-based role had set him apart from his colleagues, to have sabotaged even that role leaves him completely isolated, even if morally vindicated. His mournful expression here also contains anger and frustration, seeming closer to breaking down in a way far more justified than *Solaris* or *Syriana*. Like his speeding away from Greer's house, he declares to his brother to whom he hands the phone, "I need some air."

The final shot, a nice way to encourage cinema audiences to stay in their seats and read the credits, and our last view of Michael, is not akin to the fist-thumping elevation of a *Rocky*-style narrative; we are not celebrating the victory of the underdog. Rather we are closer to the end of *The Long Good Friday* (John Mackenzie, 1980), where gangland boss Harold Shand (Bob Hoskins) is shown also in the backseat of a car, albeit at gunpoint, and we see a similar range of emotions (self-loathing, resignation, and grief) pass over his face and do not need to see the end of either journey to realize that both men are, to some extent, broken. Clayton has been brought to the realization articulated by Arthur at the beginning. He has become Arthur's heir, "Shiva, the god of death," bringing down two of the most immoral figures that he works with but many, and the system that produced and supported them, still remain. He has betrayed the company that just lent him $80,000, which they will no doubt want back, the basis of his trade (trust) may be lost by his openly acting as a whistle-blower, and there is no clear sign of how he can function professionally as he is still caught between the legal and criminal worlds, fitting securely in neither. His instruction to the driver (an uncredited vocal contribution by Gilroy himself) to just drive suggests this aimlessness.

Michael Clayton has a slight feel of conspiracy theories like Alan J. Pakula's *The Parallax View* (1974), in its depiction of faceless corruption and a willingness to kill anyone to maintain economic (and political) power. In *Michael Clayton*, it is not a matter of a corporation having to seek out alternative criminal worlds for the assassins. We see Verne and Iker at the golf course, sporting U-North logos on their bags. They are the company. On the film poster, the *X-Files*-style slogan ("The truth can be adjusted") is more central and in larger font than the title of the movie itself and placed over a slightly blurred image of Michael.

Clooney originally rejected the role, deterred by Gilroy as a first-time director, but the status of the producers here (Soderbergh, Pollack, and Anthony Minghella) is very impressive, reflecting the strength of their belief in Gilroy's script and his ability to realize it on-screen.

Legendary scriptwriter William Goldman described Clooney as "giving the performance of his career," and certainly there is a strongly mournful, elegiac quality to the film, largely implicit in Michael's character and brought out in Clooney's delivery of it.[4] As a fixer, he solves people's problems, taking their guilt away, a role performed by priests in former times. As Arthur says to him about the "burden" such work creates, he is a social purger of sins, a role that takes a toll on his own soul in the carrying of knowledge about the sins of others. The role works only if he keeps this knowledge and does not pass it on, but to keep it exacts a heavy price, etched on his careworn features.

THE AMERICAN (ANTON CORBIJN, 2010)

> Keeler: It is like entering a different time zone. You're an outsider, isolating yourself. You're condemned ... You have become mere sadness and live in a different state of mind.
>
> —*Confessions of a Dangerous Mind*

The opening prologue in Sweden sets the stylistic markers found in the body of the film. Our first sight of Jack (George Clooney) shows him sitting forward, unsmiling, drinking whisky, next to a naked girl, Ingrid (Irina Björklund). It may be a theoretically romantic cliché with an isolated situation, a log cabin, and a roaring fire, but Jack's look of melancholy and need for tense shoulders to be massaged suggest he is not at ease. Handheld, shaky point-of-view shots, like the slow tracking shot toward the cabin, suggest the presence of a would-be assassin but there is no attack on them at this point (denying us an action-based opening such as in *The Spy Who Loved Me*, Lewis Gilbert, 1977). Similarly, as Jack subsequently outsmarts the second killer, circling behind him, we have a point-of-view shot from behind the car but this is not immediately followed by Jack's surprise attack. We are denied viewing positions that can be easily identified simply with an antithetical force, creating a sense of unease from the outset. The editing pace is leisurely, almost ponderous (Jack is held in shot, motionless, staring out from the car ferry for 10 seconds), action scenes are shown in long or extreme long shot (there is no cutting to close-ups for dramatic effect), and there is little or no use of a soundtrack to heighten the drama of physical action.

As a character, Jack is also far from simple. For the first time, we see Clooney play a character that shoots an apparently innocent girl (with whom he had some form of relationship), and yet via a blend of performance, direction, and script his character retains an element of viewer sympathy. It is not until he meets Clara (Violante Placido) that he addresses another character face-to face at length. He avoids direct eye contact where possible, denying himself the kinds of human contact that he knows his chosen profession makes impossible to sustain. As Pavel (Johan Leysen) tells him, "Don't make any friends." However, either by luck or simply that others respond to a need they feel in him, other characters do reach out to him, most obviously the priest, Father Benedetto (Paolo Bonacelli). Invited to the priest's house, Jack sits at a table with him but does not look at him; and in making contact with Mathilde (Thekla Reuten), the pair sit at adjacent tables at an outdoor café again avoiding direct glances. The opening credits, played out over a lengthy shot as Jack drives down a road tunnel, suggest a shadowy character whose destiny is set on a particular course.

Once in Castel del Monte, Corbijn takes this a stage further with a large number of tightly framed shots of Jack, often from directly behind him, which might be the point of view of an assassin about to stab him in the back, but since Jack frequently twirls around as he walks, it suggests the presence of an entity, closely following, almost like a notion of con-science. The geography of the town is never made clear. Jack approaches his small apartment from different routes, and in several scenes we see him walking at night shot from in front and behind with tight shots that do not allow us to see clearly where he is going or whether he is being followed. From the first time he walks through the town in daylight, the narrow medieval streets, blind corners, and steps that seem to go back on themselves form a visual fabric like an Escher picture, creating a Kafkaesque, paranoid sense of being watched and followed. This creates ambiguity from the outset, like the backfiring scooter, before it is clear there are specific assassins seeking to kill Jack. As the pressure mounts, we have a slowly rotating top-shot above the rooftops of the town, still denying us a sense of precise geography, and cut with a soaring bird of prey, suggesting the gathering of forces against him.

Corbijn's former profession surfaces not just in his picture composition or the choice of photographer as an alibi for Jack but in the numerous spectacular long shots of Castel del Monte, sometimes at night or with mist rolling in. There are many, many shots of a single car winding through the landscape, mostly in extreme long shot, both day and night, emphasizing just how alone Jack is but also creating something of the cold aesthetic of car commercials or pictures used for calendars. This is reflected in the tie-in publication, *Inside the American* (2010), which showcases Corbijn's extraordinary eye for minor detail and the relation-ship of framing and available light.

Gradually, through glimpses of his tattoo, the book that he drops on waking, and the nickname given him oddly by both Clara and Mathilde ("Mr. Butterfly"), suggesting some kind of link between them, we realize that Jack does have an interior life, albeit one starved of the oxygen of human contact. He takes Mathilde to the riverside spot as much for its nature as for the isolation it affords them. The romantic connotation in the notion of a riverside picnic is destroyed by his profession. On dropping Mathilde back at the station, she thanks him for a lovely day at which his head drops. This is the best he seems able to hope for. A beautiful woman and a romantic setting (opportunity and motivation in crime terms) are not enough. He is suppressing his need for human contact and we see its toll on his spirit, writ large in his careworn face and tears welling up.

At dinner, he buys Clara a rose, which she says make them look like a couple, at which Herbert Grönemeyer's piano theme cuts in (used relatively sparingly throughout) to underline that, as Jack tears up again, he realizes that they can never be like that. His profession makes him suspect everyone, poisoning relationships so that he imagines Clara is carrying a gun to kill him, leading to the tense scene by the river and destroying its potential for romance. The first time the scene was spoiled by the presence of active evil, the second time by the suspicion of evil, and the third and final time because it arrives too late for Jack to exploit.

Clooney appears in virtually every scene. With a relatively small cast, the appearance of other characters matters only as they relate to him, almost as aspects of his own personality. We are offered some new sides to his film persona. His naked torso is seen performing press-ups, chin-ups, and some impressive stretching exercises. His body here seems functional rather than in condition to be looked at. He also has a previously unseen profession: not just that of killer but of gun maker. Despite protesting the contrary, Father Benedetto notes that Jack is good with machines, perhaps in lieu of human contact. The speed with which he manages to find useful components from the junk in the garage of Benedetto's son, Fabio, may stretch credibility, but Corbijn's cropped shots suggest Jack's hands almost act independently of his body in weighing the suitability of various tools and spare parts.

We also have the longest love scene in the Clooney canon in an extremely erotic encounter with Clara. As elsewhere, Corbijn refuses to cut to close-ups but allows his actors to pass out of shot before coming back, remaining focused for the most part on Clara's face, as she appears to be enjoying what Jack is doing. He says afterward that she does not have to act with him and that he just wants her "to be exactly who you are," which suggests both that he is tired of the phoniness of his life but also that her show of pleasure was in some measure faked. The morality of her job does not seem to trouble him, even when she says she is carrying a gun because she is scared of being attacked (there have been attacks on prostitutes nearby) and she must work that night; i.e., she is sleeping with other men for money while appearing to be in love with him. He claims earlier that he does not visit other women, reflecting an oddly chivalrous view of fidelity, but is apparently relaxed about her not doing the same. Perhaps his attitude to her job and her name, suggesting clarity, is suggestive of a forgiving nature, interested in souls more than physical actions.

It is clearly a tale of sin and redemption, most obviously in the dawn exchange between Jack and the priest but from the outset too in the cross seen in the foreground of the shot of Castel del Monte, the priest looking down benevolently above Jack as he walks down the steep alleyways for the first time and the doleful bell that punctuates the narrative. However, Jack does not heed the call to prayer, using the bell sound to cover his action in hammering a part of the gun he is making. At the moment he finishes the gun and later the fake briefcase, he lays his hands on it in an act of apparent blessing or finds a moment of peace. Unlike Father Benedetto, who crosses himself before eating, this small act suggests Jack finds the possibility of grace in his everyday actions, as if his body is instinctively looking for spiritual peace, even if he does not consciously recognize it. By the end despite being offered the chance to confess and purge his soul, Jack bypasses orthodox religion, noting earlier "I don't think God's very interested in me." Looking down at Mathilde as she lies dying from the rifle misfire he instigated, it is he who administers a form of the last rites, demanding who she works for. In his naiveté, he still has not realized the source of his betrayal (or in some sense is in denial). His redemption is in the form of preventing an assassination by sabotaging the rifle, killing his betrayer (Pavel), but most of all struggling to meet Clara by the river.

With overtones of a cleansing baptism, his angrily thumping the steering wheel reflects the frustration of the timing. He finds someone whom he can love and who loves him at exactly the point that his past catches up with him. Just as Clara treads on the bullets discarded from the scene trying out the rifle, so he cannot escape his past. Whether he likes it or not, he is a product of his history. He has tried to live solely in the present but he cannot. However, the fact that he can appreciate such fragile beauty in his love of butterflies among the brutality of a world of killing (albeit partly at his instigation) suggests that he still has the capacity for redemption. Corbijn pans away from Jack's actual moment of death and focuses on a nearby tree upon which a butterfly (his soul perhaps) seems to be fluttering. As Jack noted earlier, the creature, like his state of grace, is "endangered."

Corbijn, in interviews, makes much of the attempt to follow the basic structure of a western, and certainly there are elements here, particularly of the spaghetti westerns of figures like Sergio Leone, like the rugged landscape, the presence of a stranger in town who must atone for past sins of living by violence, a hero torn between the demands of the flesh (the prostitute) and the spirit (the priest), a final shoot-out, as well as a leisurely shot length and pace of narrative action. Sitting alone in a bar,

Leone's classic western, *Once upon a Time in the West* (1968), is on-screen, at the point where the killer, Frank (Henry Fonda), callously shoots an innocent small boy just because he heard a name. It is a reminder of the forces that are gathering against Jack but also of his own callous murder of Ingrid. He will have to atone for his sins as a killer too (also at the hands of a fellow assassin who arrives by train like the characters in the Leone film).

However, we do not have the exchange of direct looks that Leone is also famous for, there is minimal backstory, and in a sense the nationality of Jack is not central (Rowan Joffe's script changes him from the Englishman in Martin Booth's 1990 novel, *A Very Private Gentleman*). It is the state of his soul that is paramount. Whereas most westerns make it clear exactly what is being fought over, here the relative scarcity of narrative information converts Jack's increasingly paranoid existence into an existential drama. As Father Benedetto sees, Jack is in a hell of his own making in which he destroys everything he comes into contact with, which is why he does not tell Clara his secret so that she remains spiritually pure, despite her profession, and why he is attracted to butterflies as the sole symbol of fragile beauty and potential metamorphosis in his world. This is change at a profound level, not the kind symbolized by Mathilde's changing hairstyle at every meeting.

Most powerfully, in the final sequence as he struggles to control the car despite being wounded, Clooney's face manages to capture not just physical pain but the spiritual pain of having his final chance of happiness snatched away from him at the last. It makes the manner of his death deeply tragic, and the riverside location, the place Clara terms "paradise," gains its fullest meaning from his final entrance, his hand raised in greeting.

Although *The American* might seem a watershed in Clooney's acting, reflecting a more somber, elegiac mood in which a sense of sorrow and loss infects the present, this is present in earlier work too. Personal grief in *Solaris* is partly modulated into political grief in *Syriana* at the corrosion of principles to religious grief here. From the opening shot where Clooney is slumped by the bed to his car scene with Clara after the picnic, he is framed looking down and needing the physical (and apparently spiritual) comfort of another. He is a lost soul, one who can maintain his body via exercise—it is his weapon after all—but who cannot gain any mental peace. This is present even in apparently minor scenes, such as his dinner with the priest, where we see Jack toying with a small crucifix and a version of "Madam Butterfly" is being sung in the background.

Cinematic trailers played up the action scenes, and with the dominant icon on posters and DVD cases being Jack in midstride, carrying a gun, the impression is of an action thriller. However, in this the film was mis-represented, in part contributing to some audience disappointment. The film is a study of the interior price paid by one man's soul for the sinful life he has led. Guns are present, but even in the scenes where they are assembled, they are not fetishized (the riverside scene where Mathilde puts the rifle together focuses on Jack's reaction, and the assembly process is conveyed almost entirely by sound effects).

Corbijn and Clooney wanted to keep to the agreed location despite the earthquake in the region in Abruzzo five months before shooting was due to begin, in order to help support regeneration efforts. It is hard not to see Clooney the man here, at home in Italian cafés, being able to understand the language around him, watching and attracting the attention of beau-tiful young women. When he smiles and invites Clara for a coffee (or, in a deleted scene, she offers him a strong coffee to ease his shoulder pain), the crossover into a Nespresso commercial is almost complete. For the Italian public, familiar with Clooney's commercials for Fastweb and Fiat along-side his film career, allowing him great wealth, a luxurious home, and global fame, he personifies the possibilities of American life.

CONCLUSION

Clooney's breakdown at the end of Alexander Payne's *The Descendants* (2011) may seem new, but that level of emotional complexity has been present in his performances reaching back as far as *Solaris* (2002), through *Michael Clayton* (2007), *Syriana* (2008), *Up in the Air* (2010), and *The American* (2010). Chris Kelvin, Michael Clayton, Bob Barnes, Ryan Bingham, Jack in *The American*, even Harry Pfarrer in *Burn after Reading*—all of these characters are inches away from mental collapse. Perhaps reflect-ing this growing sense of interiority, *The Descendants* uses voice-over exten-sively, like Payne's *About Schmidt* (2002) (and in the early sections of *Up in the Air*), which is perhaps justifiable initially given the amount of backstory about the legal question of the land as well as following the first person nar-rative of the source text, but it may still seem intrusive to some viewers.

Based on the debut 2008 novel of Kaui Hart Hemmings (the author can be glimpsed in a cameo as Clooney's secretary), *The Descendants* manages to tread a very delicate balance between mawkish sentimentality as absent father Matt King (Clooney) has to return to Hawaii to deal with a comatose wife and a fragmented family. Although it may seem that we are seeing a brand-new side to Clooney's art, his character, unequal to the pressures of fatherhood mixed with a subtle mix of grief and anger at his wife (whom he discovers was adulterous), is evolutionary rather than revolutionary. Like *Michael Clayton* and *Syriana*, he is a father distanced from his children by marital breakdown and the demands of a particular career, respectively. Tearfulness in earlier work develops into open crying both at discovering the name of his wife's lover and at her bedside at the end, in an outburst of grief that perhaps excuses some of his character's decisions elsewhere (the island trip in particular).

What is new here is the gender balance: he is father to teenage girls. Far from his usual predominantly male environment (*Ocean's, Three Kings, Perfect Storm*) he must struggle to understand not just his own flesh and blood but the female side of his family (his wife included). What is also new is that, apart from parodies like *Collinwood*, this is the first time we have seen him play a character lacking expertise. Unlike Clayton, Kelvin, or Jack in *The American*, we do not see professional competence, only a private insecurity in coping with two wayward daughters, Scottie (Amara Miller) and elder sister Alexandra (Shailene Woodley). He describes himself as "the backup parent," and part of the muted comedy and dramatic pleasure comes from the understudy being thrown into the main role with minimal preparation, especially in scenes between Matt and Alex, who has a greater sense of the reality behind the façade of their family bonds.

Unlike his measured exercise regime in *The American*, we see him running breathlessly in flip-flops (in a scene added from the novel and with a close-up of his distraught face): he is not in physical, familial, or emotional control. Like Ryan in *Up in the Air*, family life has continued without him. He is forced to catch up fast on the emotional nuances of relationships he has neglected to find a place for, not just within the family but in relation to his past and potential future. This latter point is implicit in the final decision to keep the land; but also perhaps there is an element of Matt as a calculating lawyer, refusing to sell to a Hollitzer, since Speer, Hollitzer's brother-in-law, would benefit from the deal. There is almost a road movie element in that the family, together with Alex's boyfriend Sid (Nick Krause), takes a trip, ostensibly to help heal emotional wounds but also to allow Matt to confront his wife's lover, Brian Speer (Matthew Lilliard). This ulterior motive diminishes Matt as a caring father, prepared to drag his children into a marital dispute. As a rich lawyer, Matt King is an urban animal out of his usual element, signaled by shift from business suit to Hawaiian shirt, although the use of the landscape remains an urban version of paradise, i.e., a lived form of a popular ideal. Hemmings's novel does not feature any specific physical description of Matt's appearance, allowing for some debate over Clooney's casting but also giving him freedom in interpreting the role.

Ironically, before the film went into production, in one of the early hospital scenes in the book, Scottie wears a T-shirt emblazoned with the words "Mrs Clooney."

All of the films in this chapter require a shock to a middle-aged male living a financially comfortable existence, often administered by a collision with a spiritual or emotional loss experienced outside the character's usual environment (a space station in *Solaris*, a hillside in *Michael Clayton*, and a small picturesque Italian town in *The American*). Clooney seems increasingly comfortable with portraying characters on the edge of emotional breakdown and even sanity at times. There is no other actor in contemporary Hollywood who so powerfully articulates masculinity in crisis but with enough wit and humor to carry mass audiences with him.

CHAPTER 9

Time for a Commercial Break: "What Else?"

As an actor with a very distinctive voice, Clooney is often in demand for work where audiences only hear him. I have discussed his contribution to *Fantastic Mr. Fox* elsewhere, but in terms of commercials, Clooney has starred in TV and radio ads for Arthur Andersen, AT&T, British Airways, and Budweiser among many others.[1] He has been criticized for making commercials at the same time as speaking out on humanitarian issues, but it is a charge that could be leveled at many actors. Even before the soap opera developed in the 1930s via short radio adverts, commerce and mass media have been closely entwined. It is hardly a sign of the corruption of contemporary culture. More interesting is exactly what Clooney does in the adverts and how they work with or against his star image.

MARTINI (2000)

"No Martini, no party"

The ad opens with a fantasy set, filled only with attractive women dancing by a pool. Clooney, playing himself, rings the bell but is not allowed in with the closing slogan, "No Martini, no party." Playing against his romantic image, he is rejected in a series of variations on the same theme. There is even a closing shot of him at the door with cases of Martini and a clichéd wordless popping of a cork. "Night over Manaus" by Boozoo Bajou reflects the shift to sophisticated lounge music and music channels like Deluxe, aimed at a slightly older demographic than MTV. We occupy the space outside the door as Clooney is rejected and his surprise is registered by looking down.

A subsequent ad shows Clooney downstairs from a noisy party, disturbing the mood he is hoping to create with a woman whose glasses (and by implication, much else besides) he is about to remove. Going upstairs, he walks around collecting drinks from partygoers like an overzealous waiter in reverse, before delivering the familiar "No Martini, no party" punch line, now with the ring of a punishment about it. However, before he seems too much of a killjoy, he switches the music from pop to classical, suggesting a slightly more mature persona.

"BELLISSIMO" (2007)

Like a later Nespresso ad, there is a false element of tension here as the two leads (Clooney and Shannyn Sossamon) both make for the last serving of the product at a party as if their lives depend on it, although there is clearly more available. She takes the more direct route while he has flashbulbs going off in his face. Although she is walking through fountains in slow motion, the element of glamor is undercut by the statue that appears to be peeing on her and also Clooney's absurd expressions and his final gestures for her to wipe her face on the handkerchief he gives her. Although supposedly set by the sea, this is a parody of the excesses of a Hollywood party.

As someone known to have a home and an interest in Italy, the idea of Clooney as a fake Italian fits with his image well. With the fake moustache, the exaggerated facial expressions, and the delivery of the single word "Bellissimo," he comes across like a wannabe Casanova, still struggling with the language. It also reflects Clooney's vain character of Miles Massey in *Intolerable Cruelty* and McGill (with a similar moustache) in *O Brother*. Clooney seems happy to mock his own image: a monographed "G" is briefly visible on his handkerchief.

"EL TORO" (2007)

Clooney plays the same character again, here identified as a film star, named as "Giorgio" in a large poster, at a film festival, greeted by screaming fans at a premiere or an after-show party. However, the sense of glamor is undercut by some fairly crude humor: lacking ice cubes, Leonor Varela dressed as a matador provides two by cutting an undisclosed part from an ice sculpture of a bull. Culturally, there is some conflation of stereotypes here since Varela's costume and the title point to a Spanish theme and yet the name "Giorgio" is Italian. The music is provided by Mark Mothersbaugh's band, Mutato Muzika, who had contributed to *Collinwood*, and Mothersbaugh would go on to score *Fantastic Mr. Fox*. Like "Bellissimo," this is shot in black-and-white (except for the product), features only a single word at the end ("Magnifico"), and is more a carefully choreographed example of melodramatic pastiche.

In a further Martini commercial, in brilliant color, we see Clooney running out of gas on his speedboat and having to choose between rescue and giving up a case of Martini, at which point we cut to the final shot of him marooned with the Martini by his side. Clooney is playing a less exaggerated version of himself here, running out of gas on a date cliché of running out of gas transferred to the life of a Hollywood star with unnamed female beauty attached. Rather than keeping his boat (and the girl), this hero chooses the product.

EMIDIO TUCCI (2003)

Clooney shows his sartorial side here, donning a light suit for a change and definitely outside his usual color range: a light brown, with matching tie and shoes. His character is seen approaching a house, apparently guarded by burly bodyguards. Climbing a fire escape and hopping across a roof and in through a window, he meets the object of his quest (his mother), whom he presents with flowers. Clooney here blends his persona as master spy, deftly able to avoid detection, but also associations of an honorable son, who still has time for his mother (particularly important in Mediterranean culture perhaps). He even has time for a telltale nod down the lens at the viewer at the end.

An earlier ad (2002) shows him playfully riding a bicycle backward and forward on a seaside promenade while performing various feats of balance. The more daring moves in longer shot look like a stunt double, but tighter shots are Clooney himself. Like the later Nespresso ad, the voice-over lists adjectives, ambiguously referring to both the product and Clooney's persona in endorsing them: elegant, natural, distinctive, attractive, with character. The pseudo-martial arts moves he performs on the bike and the final shot of him still playing at dusk have a slightly *Karate Kid*-feel, perhaps pushing his action more toward the childish than playful.

An earlier ad still from 1999 shows him coming home and slipping into something more comfortable: a Tucci suit, complete with rust-brown tie. We might assume he is getting ready to go out, but the implication is as he slumps in front of the TV that such stylish clothing is more comfortable than sweatpants.

TOYOTA (2001)

In a Mark II, we see Clooney enjoying driving a particular car, but the opening "Let's go" almost has the effect of parody when we see what he is actually driving. As ever, his chivalrous credentials are underlined, driving around a puddle rather than splash an attractive woman walking past. Another ad shows him called to hurry as "We have a situation," followed by similar footage through surprisingly empty urban streets. His gentlemanly nature allows a woman into an elevator first with the clichéd "After you," picked up again later as he gives her a lift, in another chivalrous act or an open pickup. A further ad shows him as "Uncle George" taking a little girl supposedly to school but he takes her to work instead (an office rather than a film set). He seems content (as Michelle Pfeiffer noted during the shooting of *One Fine Day*) playing the "fun dad." The Toyota ads, unseen by U.S. audiences, might seem open to parody, and offer the thrills of an action narrative but fail to deliver. Even the slogan, "Drive your dreams," suggests your dreams must be quite tame.

FIAT (2004)

Fiat uses Clooney to promote their small minivan, named the Idea. We see a woman stopping next to an Alpine villa but leaving the door open. Clooney, known for his love of sports, jogs past in typical black T-shirt (a premise used in a later Fastweb ad). Attracted by the car, he gets in and finds it so comfortable that he reclines, at which point the woman returns (shot in slow motion), locks the doors, and traps him inside, before driving off with her prize. The ad is almost a parody of the notion of a Venus flytrap (with "Fever" chosen as the soundtrack), a tongue-in-cheek notion that female drivers (the ad's apparent target audience) might ensnare the man of their dreams if they too had such a car. Clooney, now with a house in Italy, is shot in an Italian setting and interested in an Italian car. There is a deprecating wit in evidence (and a playful nature, fooling around in the car, trying on sunglasses, and putting his feet up), not about his lady-killing prowess but his desirability to a wily female, setting and springing an effective trap. However, with a typical head tilt, this time sideways, a gesture mirrored by the woman, it is clear he is not too concerned. The setting, identified by caption as Lake Como, implying the trap is for Clooney specifically, is underlined by the slogan "George not included" as if he is on first-name terms with his public.

NESPRESSO (2007–PRESENT)

The Nestlé-owned company Nespresso engaged the services of the agency McCann Paris to use Clooney in rebranding their product as upmarket but accessible. "George Who?" shows Clooney approaching a

Nespresso store, establishing his identity for the first of the series of commercials. He passes mother and son as they come out, looking longingly perhaps at her or at the family life they represent, both part of Clooney's interest for the tabloid media as well as underlining his chivalrous credentials in holding the door open for them. Another woman passes out, whom he also watches, so that by the time a third woman comes in and she hands her keys to him, the gag that he is some sort of parking valet seems vaguely plausible. His look at this third woman, right down the camera lens, is a very direct link with the viewer (this first ad was filmed in the Milan area, close to Clooney's Lake Como home). Whip pans juxtaposed with leisurely tracking shots of luxurious furniture with couples sitting suggest an exciting yet chic hangout for the super-rich but also accessible to anyone walking in off the street. In terms of soundtrack, there is a heavy bass line and a few chords from an electronic piano (Karma Leon's track "Eternal Bliss"), suggesting something quirky and off-beat, returning at times to counterpoint the gags. It acts like a theme tune for a favorite TV show, bookending the ad and alerting fans to its presence.

He is approached by a succession of attractive young women, all with dark brown hair and eyes to match the dominant décor of the store and the product itself. Clooney assumes that one in particular (Camilla Belle) wants an autograph before realizing that she either does not recognize him or is not interested. The woman who demanded that he park her car reappears and shows surprise ("I didn't recognize you . . . ") before the second punch line that it is the other woman, not Clooney, whom she is talking about. He turns away, having been unrecognized twice, but is perked up at the feel of the car keys in his pocket and walks out of shot. Clooney is playing with the notion of fame and visibility and both perpetuates his notion as a recognizable star while gently poking fun at himself for taking it too seriously.

"What Else?" shows Clooney sweeping into a Nespresso store, waving to an Orlando Bloom-lookalike serving behind a counter as if he is just entering a club, restricted to beautiful people. While he loads up his shot of Nespresso, two women start listing adjectival phrases ("dark, very intense, balanced, unique, mysterious, an intense body, delicate and smooth, with a strong character, rich . . . very rich") at which point we zoom in to Clooney looking straight at the camera. They continue with "Latin-American temperament, deep and sensual, a delicious aftertaste." He sidles up to them and just checks that they are talking about the coffee, to end with the catch phrase "What else?" The final shot shows him still eavesdropping, peering around a partition, conveying the sense of an egotistical star, flattered to be described like this but realizing he is second best to the coffee.

A following Nescafé ad features him being recognized positively by a young woman who raves about him before walking off with the last Nespresso pod. Approached by a second woman, he assures her that she must be mistaken, denying his identity in order to secure the coffee for himself. However, since we see a plentiful supply of pods in a dispenser nearby, the precise logic of this does not quite work. The Nespresso monopoly on its pods adds an overt element of exclusivity and belonging to a select club, a club you implicitly share with Clooney.

The premise of the later Nespresso ads is strikingly similar to the series run by rival Italian company, Lavazza, set in heaven and featuring an ongoing dialogue with a white-haired St. Peter character, although the light, conversational tone lacks the wit and star power of the Nespresso commercials. It is not simply a matter of budget, recognizable stars, and big-name director, but the Nespresso commercials with slicker editing and use of close-ups feel like they are made for the big rather than the small screen. The idea of a white-suited figure from heaven who can appear and disappear at will and play jokes on the living feels a little like a mixture of Casper the Friendly Ghost and the British cult TV series *Randall and Hopkirk (Deceased)* (ITV, 1969–70) as well as tapping into Clooney's star persona, placing him opposite John Malkovich (his costar in *Burn after Reading*).

The Nespresso ads feature Clooney performing an action any viewer might copy (walking into a store, operating a machine, enjoying the coffee, and buying a Nespresso machine), but it also invites us to partake in a lifestyle choice in which beautiful young men and women can meet and flirt, drink luxurious coffee (shown in slow motion), and buy products packaged like items of chic clothing (particularly his favorite gold Cru flavor).

The longer version with Clooney trying to persuade St. Peter to take his Porsche or house also taps into known icons of his life, but the commercial essentially does not need this and is usually shown cutting straight from Clooney's surprised look at Malkovich's nod toward the Nespresso bag to finding himself empty-handed outside the store once more, turning just in time to miss the piano. A further scene shows him asking about a back way out of the store.

A second version shows him walking proudly into heaven with his Nespresso machine and then we cut to a very static scene of Clooney, Malkovich, and two attractive angels with overlapping dialogue, about the nature of heaven (whether they always wear white, what they eat, and whether there are there other angels). A series of fade-to-whites suggest edits from improvised conversation rather than scripted lines and include Malkovich's gag, which makes Clooney laugh, about not making films as there are no producers in heaven.

"Cab Driver" (Grant Heslov, 2010) uses the standard shots of a Nespresso store but with a rack focus between Clooney and some attractive women looking his way. A pan following one of them cuts across the white-suited figure of Malkovich, who disappears just as magically in the next cut. Clooney still uses the head tilt here, like a throwback to an earlier era in his career. Series of ads can start to refer to their own structures, so Clooney gives a nervous look up when he steps outside but there is no piano there. He gets in a taxi, at which point the driver, Malkovich, demands all the capsules that Clooney has. Clooney's on-screen persona as a loveable rogue is evoked as begrudgingly he hands them over but has to be prompted by a show of heavenly power as Malkovich causes rain to suddenly pour on the car to empty a few out of his sleeves. Nespresso not only exploits the star image of Clooney, always in a smart suit even if not wearing a tie, but also extends it, allowing viewers to download a template of "Cab Driver" and then make their own versions. Members of their so-called Nespresso Club even have the chance to submit film proposals for future commercials.

In "The Swap" (2011) we see Clooney alluding to his character in *Up in the Air*, mistakenly taking the minimalist luggage of an unknown woman (Nazanin Boniadi) and swapping back at a Nespresso store. Clooney is dressed in black as usual and assumes he has been recognized (which he may have been), but rather than the error being about assumptions about his height, it is that he is "Mr. Decaffeinato" rather than "Ristretto." It conveys the sense not only that your choice of coffee type defines your personality but that Clooney is so closely associated with this product it almost literally defines him now.

All of the Nespresso commercials, like his experiments with screwball, promises and then denies a sense of consummation. The Clooney character repeatedly does not get the girl, and banter and innuendo replace direct presentation of sexual matters. In advertising terms, it is the perfect creation of almost infinite deferral.

HONDA (2008)

This seems a fairly straightforward 30-second spot, shot in a single take. We see Clooney pull up in a Honda, get out, buy a parking ticket, and walk off down a busy western city street. As such he is the extraordinary (a Hollywood star) performing the ordinary (parking his car). The slogan, "The Power of Dreams," is reflected in the notion that you might meet Clooney in everyday life (or that he can find a parking space so easily perhaps). However, it is also part of the Clooney brand: he is smartly dressed (in the familiar dark suit, minus a tie), law abiding, careful to pay for what he uses, and civil, smiling to a passing stranger. However, the use of the Bee Gees' "Staying Alive" undercuts this star image, reminding viewers of John Travolta's often-parodied strut down a street over 40 years ago in *Saturday Night Fever* (John Badham, 1977). The implication is that here is a more modest version of someone who knows how to "use his walk" as the song says, but perhaps the line that he is "a woman's man" is more telling. It is an attractive female stranger who he chooses to smile at.

FASTWEB (2011)

"Jogger"

Italian telecommunications firm Fastweb uses Clooney to promote its Fibra 100 broadband service. We see him joining a friend to jog in a park and chatting in apparently passable Italian. His friend is heavily built, bald, and sweating, whereas Clooney is not. Clooney's character pats the other man as they pass a lamp post, pushing him into it so that he falls stunned behind a low hedge, just at the moment an attractive female jogger passes by, whether by accident or design is unclear. Dressed in his trademark black, Clooney is still charming the ladies, throwing a "Ciao" after the woman, who does not stop, but showing loyalty in finding his friend via the web-based technology being promoted and asking if he needs a hand up. We see Clooney integrating with his adopted culture (and possibly opening some new revenue streams), pursuing commercials with humor that still play on his lady-killing reputation. So far, these have aired only in Italy.

"Airport"

The camera follows behind a man arriving in an Italian airport, causing a stir of reaction among onlookers before being met by a representative from Fastweb, who addresses Clooney by name. Outside, he is approached by an older woman who assures him that he could pass for Clooney's stand-in, to which he agrees. Here we see him integrating still further, listening and apparently understanding colloquial Italian spoken at normal speed, while still playing with notions of his public persona, in particular how recognizable he is. There is a nod to the dominant setting in the first half of *Up in the Air*; and in showing Clooney pause to sign autographs and speak to his public, this could almost be an advert for Clooney Plc. and part of a charm offensive for his adopted second home.

"Manhole"

As cables are being laid at night, just outside the iconic Coliseum in Rome, Clooney appears from a manhole, complete with hard hat. A woman spots him and cannot believe her eyes, but he declares "Sono io" ("It's me") before disappearing again. The idea is so unbelievable that a passing policeman leads the woman away, clearly thinking she is mad. Again, it is issues of identity that dominate, but the surprise of his appearance obscures the illogical nature of the premise. Apart from the fact that he emerges from the hole and the woman's car screeches to a halt almost simultaneously or that she recognizes him at night, Clooney not only is playing himself endorsing a product but is also strangely a character, who seems to be actively working for Fastweb (why else would he be down the hole?).

"Bookshelf"

Here Clooney manages to make a piece of furniture collapse just by touching it (hardly an endorsement of quality if it was bought via Fastweb) and casts a reproving glance at a worker who seems to accept the blame. His single word on admiring the craftsmanship before this happens ("Magnifica") seems a reference back to his previous Martini ad (with the correct grammatical ending here).

DNB NOR (2011)

A tousled bride wakes to find she has apparently married George Clooney, who emerges from a side room to gallantly announce that he did not want to wake her. However, why the woman is apparently hungover is somewhat confusing given the premise of a dream husband come true, and it does not seem a particularly romantic situation. Clooney points out some places where they might live (linking with the financial services of the Norwegian bank being promoted), but the woman is denied any lines, and a Danish (Julie Agnete Vang) rather than Norwegian actor is cast, suggesting perhaps that Norwegians might not approve of such behavior in one of their own citizens.

CONCLUSION

Clooney's commercials have a number of similarities. They are uni-
formly high in production values and seem as much at home on the big
screen as on television. They are all effectively mini-movies, featuring
stars (Clooney obviously but Malkovich too) and helmed by big-name
directors like Robert Rodriguez ("El Toro" for Martini) and Michel
Gondry (for the "Boutique" episode in the Nespresso series). Most feature
an element of tongue-in-cheek, sometimes even earthy, humor and all
feature a satirical playing on Clooney's own star image. Clooney is ideal
for commercials, which must establish situation and characterization
within seconds, particularly so since he is always playing himself or
versions of his cinematic selves.

Clooney is certainly open to the criticism of so-called "japandering"
(a blend of "Japan" and "pandering"): the practice of making lucrative
commercials outside the United States, which will not be seen by a star's
prime fan base and thus not damage their core brand image. His South
Korean print ads for Lancelot whisky seem oddly reminiscent of Bill
Murray's role as depressed movie star Bob in *Lost in Translation*. Such
activities are often attacked as crude exploitation and a sign of a career
on the wane, but Clooney's efforts in this sphere complement rather than
tarnish his image. Besides, in a global marketplace and with video capture
sites like YouTube or TV shows that compile foreign commercials for
entertainment, it is hard to keep any such work secret for long. It is
safe to assume they will be seen by everyone, sooner or later. The
DnB NOR commercial had over 1.5 million YouTube hits within a week.
Distinctions in how stars are perceived may be affected less by geography
than by Internet access. On a more philanthropic note, Clooney has
appeared, along with several other celebrities, in a public service
announcement as part of the ONE Campaign, fighting African poverty,
and in another called "Peace is Hard" in 2008 to raise awareness about
UN peacekeeping.

Conclusion

Anything I've done, I've had good cause to do.

—Jack in *The American*

Clooney has starred in (and sometimes written and directed) an average of two films a year for nearly 20 years. His Oscar wins and nominations reflect a growing depth and maturity to his work that he might justifiably feel has been neglected. Having reached a certain level of financial security in the mid-1990s and after the disappointment of *Batman*, Clooney has made a concerted effort to make only scripts that pass a certain quality threshold, and found that certain figures largely working in independent film, the Coen brothers and Soderbergh in particular, represent the kind of films he is trying to make. *Out of Sight*, nominated for Oscars for its screenplay and editing, was a turning point in Clooney's career, linking him for the first time with Steven Soderbergh and signaling a shift to more thoughtful, generically rich styles of filmmaking. The result has been that although the films he has made since have not always made a great deal of money, most break even, and some, like the *Ocean's* franchise, produce valuable revenue, which is then plowed back into more esoteric projects.

He seems to have taken from his collaborations with the Coen brothers and Soderbergh the notion that a film set should be a place where actors want to come and do good work; a relaxed environment where it is positive to laugh and joke. In a sense, the serious business is at the casting stage, and once actors have been selected, Clooney prefers to give individuals sufficient respect for their own professionalism so that they do not need to be badgered and hectored to produce their best work.

Perhaps a key factor in Clooney's development is that his break in movies came relatively late, when he was already 35 (and looked older) so that placing him in an ultra-hip contemporary setting, surrounded by other actors of the 16–34 demographic, would not work. The process of ageing possibly holds fewer threats for his image than for other actors and less of a mind shift for audiences to accept him in more mature roles. We have already seen him on screen as a middle-aged man who refuses to wear makeup on camera, so we do not have to wonder how he will cope with gray hair and a few more wrinkles.

He could have remained stuck as a romantic lead (*One Fine Day*), as an action hero (*The Peacemaker*), or as part of a single franchise (*Batman*), but he decided to shift between the young guns of the indie world (Tarantino, Russell), the innovative, politically engaged face of nonlinear narratives (Gaghan, Gilroy), the quirky but ever-more-mainstream (Coen brothers), and occasional personal pet projects with friends (Heslov). Soderbergh's own career has huge peaks and troughs, and Clooney seems to have chosen to collaborate on the more successful ventures (possibly making them so). *Solaris* showed that he was secure enough to take a financial loss, a major one, and still survive as a star and a filmmaker.

Clooney's belief that real figures should not be played by big stars reflects an assumption about what a star is. For the most part his theory holds true, but there are a small group of actors who can transcend their stardom and inhabit a role rather than just carry their star persona from film to film, even when portraying figures in the real world—for example, Meryl Streep as Julia Child in *Julie and Julia* (Nora Ephron, 2009) or Margaret Thatcher in *The Iron Lady* (Phyllida Lloyd, 2012); or *Invictus* (Clint Eastwood, 2009), which is fronted by two examples of such performances: Matt Damon as South African rugby captain Francois Pienaar, and Morgan Freeman as Nelson Mandela. David Strathairn's competition for the Best Actor Oscar of 2005 included Philip Seymour Hoffman in *Capote* (Bennett Miller) and Joaquin Phoenix in *Walk the Line* (James Mangold), both playing real famous figures. Playing known figures from the real world is exceedingly difficult but not impossible. The fact that Michael Sheen has credibly played David Frost (*Frost/Nixon*, Ron Howard, 2008), Tony Blair (*The Queen*, Stephen Frears, 2006), and Brian Clough (*The Damned United*, Tom Hooper, 2009) within a few years of each other underlines the point (although one might debate at what point Sheen has moved from a character actor to a star).

The films of George Clooney might be seen to convey values of the American Dream, where his character strives to succeed and eventually does (*O Brother*), where his character has a certain raffish charm, suggesting that women wish to be treated courteously (*One Fine Day*), that not all problems can be solved with physical force but some can (*From Dusk Till Dawn* and *The Peacemaker*), and that wit and charm can be of greater value (*Out of Sight* and the *Ocean's* series). At the same time, his persona can suggest that it is acceptable for a hero to feel and look vulnerable (*Solaris*), that the values of a liberal democracy that questions authority are important (*Good Night, and Good Luck*), and that an intellectual engagement with a complex world in which the United States is no longer always the most powerful player is essential (*Syriana*). As the strongest cinematic icon of his age group and with the ear of the president, he is probably the most famous face of liberal America.

Now into his 50s, Clooney still rides motorbikes, likes a drink (in moderation), and enjoys the company of beautiful women. As a fantasy bachelor and as an American, he is still living the dream. Madame Tussaud's Wax Museum in Las Vegas has a model of Clooney, all dressed in tuxedo, that visitors can pose next to in a wedding dress as a fantasy wedding photo.

In *Confessions*, the visual gag of newlyweds Barris and Penny coming out of the front of the church, just as a coffin is entering by a side door, may be how Clooney sees marriage, but the popular press will undoubtedly keep linking anything he says or does in the direction of a news narrative that would interest their readers. A rarity in the Clooney canon (until *Up in the Air*), we see him pursuing a woman with a proposal of marriage, with the quick downward glances and self-deprecating knowing smiles more visible in *One Fine Day*.

In his overtly romantic roles (like *One Fine Day* or *Up in the Air*), he is mostly paired opposite a prime female antagonist (Michelle Pfeiffer or Vera Parminga, respectively), but most of his film roles place him in an ensemble cast, often in a predominantly male environment. He is often head of a team, which might be work related (*The Perfect Storm*) but is more often military (*The Men Who Stare at Goats*) or criminal (the *Ocean's* series) or a mixture of all three (*Three Kings*). Clooney is nearly always a figure of authority: captain in *The Perfect Storm*, a major in *Three Kings*, mastermind of the escape in *O Brother* (although the others in his group are hardly leadership material), a colonel in *The Peacemaker*, and the eponymous superhero in *Batman and Robin*. Only rarely (*Syriana* and *Michael Clayton*) has Clooney played a role involving a family and more particularly children (in both cases with relationships that are distant or strained). The predominantly male groups that he leads act in a sense as a surrogate family with him as a paternal figure (in *O Brother*, *Three Kings*, and *The Perfect Storm*, for example). Very little of his brief cameo in *The Thin Red Line* (Terrence Malick, 1998) survived the cutting room floor, but as Clooney's character, Captain Bosche, states, addressing a group of raw recruits: "We are a family. I'm the father." As he ages, it may be that future roles, such as *The Descendants*, extend this aspect of his on-screen persona, and like Ryan Bingham in *Up in the Air*, that his character is brought into greater contact with family members.

He is often portrayed as just on the wrong side of the law (*Out of Sight*, *Collinwood*, or *O Brother*) but usually with a fair degree of incompetence. Only in the overt caper movies of the *Ocean's* series does he show more confident criminal ability. In more mature films he plays isolated, introspective loners at a distance, not just from a romantic partner but from humankind itself (*Solaris*, *Michael Clayton*, and *The American*). It is in these latter, more elegiac roles that Clooney has had the chance to show a darker side to his persona, which has actually always been there since *Red Surf* and *From Dusk Till Dawn* but now seems to carry serious conviction. Through these latter films, there is an increasing use of moments of silence, especially in *The American* but even present in less obviously contemplative work like *Leatherheads*, such as when the huge boy from high school sits down in the train, Dodge opens his mouth to speak but then stays silent.

In Clooney's movies, memory is equated with film. In *Three Kings*, Gates replays mental images of the first entrance to the square (in slow motion) and realizes the boot-wearing figures around the well were soldiers in disguise. *Leatherheads* uses the motif of a camera tracking across black-and-white or sepia-toned photos capturing iconic moments from a past, thus given a hazy tone of nostalgia, a feature of films as diverse as *Butch Cassidy and the Sundance Kid* (George Roy Hill, 1969) through to the credit sequence for *Cheers* (NBC, 1982–93). Often the past that is evoked in Clooney's films is openly reminiscent of, and even nostalgic for, the period 1965–75, in particular the so-called American New Wave, dramatizing criminality and corruption but in which journalism is seen as moral, crusading, and principled before the advent of 24-hour celebrity-driven media.

There are very few films in which he dies. *The Perfect Storm* underlines its credentials as a true story and to have Bobby survive would undermine the elegiac tone of the whole film; and in *Red Surf* and *The American*, he plays a character that cannot be morally reintegrated into society. Both at least allow the dignity of a death off-screen. Exactly whether he dies at the end of *Solaris* is open to question, depending on your reading of the final scenes where his spacecraft plunges into the planet's surface; and in *Confessions*, his character may be no more than a delusion of the hero.

If there is a threat to his image, it may lie in reaction to his public announcements. This may even come from previous collaborators. In *South Park*, season 10, episode 2 (2006), Trey Parker and Matt Stone parody attitudes to hybrid vehicles but also tap into some residual audience hostility toward apparent smugness in Clooney's Oscar acceptance speech for *Syriana*. A so-called "Smug cloud" appears over the town and threatens to create "a perfect storm of self-satisfaction."

Is Clooney the greatest male actor of his generation? Probably while Philip Seymour Hoffman, Daniel Day-Lewis, or Sean Penn are active, such a title would be hotly contested. In terms of Clooney's work as a director, while *Leatherheads* may seem clunky as a screwball comedy it is thoughtful in its evocation of an era, *Confessions* is remarkable for its ambition, and *Good Night, and Good Luck* powerful in its claustrophobic sense of theater. Kimberly Potts terms him "the last great movie star," which may be a little disrespectful to figures like Clint Eastwood, who has had an amazing resurgence in the latter part of his career. What makes Clooney distinctive is his unmatched ability to blend unequalled leading man credibility with an on-screen wit, extending from comedy to action and hybrid forms between the two (the heist move especially). With astute decisions about whom to work with and accepting only literate, and sometimes literary, scripts, he has carved a niche for himself blending art-house sensibility with commercial potential. Except perhaps in *Syriana*, he is instantly recognizable as George Clooney, so unlike Hoffman, Lewis, or Penn, he cannot easily disappear completely into a role. What he does instead is expand the dramatic possibilities, the range of contexts in which audiences will accept him, blurring generic boundaries and bringing politics into the mainstream. Even in his caper movies, there is an element of liberal politics at play. As Danny Ocean he is directing an operation to redistribute capital and exact revenge against richer, more powerful individuals; and in *Three Kings*, his robbery plan is diverted into funding resistance against Saddam Hussein's regime and saving a specific group of dissidents trying to cross the border. Positions of authority no longer allow his character to remain aloof from criticism of the bodies of which he is part. *Up in the Air* portrays America undergoing painful downsizing, of which Ryan is initially the agent but eventually also its victim, and as Governor Mike Morris in *The Ides of March*, he represents a political system that leads Meyers from optimism to power-brokering cynicism.

Perhaps Clooney is still searching for a single career-defining role, but as he disappears further into characters and expands generic and dramatic possibilities, it becomes increasingly harder to predict what a George Clooney movie might look like. Stars of previous eras were tied much more closely to specific genres, but Clooney has extended the life of his career by diversifying his brand and not tying his colors to any one particular generic mast. In a sense, Clooney's roles have moved from the exception to the rule; from Superman to Everyman. He began his film career as a fantasy gangster (Seth Gecko), fantasy action figure (Thomas Devoe), and literal fantasy cartoon figure (Batman). A decade later, he is a legal "janitor" (*Michael Clayton*), an intelligence operative (*Syriana*), and a failed husband facing divorce (*Burn after Reading*). So far, Clooney has had to play an on-screen role to attract finance and be part of the marketing of a film (even if this distorts the design of promotional material, as in *The Magic Bubble* and to a lesser extent in *Collinwood*). Perhaps the next benchmark in his career is when he can disappear behind the camera completely.

Notes

INTRODUCTION

1. Richard Dyer, *Stars* (London: BFI, 1979).
2. Susan Hayward, *Key Concepts in Cinema Studies* (New York: Routledge, 1996), 340.
3. Christine Gledhill, *Stardom: Industry of Desire* (New York: Routledge, 1991).

CHAPTER 1

1. George Clooney cited in David Gritten, "The Morals of King George," *The Telegraph*, March 8, 2003, http://www.telegraph.co.uk/culture/film/3590882/The-morals-of-King-George.html.
2. See Mark Browning, *Stephen King on the Small Screen* (Bristol, UK: Intellect Books, 2011), 63–65.

CHAPTER 2

1. Walter Kirn, *Up in the Air* (New York: Random House, 2001), 41.
2. Andrew Sarris, "The Sex Comedy without Sex," *American Film* 3, no. 5 (1978): 13.
3. Ellen Cheshire and John Ashbrook, *Joel and Ethan Coen* (Harpenden, Herts., UK: Pocket Essentials, 2005), 124–26.
4. Kirn, *Up in the Air*, 272.
5. Ibid., 8.
6. Ibid., 34 and 47.
7. Ibid., 201.
8. Ibid., 242.
9. Ibid., 168.

CHAPTER 3

1. Joel Schumacher, cited by John Glover in *Shadows of the Bat: The Cinematic Saga of the Dark Knight, Part 6—Batman Unbound*, 2005, Warner Home Video.
2. George Clooney, "Behind the Masks," *Boston Globe*, June 12, 2005.
3. Sebastian Junger, *The Perfect Storm* (London: Fourth Estate, 1997), 168.
4. Ibid., 15.
5. Ibid., xi.
6. See ibid. 55, 56, 71, 109, and 125.
7. See ibid. 155 and 104.

CHAPTER 4

1. Jami Bernard, *Quentin Tarantino: The Man and His Movies* (London: HarperCollins, 1995), 133.
2. See Mark Browning, *Stephen King on the Big Screen* (Bristol, UK: Intellect Books, 2009), 135–37.
3. See Mark Browning, *Wes Anderson: Why His Movies Matter* (Santa Barbara, CA: ABC-CLIO, 2011), 139–40.

CHAPTER 5

1. Derek Hill, *Charlie Kaufman and Hollywood's Merry Band of Pranksters, Fabulists and Dreamers: An Excursion into the American New Wave* (Harpenden; Herts., UK: Kamera Books, 2008), 75.
2. Wahlberg would later go on to star in F. Gary Gray's remake in 2003.
3. See Mark Browning, *David Fincher: Films That Scar* (Santa Barbara, CA: ABC-CLIO, 2010), 75–76.
4. Hill, *Charlie Kaufman*, 76.
5. Ibid., 77.
6. Scott Frank, *Out of Sight* (Eye, Suffolk, UK: Screenpress Books, 1999), 57.

CHAPTER 6

1. George Clooney and Grant Heslov, *Good Night, and Good Luck: The Screenplay and History behind the Landmark Movie* (New York: Newmarket Press, 2006), 79.
2. See Joe Wershba in ibid., 30.
3. Ibid., 72.
4. Ibid., 28.
5. Ibid., 92.
6. Ibid., 91.
7. Ibid., 75.
8. Ibid., 146.

CHAPTER 7

1. Robert Baer, *See No Evil* (New York: Three Rivers Press, 2002), 33.

2. Ibid., 14.

3. Ibid., 257.

4. Ibid., 270.

5. Ibid., 81.

6. Ethan Coen, cited in Susan Wloszczyna, "Fall Movie Preview: Coens Dumb It down with 'Burn,'" *USA Today*, September 2, 2008.

7. George Clooney speaking at the Venice Film Festival, August 26, 2008.

8. Baer, *See No Evil*, 74.

9. Jon Ronson, *The Men Who Stare at Goats* (London: Picador, 2004), 41 and 45.

10. Ibid., 78.

11. Ibid., 159.

12. Baer, *See No Evil*, 132.

CHAPTER 8

1. See Tzvetan Todorov, *The Fantastic: A Structural Approach to a Literary Genre*, trans. Richard Howard (Ithaca, NY: Cornell University Press, 1975).

2. Steven Soderbergh, cited in Hugh Hart, "Partners in Angst," *San Francisco Chronicle*, November 24, 2002, http://articles.sun-sentinel.com/keyword/steven-soderbergh.

3. Tony Gilroy, *Michael Clayton* (New York: Newmarket Press, 2007), 81.

4. William Goldman in ibid., viii.

CHAPTER 9

1. See Mark Browning, *Wes Anderson: Why His Movies Matter* (Santa Barbara, CA: ABC-CLIO, 2011), 89–102.

Bibliography

Baer, Robert. *See No Evil*. New York: Three Rivers Press, 2002.

Bernard, Jami. *Quentin Tarantino: The Man and His Movies*. London: HarperCollins, 1995.

Biskind, Peter. *Down and Dirty Pictures: Miramax, Sundance and the Rise of Independent Film*. London: Bloomsbury, 2004.

Browning, Mark. *David Fincher: Films That Scar*. Santa Barbara, CA: ABC-CLIO, 2010.

Browning, Mark. *Stephen King on the Small Screen*. Bristol, UK: Intellect Books, 2011.

Browning, Mark. *Wes Anderson: Why His Movies Matter*. Santa Barbara, CA: ABC-CLIO, 2011.

Cheshire, Ellen, and John Ashbrook. *Joel and Ethan Coen*. Harpenden, Herts., UK: Pocket Essentials, 2005.

Clooney, George, and Grant Heslov. *Good Night, and Good Luck: The Screenplay and History behind the Landmark Movie*. New York: Newmarket Press, 2006.

Dyer, Richard. *Stars*. London: BFI, 1979.

Frank, Scott. *Out of Sight*. Eye, Suffolk, UK: Screenpress Books, 1999.

Gilroy, Tony. *Michael Clayton*. New York: Newmarket Press, 2007.

Gledhill, Christine. *Stardom: Industry of Desire*. New York: Routledge, 1991.

Hayward, Susan. *Key Concepts in Cinema Studies*. New York: Routledge, 1996.

Hemmings, Kaui Hart. *The Descendants*. London: Vintage Books, 2011; first published in 2008.

Hill, Derek. *Charlie Kaufman and Hollywood's Merry Band of Pranksters, Fabulists and Dreamers: An Excursion into the American New Wave*. Harpenden, Herts., UK: Kamera Books, 2008.

Hudson, Jeff. *George Clooney*. London: Virgin Books, 2003.

Junger, Sebastian. *The Perfect Storm*. London: Fourth Estate Ltd., 1997.

Kanon, Joseph. *The Good German*. London: Sphere Books, 2007; first published in 2001.

Keenleyside, Sam. *Bedside Manners: George Clooney and ER*. Toronto: ECW Press, 1998.

Kemp, Philip. "*Michael Clayton*: A Review." *Sight and Sound* 17, no. 10 (October 2007): 61–62.

Kirn, Walter. *Up in the Air*. New York: Random House, 2001.

Potts, Kimberley. *George Clooney: The Last Great Movie Star*. New York: Applause Books, 2007.

Ronson, Jon. *The Men Who Stare at Goats*. London: Picador, 2004.

Sarris, Andrew. "The Sex Comedy without the Sex." *American Film* 3, no. 5 (1978): 13.

Todorov, Tzvetan. *The Fantastic: A Structural Approach to a Literary Genre*. Translated by Richard Howard. Ithaca, NY: Cornell University Press, 1975.

Wood, Jason. *Steven Soderbergh*. Harpenden, Herts., UK: Pocket Essentials, 2002.

Index

About the Author

After receiving a First Class English degree at Manchester University, Mark Browning attended universities in Leeds, London, and Kent and gained a PGCE, an MA, and a PhD respectively. He has taught English and Film Studies in a number of schools in England and was a Senior Lecturer in Education in Bath. He has published study guides for Film Education, academic articles on the processes of adaptation, and also written comedy sketches for BBC Radio 2.

He has published a number of film-related works: *David Cronenberg: Author or Filmmaker?* (Intellect Books, 2007), which has also been translated into Serbo-Croat; *Stephen King on the Big Screen* (Intellect, 2009); *David Fincher: Films That Scar* (ABC-CLIO, 2010); *Wes Anderson: Why His Movies Matter* (ABC-CLIO, 2011); *Stephen King on the Small Screen* (Intellect, 2011); and *Danny Boyle: Lust for Life* (Chaplin Books, 2011).

He currently lives in Germany where he works as a teacher and freelance writer.